MEXICO'S ILLICIT DRUG NETWORKS

AND THE STATE REACTION

MEXICO'S ILLICIT DRUG NETWORKS

AND THE STATE REACTION

NATHAN P. JONES

Georgetown University Press
Washington, DC

Library of Congress Cataloging-in-Publication Data

Jones, Nathan P., author
  Mexico's illicit drug networks and the state reaction / Nathan P. Jones.
    pages cm
  Includes bibliographical references and index.
  ISBN 978-1-62616-294-5 (hardcover : alk. paper) —
  ISBN 978-1-62616-295-2 (pbk. : alk. paper) — ISBN 978-1-62616-296-9 (ebook)
  1. Drug traffic—Mexico. 2. Drug control—Mexico. 3. Organized crime—Mexico. I. Title.
  HV5840.M4J66 2016
  363.450972—dc23
                        2015024224

♾ This book is printed on acid-free paper meeting the requirements of the American National Standard for Permanence in Paper for Printed Library Materials.

17 16   9 8 7 6 5 4 3 2
First printing

Printed in the United States of America

Cover design by Naylor Design, Inc. Cover image by shutterstock.com.

To my family: Sofia, Ethan, and Sean.

Contents

Illustrations

Acknowledgments

ALONG THE WAY A YOUNG scholar writing his dissertation and converting it into a book receives help from more people than he can possibly thank. If I forget anyone, forgive me.

Much of the editing/rewriting for the initial manuscript drafts was done at Rice University's Baker Institute, where I spent two years proudly as the Alfred C. Glassell III postdoctoral fellow in drug policy funded by the Glassell Foundation. The Center for Global Peace and Conflict Studies (CGPACS) and the UC Irvine Political Science Department funded preliminary research trips to Tijuana. I learned much from my participation with the National Defense Intelligence College (NDIC, now the NIU) collaboration with the University of San Diego, which was spearheaded by Professor Emily Edmonds-Poli of the University of San Diego. The Institute for Global Conflict and Cooperation (IGCC) funded my dissertation fieldwork in Mexico City and Tijuana. The Colegio de la Frontera Norte, Tijuana (COLEF), allowed me to spend my fieldwork in *estancia* (in affiliation with) with an office (with an ocean view) provided to me by Rocio Barajas. While at COLEF, I was lucky to be advised by José Maria Ramos who provided amazing feedback and allowed me to pick his brain for hours. Patricia Escamilla Hamm and Lorena Pérez Floriano have both been true friends and colleagues. Thank you to the faculty at COLEF who allowed me to ask questions and work among them. Federal judge David Carter, Richard Marosi of the *Los Angeles Times*, Sandra Dibble of the *San Diego Union-Tribune*, and *Zeta* magazine reporters all assisted me along the way.

Special thanks must go to my dissertation advisers, Caesar Sereseres and Etel Solingen. You both made me a better scholar and person. Thank you both for getting me through the rigorous process. Thank you to the other dissertation committee members, Kamal Sadiq and Louis Desipio, who provided rapid feedback and support.

I owe a debt of gratitude to the following scholars in Mexico, the United States, and Canada who took the time to speak with me and point me in the right directions: Raúl Benítez Manaut, Samuel Gonzalez Ruiz, Luis Astorga, Guadalupe Correa-Cabrera, Viridiana Rios Contreras, Tony Payan, Vanda Felbab-Brown, Margaret Daly Hayes, Ashley Ross, Clayton Wukich, Desmond Arias, Carlos Flores Pérez, Inigo Guevara Moyano, Paul Chabot, Daniel Sabet, Tom Marks, Emily Edmonds-Poli, David Shirk, James Creechan, Robert Bunker, John Sullivan, Col. J. Cope, Eduardo Guerrero Gutiérrez, Michael Kenney, H. Brinton Milward, Duncan Wood, Eric Olson, and Randy Willoughby. Special thanks to InSight Crime director Steven Dudley and Patrick Corcoran for helping me in Tijuana and to the prolific InSight Crime team for letting me contribute.

At Sam Houston State University, numerous research assistants assisted me by tracking down articles and tolerating my immediate demands for facts, documents, and assistance with formatting. First and foremost, I must thank my TA/RA, Joshua Mareel, who tolerated my last-minute formatting efforts and assisted with visuals and research. Adriana Guerra assisted with conversions of visuals. I must also thank student assistants Sarita Benavides, Iain Dewar, and Tyler Reese and McNair Scholar Luis Morales.

The esteemed Dr. Bill Martin tolerated my initial drafts, provided excellent feedback/edits, and taught me how to be a better husband and father. The drug policy interns at Rice University's Baker Institute, including Danny Cortez, Taylor Britt, Vicky Comesañas, Myrna Garza, and Sussy Aguirre, also assisted me.

I am eternally grateful to US and Mexican government/law-enforcement interviewees, many of who cannot be named. Steve Duncan of the California Department of Justice has been an invaluable resource and true friend. Former DEA Houston intelligence chief Gary Hale has also been a great friend and resource.

Georgetown University Press reviewers provided incredible feedback, and Don Jacobs and the Georgetown University Press team helped to make this book a reality. I cannot thank them enough.

Special thanks must go to those who gave feedback on drafts of various chapters in the book and dissertation phases: John Bailey, Irina Chindea, Russell Lundberg, Caesar Sereseres, William Martin, William Dittman, Cathy Wogan, Michael Hampson, and John Sullivan. Any errors are my own.

We lost an amazing scholar in George W. Grayson in March 2015. So many of us knew him for his work on Mexico and were surprised to learn that he was as equally prolific in every facet of his life. George, thank you for teaching us how to stay friends with critics, write well, and have a sense of humor. We still laugh at your jokes.

Most important, thanks must go to my wife for tolerating my long work hours and constant focus on the book and to my sons Ethan, who was still excited to see his dad after long days, and Sean, who came early and let me work on the book beside his incubator.

Abbreviations

AFI	Agencia Federal de Investigación
AFO	Arellano Félix Organization
ATF	Bureau of Alcohol, Tobacco, Firearms, and Explosives
AQI	Al Qaeda in Iraq
AUC	Autodefensas Unidas de Colombia
BLO	Beltrán Leyva Organization
CFO	Carrillo Fuentes Organization
CI	confidential informant
CIA	Central Intelligence Agency
CISEN	Centro de Investigación y Seguridad Nacional
COLEF	Colegio de la Frontera Norte
COPARMEX	Confederación Patronal de la República Mexicana
CPOT	consolidated priority organization target
CT	Los Caballeros Templarios (Knights Templar)
DEA	Drug Enforcement Agency
DFS	Dirrección Federal de Seguridad
DHS	Department of Homeland Security
DTO	drug-trafficking organization
FARC	Fuerzas Armadas Revolucionarias de Colombia
FBI	Federal Bureau of Investigation
FSO	Fernando Sánchez Organization
GAFE	Grupo Aeromóvil Fuerzas Especiales (Mexican military special forces)
GDP	gross domestic product
HIDTA	high-intensity drug-trafficking areas
HVT	high-value target
ISIS	Islamic State in Iraq and Syria
IMCO	Mexican Competitiveness Institute
LFM	La Familia Michoacána

MS-13	Mara Salvatrucha
NAFTA	North American Free Trade Agreement
OCDETF	Organized Crime Drug Enforcement Task Force
OFAC	Office of Foreign Assets Control
PAN	Partido Acción Nacional (National Action Party)
PEMEX	Petróleos Mexicanos (Mexican national oil company)
PGR	Procuraduría General de la República (Mexican Attorney General's Office)
PRD	Partido de la Revolución Democrática (Party of the Democratic Revolution)
PRI	Partido Revolucionario Institucional (Institutional Revolutionary Party)
PSIN	profit-seeking illicit network
SEDENA	Secretaría de la Defensa Nacional
SEMAR	Secretaría de Marina
SIEDO	Subprocuraduría de Investigación Especializada en Delincuencia Organizada (Attorney General's Special Investigations Unit for Organized Crime)
SSP	Secretaría de Seguridad Pública (Secretary of Public Security)

Introduction

I WILL BE DISCUSSING PROFIT-SEEKING illicit networks (PSINs), which I will refer to as drug networks (though I acknowledge that not all PSINs are solely in the illegal drug industry), and their resilience in the context of Mexico's battles with organized crime. Drug networks come in two incarnations: "transactional" and "territorial."[1] Let me explain. Trafficking-oriented drug networks focus on "transactional" activities, such as the trafficking of drugs and the logistics involved in moving commodities from point A to point B.[2] Territorial drug networks, in contrast, focus on the control and taxation of territory.[3]

Territorial drug networks and states are enemies because they are so much alike. Both are territorial, hierarchical, resilient, prone to violence, and funded by taxation.[4] Territorial drug networks threaten the state's underlying raison d'être—the ability to govern through the taxation of territory. The "predatory" "alternative governance structure"[5] these drug networks establish through extortion and kidnapping directly challenges states by illicitly taxing the local population and exercising violence within state territory.[6] The networks thus become the primary targets for "territorially sovereign states,"[7] and this state targeting of territorial-drug-network leadership figures helps to explain their increased risk and reduced resilience over time.[8]

Transactional drug networks that focus their illicit activities on the trafficking of narcotics, money laundering, front businesses, the provision of protection from the predatory aspects of the state,[9] or other nonextortionist activities become secondary targets for states and are more capable of forming alliances with states through corruption and even with other illicit networks. Because civil society prompts violent state reactions against territorial drug networks, they tend to be less resilient than their transactional or trafficking-oriented counterparts.[10] The transactional drug networks that survive these periods of conflict between states and territorial networks form alliances with states against their territorial rivals,[11] thus institutionalizing cooperation between the state and drug networks that hinders long-term democratic consolidation. The threat

I

that transactional drug networks pose to states is more subtle and insidious than that posed by territorial or insurgent illicit networks that seek to supplant the state or weaken it in crucial territories through brute force. Transactional drug networks constrain and pervert democratic consolidation, economic development, and the rule of law. While the long-term effects of trafficking networks are significant, they tend to be far less violent and threatening to states than territorial networks. States thus consider transactional drug networks the lesser evil.[12]

There is evidence to suggest that the Mexican state views organized crime through this lens. In 2010, an anonymous Mexican government official quoted in the *Economist* volunteered that Mexico was targeting Los Zetas because it was a more "territorial," and therefore more violent, drug network. Further, the official continued, the Mexican state was putting less emphasis on targeting the Sinaloa cartel because of its "transactional" character.[13] That brief statement inspired the first part of the conceptual argument presented in this book. While the term "transactional" encapsulates much of the idea, the term "trafficking-oriented" emphasizes a portion of the business model that is more relevant to this argument. A trafficking-oriented network could increase its vertical integration into various aspects of the drug markets, thus becoming less transactional but still remain trafficking oriented and minimizing territoriality. Further, the Sinaloa cartel, a largely trafficking-oriented network, does engage in extortionist or territorial activities despite being more heavily weighted toward drug trafficking in its business model. When the Sinaloa cartel engages in extortionist activities, there is typically a higher degree of "complexity of criminal act," as Bailey has conceptualized, thus masking these activities.[14]

I add to this understanding of illicit network structures by elucidating the territorial and trafficking drug-network business strategies and demonstrating empirically why civil society forces the state to react so viscerally to territorial drug networks. Further, in the appendix I provide a 26-point typology of the expected behaviors of each business strategy.

While my explanation is simple, it requires an understanding of the raison d'être of states and of the structure of drug networks. I use the historical case study of the Arellano Félix Organization (AFO), better known as the Tijuana cartel, to illustrate my "state reaction argument." Later, I use George and Bennett's method of structured focused comparison on three minicases (Los Zetas, Los Caballeros Templarios, and the Sinaloa cartel) to test the argument across cases and maximize validity.[15] My argument goes beyond the idea that governments simply attack the most violent drug networks, to explain why these networks are more violent and why some elicit visceral reactions from the state, while others appear ignored at best and "favored" at worst.[16] In the conclusion, I will also discuss whether or not the process is an artifact of a particular stage of the "competitive adaptation" between drug networks and the states involved.[17]

The analysis began with a simple question: What makes illicit networks resilient? As the research continued, the answer to that question was found largely in the answer to another: Why do states attack some illicit networks more aggressively than others?

Nothing could be more relevant for Mexico today than an understanding of why the state, at various levels, tends to target certain drug networks over others, and answering this question has implications for the resilience of drug networks and their relationships with states. This understanding provides insight on how best to combat drug networks and points to long-term issues that may arise as some drug networks prove resilient. Mexican drug networks are present in at least sixteen countries and are widely considered to be the world's premier illicit networks.[18] For example, recent reports have shown the Sinaloa cartel has attempted to establish a presence in the Philippines, much to the chagrin and fright of that country's government.[19] Perhaps most importantly, the resilience of Mexican drug networks has important implications for Central America. Because Central America comprises seven small states, the region is ill equipped to respond to the presence of large, violent, and highly profitable Mexican drug networks. Unfortunately for Central America, Mexican drug-network profits compare favorably to total gross domestic products of the individual countries in the region.[20]

Before I continue, let me discuss the myriad reasons why I prefer the term "profit-seeking illicit networks" (PSINs to "cartels," though I do use the latter, as well as the less jargon-laden term "drug networks." To the best of my knowledge, this is the first formal use of the term, though "profit-seeking" and "illicit network" and "dark network" have appeared in the work of authors such as Kenney, Van Schendel, Abraham, Sadiq, and Milward and in formal government reports on organized crime.[21]

First, the term "PSIN" positions my analysis within the literature on "illicit networks" and "illicit flows."[22] The qualitative sociological network literature provides useful concepts that can explain the ability of criminal actors to create "networks of complicity" within the state apparatus.[23] The term "illicit network" also connotes their transnational character because the term is not constrained by "state-centric discourse" and allows for nonstate actors.[24]

Second, "profit-seeking" separates these illicit networks from broader insurgent illicit networks with political aims. While profit seekers may at times have political aims, those aims generally serve their profit-seeking ends. In contrast, insurgent networks sometimes spend a great deal of time fundraising through criminal acts to fund their politically motivated attacks. At what point does an insurgent network spend more time seeking profit than seeking political change? I don't seek to answer the question but to acknowledge the "crime–terror continuum" identified by others and the dark-network research that discusses when insurgent or territorial groups are likely to expand heavily into drug trafficking.[25] Explaining why states attack insurgent networks is obvious. They are political entities seeking to overthrow and supplant the state. Explaining why states attack some profit-seeking illicit networks and not others is thus far more interesting and important.

Finally, "PSIN" is more accurate than "drug cartel" because these networks have not proven capable of controlling the supply and price of a given commodity. Thus, they are not cartels in the economic sense.[26] As Kenney argues, the term "cartel" also implies a hierarchical organizational structure that drug networks may not possess.[27] PSIN is also superior to the term "drug-trafficking organization" (DTO) because drug networks are neither limited to trafficking illicit narcotics, nor are drugs always their primary source of profit.[28] Unfortunately, "profit-seeking illicit network" is a mouthful, and we have enough acronyms in our lives already. I will refer to PSINs as "drug networks" for the sake of simplicity.

Globalization and Illicit Networks

The rise of drug networks must be understood in the context of globalization, including the expansion of licit trade and the spread of technology. Illicit-network flows are a burgeoning area of study in international relations and comparative politics.[29] Globalization has meant increased international trade. Increased licit flows have allowed increased illicit flows to hitch a ride.[30] In turn, the power and profits of organized-crime actors has increased. In many ways these illicit flows predate states. States have simply attempted to superimpose their borders and their rules upon them.[31] In so doing, states have increased the profits of organized crime by increasing the risk premium paid for subverting state controls.[32]

In some cases, the very attempt of states to impose rules and regulations leads to the illicit flow itself. Drugs are a perfect example. The United States has pioneered an international drug prohibition regime with roots in the early twentieth century. The Richard Nixon administration (1969–74) declared a "war on drugs" that has lasted more than forty years, though in reality it began much earlier. While the Barack Obama administration has jettisoned the term, the policies of prohibition continue unabated at the federal level with increasing exceptions for states experimenting with medical and recreational marijuana,[33] and the United States has continued as the world's largest drug-consuming nation.[34] This has been particularly damaging for Latin America, which is the source and transit zone for much of the drug flow into the United States.[35]

The prohibition regime itself has driven drug prices up by creating what economists call a "risk premium" that increases profits and puts the market in the hands of organized crime.[36] Today we see this most potently in Mexican drug networks that took the place of Colombian cartels in the mid-1990s, following US–Colombian collaboration against the Medellín and Cali cartels. We have also witnessed the Felipe Calderón administration's militarized onslaught against the cartels result in Mexican drug networks shifting operations into Central America.[37]

This is known as the "balloon analogy."[38] As states pressure drug networks at one point, their operations expand in another, much like a balloon. The "cockroach analogy" is similar.[39] When one shines a light, cockroaches scatter to darker areas. For example, as the Calderón administration pressured Mexican drug networks, they moved their operations into Central America, a region poorly equipped to address the threat because of weak state capacity. Similarly, in Colombia two large drug networks were replaced by three hundred separate and highly specialized networks and cells, sometimes called *cartelitos*, that transported, processed, and provided protection in a highly sophisticated market.[40] None of these "successes" in combatting drug networks has resulted in reduced drug trafficking or flow. Even when the purity of one drug goes down, indicating a reduction of supply, drug networks simply adapt by moving to other products or by diversifying criminal activities.[41] A broader discussion of how to address the underlying political economic forces driving violent organized crime through alternative drug policies will be provided in the conclusion.

The Illicit-Networks Literature

The existing literature on illicit networks can be divided into three types: (1) works that focus on the internal structure of illicit networks, (2) those that focus on the domestic structure of the illicit network in relation to its host state, and (3) those that focus on the global structure of illicit networks, assessing their structure based on the changing structure of the international state system, often referred to as "globalization." The global-structure illicit-network literature often includes broader political economic arguments that take markets, sovereignty, and borders into account.

This tripartite division of the literature highlights the various levels of analysis in assessing illicit networks. By levels of analysis, I refer to the unit of analysis under study. Are we (1) assessing the smaller nodes involved in trafficking, such as smugglers, logisticians, cultivators, processors, producers, distributors, and protection rackets? Are we (2) assessing the "collusion," "confrontation," or "tolerance" of the state as part of the network?[42] Or are we (3) assessing the network structures under the conditions of globalization that have fueled the capabilities of illicit networks and the implications for international relations? While some scholars straddle these divisions, each has a theoretical focus placing them at one of these levels. I will briefly point to some of the ways these varying analyses can be synthesized to complement one another.

The first level of analysis assesses the internal structures of illicit networks. The central question in academia and policy debates following the attacks of September 11, 2001 (9/11), was whether "network forms of organization" in illicit networks convey some advantage over hierarchically organized states.[43] In addition, are illicit, or "dark," networks challenging states in new ways in an era of rapid technological improvement? How can states react?[44] Before we can answer those questions, we must understand what networks are.

Networks are conceptually defined as the space "between markets and hierarchies."[45] We can imagine a continuum. At one pole of the continuum is the ideal market with its perfect information: Buyers and sellers come together through the price mechanism, driven purely by the forces of supply and demand. One may associate this pole with the image of a bazaar. At the opposite pole, we can envision the perfect bureaucratic hierarchy, with many "layers of management,"[46] organizing vast resources toward singular goals that are not always addressed by markets. The image conjured might be of the Roman legion or even the highly bureaucratized US military with its many ranks or "layers of management."[47] Between these idealized poles, networks reside.[48]

Networks are relationships between "nodes" or "actors" that can reduce "transaction costs"[49] and resolve "collective action problems" "in the absence of central authority"[50] in both licit and illicit business.[51] For example, filial "networks of trust" can protect illicit networks from law-enforcement infiltration by the state or rival drug networks.[52] Some network theorists, such as Podolny and Page, reject the tripartite division of markets, networks, and hierarchies, arguing instead that hierarchies are simply highly centralized networks, while markets such as perfect "spot markets" are network nodes with no ties.[53] According to Podolny and Page, networks are defined as "any collection of actors $(N \geq 2)$ that pursue repeated, enduring exchange relations with one another and, at the same time, lack a legitimate organizational authority to arbitrate and resolve disputes that may arise during the exchange."[54] Illicit networks survive in an evolutionary and market-based fashion.[55] When a node is removed from the network, either another eventually takes its functional place, or the network restructures entirely to accommodate when sufficient profits are available. Nodes can be individual actors or organizations in networks.[56] Internally they can vary in their degree of hierarchy and be "tightly" or "loosely coupled" among each other.[57] However, in their relationships with other nodes in illicit networks, they tend to be loosely coupled.[58] Nodes and entire networks that do not adapt to exogenous factors, such as the challenge of states or other drug networks, are removed from the system to be replaced by more resilient networks in an evolutionary fashion.[59]

I view organizations as nodes within larger networks. For example, the AFO was a transport and protection node in a larger drug-trafficking and -distribution network of illicit narcotics spanning from the Andes to the United States and expanding into Europe. It has been, at various points, the central node of the network, not just geographically, but also relationally, commanding a dominant and central network position.[60] It can also be viewed as a network in and of itself with various cells functioning as nodes.

False dichotomies are drawn in the academic and policy worlds between networks and organizations. According to a 2006 Congressional Research Service report, "definitions of transnational organized crime often differentiate between traditional crime organizations and more modern criminal networks. Traditional groups have a hierarchical structure that operates continuously or for an extended period. Newer networks, in contrast, are seen as having a more decentralized, often cell-like structure."[61] Drug networks in Mexico can be characterized simultaneously by these descriptions of networks and organizations. First, while they exist for extended periods of time, they form, break, and reform relationships with other "cells," "organizations," or "nodes" to traffic drugs and engage in other criminal activities.[62] Second, drug networks have changing relationships with the Mexican state—another network node—depending upon the political party in power, the degree of democratic consolidation, and their ability to bribe officials.[63] Third, they organize themselves internally along network lines. While some Mexican drug networks such as the AFO had five or six layers of management, they were also decentralized in decision making and compartmentalized into cells. This bifurcation between networks and organizations makes little sense for the AFO and other drug networks.[64]

Arquilla and Ronfeldt have identified three ideal network "topologies" that they call "chain," "all-channel," and "star" networks.[65] The three network structures can challenge the state in different ways. Chain networks are networks in which each node is in contact only with the node before and after it in the chain. They are the most logical starting point for the development and inception of illicit networks and are empirically where most begin.[66] Over time, chain networks are consolidated into "star" or, as Kenney refers to them, "wheel networks" by "core nodes" that provide protection and enforcement services.[67] As Kenney and Williams argue, wheel networks are vulnerable to state attack because the state's coercive apparatuses can target their core nodes.[68]

In all-channel networks, all nodes are in communication with each other.[69] The all-channel network is not well suited to the illicit world because it lacks compartmentalization. Remove one node in the network and it becomes possible to discover the entire network. Thus, the all-channel network is more suited to the licit action of civil society groups that use technology to legally challenge democratic states through control of message and public opinion, rather than insurgencies or drug networks.[70]

Drug trafficking in Colombia provides the prototype for this process. The Medellín and Cali cartels consolidated into two large wheel networks during the 1980s and 1990s.[71] The Colombian state, in conjunction with the US military, dismantled the core nodes of these networks in 1993 and 1995, respectively.[72] The resulting Colombian trafficking model comprises smaller, specialized *cartelitos* more reminiscent of chain networks.[73] Recent reporting by InSight Crime and others have revealed that there may have been nodes in the Medellín market that may have provided dispute resolution post–Pablo Escobar, explaining how these decentralized networks operated with little violence.[74]

In wheel networks, a core node controls diverse cells that specialize in cultivation, processing, transport, and wholesale and retail distribution. Kenney assessed the smuggling aspects of the drug-trafficking business, which may explain his key finding that despite the description of these "cartels" by law enforcement as hierarchical and menacing, they were in reality very "flat," with only three or four "layers of management."[75] His earlier work also describes how wheel network core nodes can be easily targeted for removal by states such as the United States and Colombia. Thus, he argues that wheel networks, while efficient and profitable, may be vulnerable to attack.[76] This is particularly relevant in the Mexican context where the Calderón administration's kingpin strategy of targeting the heads of drug networks succeeds in disrupting them but increases violence because rival lieutenants fight for succession, rival drug networks perceive weakness and attack, and cells splinter to form their own networks. The same decapitation strategy that appears to have succeeded in reducing violence in Colombia has raised it in Mexico, though if the current government's homicide statistics are to be believed, violence may be plateauing.[77] And in this process an important question remains unanswered: Why does the state attack some drug networks rather than others?

At the second level of drug network analysis, scholars and analysts focus on the relationship between states and drug networks. Astorga and Shirk provide a three-part model for understanding state–drug network relations that they argue ranges from "collusive" to "tolerant," to "confrontational" as does Sabet.[78] Bailey and Godson provide "six lenses" for understanding the relations between organized crime and the state that at the highest level includes "state capture" by organized crime.[79] On the other hand, Arias points to the networked nature of organized crime, civil society, and the state in his work in Brazil.[80] My state-reaction argument makes a significant contribution to this portion of the literature by explaining why certain drug networks can establish "collusive," "tolerant," "symbiotic," or "capture" relationships, while others form "confrontational" relationships with the state, to quote the terms used by Lupsha and others.[81]

I am not the first to discuss the distinctions between territorial and trans-actional or trafficking-oriented business models. Reuter, publishing in 2009, has pointed to the distinction between transactional and territorial drug markets in Mexico,[82] using concepts likely drawn from MacCoun et al. in 2003 and Reiss and Roth in 1993.[83] Mazzitelli also distinguished between "*transportistas*" and "territorial" traffickers in Central America in his analysis of the effects of the penetration of Mexican drug networks such as Los Zetas.[84] Felbab-Brown has pointed to state-prioritized targeting for territorial drug markets over their transactional counterparts, and Kleiman has made a subtle and clever point about how consumer markets can be differentially targeted to reduce violence.[85] Bailey has distinguished between "transnational" and territorial or turf-oriented groups.[86] I do not use the transnational-versus-territorial distinction because some highly territorial drug networks such as Los Zetas are also transnational and maintain highly territorial business models in terms of extortion and taxation of legitimate businesses. My contribution here is to expand these typologies of transactional/trafficking versus territorial, apply them to in-depth, historical Mexican drug-network case studies, and put them into the context of risk, the state reaction, and resilience (which I measure through a unique proxy metric of organizational change following disruptive events).

At the broadest level of analysis in the illicit networks literature, we find authors such as Naím and Andreas. Both put forth arguments about illicit networks into the context of globalization. Naím empirically describes the rising threats of illicit networks as challenges to states and provides concepts such as "bright spots" and "dark masses" that describe where states are strong or weak in their struggles with illicit networks.[87] Andreas does the difficult work of putting illicit economies and globalization into historical context.[88] In *Border Games*, he described how illicit networks profit from subverting borders, while the institutions charged with protecting borders use them to justify more resources to combat illicit networks in a process of "escalation."[89] In more recent work, he elucidates how illicit networks contributed to US state formation, using the examples of smugglers in the American Revolution, among others throughout US history.[90]

The relationship of illicit networks to states is imperative to their survival. We should not exaggerate the threat of "flat" illicit networks to states.[91] This was common in the 1990s and the climate immediately after 9/11.[92] Scholars have since questioned the threat that illicit networks pose.[93] I concur and believe the answer is more complicated in that it depends upon the type of illicit network in question. Regardless of any organizational advantages networks may possess, states continue to have a preponderance of power and legitimacy in the international system vis-à-vis illicit networks. Mexico has a trillion-dollar economy, while total drug-network profits in Mexico are estimated at between $18 billion and $39 billion at their highest and most exaggerated.[94] While the state has other obligations such as social spending and cannot use all of its tax revenues in counternarcotics and security, sheer economic size, legitimacy, and the ability to share counternetwork capacity with other states all give states advantages in their struggles with illicit networks. Despite these advantages, some drug networks prove resilient, demonstrating the importance of the research question posed here.

Fieldwork

In addition to extensively researching archival court documents, media and government reports, and such, I conducted an academic year of fieldwork in Mexico City and Tijuana while building my historical case study of the AFO. While there, I conducted thirty-two in-depth interviews over the course of eighty hours with journalists, scholars, US and Mexican law-enforcement officials, civil-society leaders, businessmen, government officials, professionals, organized-crime victims, and, unintentionally, traffickers. Living in the region gave me a sense of the on-the-ground reality of Tijuana—a city whose level of drug-related violence was in the process of significant decline during my fieldwork.

I did not seek interviews with traffickers for numerous reasons. First, I was constrained by my Institutional Review Board proposal at the University of California, Irvine. Second, the California prison system budget made prison interviews impossible. Institutional Review Board personnel at UC Irvine warned me that due to budget constraints, the California prison system was not supporting research on prisoners and that approval would be unlikely. Third, safety was an obvious concern. Fourth, given compartmentalized networks, cell members may not know the structure of the drug network beyond their cell.

On the other hand, law-enforcement officials who have wiretapped hundreds of thousands of calls and radio conversations, interrogated former drug-network members, protected witnesses over decades, and collaborated across agencies and international borders may have a more complete historical picture of a drug network than even the cell members themselves. Anonymity was especially important for law-enforcement interviews. For example, if there were only three agents of a particular agency operating in a given locale in Mexico, mentioning their agency and area would narrow it down to three individuals, effectively destroying anonymity. I was extremely sensitive and cautious about what I included as a result. Building trust with law enforcement was critical and, as the empirical chapters will demonstrate, fruitful.[95]

My physical appearance may have impacted levels of trust in multiple ways while conducting fieldwork in Mexico. I am a white male of mixed European descent, and I appear Irish at first glance. I am an American who speaks Spanish with a slight accent, though better than the average *gringo*. I have blue eyes and do not blend physically in Mexico despite its racial diversity. Mexicans assume a *guero* (a light-skinned man) with blue eyes is foreign first and only allow the assumption to change based on the quality of the individual's Spanish. My Spanish is not good enough for that, though no Mexican would ever tell me so. Indeed, Mexicans were more understanding of my imperfect Spanish than many Americans would be of an accented English speaker. I am five-feet, ten inches tall, making me of average height in the United States but slightly tall in Mexico. I wear my hair in a short-cropped, almost military fade cut and keep my beard short and neatly trimmed.

I went to Tijuana for a preliminary research visit to get the lay of the land and establish research contacts. While talking to my landlord about my abode, I was bitten by his dog. Later, the owner told me that his thought during the incident was "Oh no! [Dog's name] bit the FBI agent!" Fortunately, the dog did not draw blood.

I was regularly accused of being a CIA agent. In one interview, this became a running joke for the subjects, which included a former politician, a former government official, and a businessman/politico. They joked that on my way to the bathroom, they would ask me to do a flip to see if a recorder would fall out. My protestations that I was not a CIA agent only emboldened their belief that I was indeed a spy. Finally, I told them that if I were a spy, I would have been able to pay them for the conversation, to which they laughed. One said, "You don't have to pay us. We always talk about this!"

Even my academic compatriots at Colegio de la Frontera Norte (COLEF), where I affiliated myself during fieldwork, were amiably suspicious. I went into the office of a Mexican researcher and friend to excitedly tell her about an intellectual breakthrough in my dissertation. She got a sad look on her face and said, "Nate, this is so disappointing. All this time I thought you were a CIA agent, but no CIA agent could fake being this excited about a dissertation."

I got the sense that the unintended perception that I was a CIA or other US federal agent did not hinder my interviews, especially in Tijuana. At this time in Mexico, there was a sense among much of the population that the Mexican government was too corrupt or inept to gather the kind of intelligence that was needed to fight Mexican drug networks. The Mexican population viewed the fact that the US government was taking an interest in Mexico with ambivalence. On the one hand, the US government could effectively combat the *narcos*; on the other hand, Mexicans feared the long-term consequences for sovereignty and were frustrated by US drug consumption and the flow of guns from the United States into Mexico. The latter views were more prevalent in Mexico City. Fieldwork allowed me to gain a rich understanding of these perceptions through firsthand experience and otherwise inaccessible interviews of people who had recently experienced the internecine conflict that was the focus of my case study.

Chapter Outline

In chapter 1, I present the conceptual framework of the state-reaction argument, which argues that the drug network–state relationship depends on the business strategy the drug network pursues. Business strategy can increase or decrease the drug network's risk, which in turn will lead to a stronger or weaker state reaction. The state reaction in turn determines the resilience of the drug network in varying ways, depending on the strength of state institutions vis-à-vis those of the drug network.

Chapter 2 provides the empirical case study of the AFO through the lens of the state-reaction argument. Critical junctures in the history of the drug network are identified, in addition to its varying network structures over the course of its history. It is a perfect case study because it was one of the first Mexican cartels to be targeted by the state and split along these trafficking-oriented and territorial lines. One survived; one did not.

Chapter 3 tells the story from the perspective of the state, detailing the resources and strategies it marshaled to combat the AFO. It is in reality the story of multiple states and multiple layers of government reacting to an illicit network. The United States as a consolidated democracy targeted the largely trafficking-oriented AFO of the 1990s early. For a series of historically contingent and structural reasons, including uneven democratization, Mexico joined that fight. The AFO was fragmented along its business-strategy fault lines into two rival factions. The chapter explains how the municipal police, federal troops, civil society, and rival networks joined forces to wipe out the territorial drug network led by Eduardo Teodoro García Simental, better known as "El Teo." The El Teo network can effectively be considered dissolved by mid-2010, though there have been reports of Los Teos (cells formerly affiliated with some of El Teo's lieutenants, such as El Muletas) continuing to operate in Tijuana.

Chapter 4 analyzes three minicases against the state-reaction framework. The cases analyzed using "structured focused comparison" are Los Zetas, Los Caballeros Templarios (CT), and the Sinaloa cartel. The analysis of these cases adds validity to the findings but also adds detail to the conceptualization of the dependent variable resilience and the organizational disruption proxy framework I use to assess it.

The conclusion applies the understanding and lessons learned from the AFO case study and the three minicases more broadly. As I will show, the AFO's story is a microcosm for the battle playing out across Mexico between territorial drug networks such as Los Zetas, insurgent-territorial networks such as the CT, and their trafficking-oriented rivals, the Sinaloa cartel. The state-reaction argument provides important lessons and predictions as to which drug networks will survive and thrive and which will be eviscerated. I will conclude with a discussion of the international drug-prohibition regime and its implications for the state-reaction argument.

Notes

1. For the earliest discussion found of transactional versus territorial DTOs in Mexico, see Reuter, "Systemic Violence in Drug Markets." Another reference to transactional versus territorial is quoted by an anonymous Mexican government official in "Outsmarted by Sinaloa." For earlier references of transactional violence, see Reiss and Roth, *Understanding and Preventing Violence*. Stratfor reports have also pointed to violent groups in relation to state targeting. Mazzitelli and Dudley separately point to the distinction between *transportistas* and territorial groups. This will be discussed further later. See "Outsmarted by Sinaloa"; Reuter, "Systemic Violence in Drug Markets," 277–79; Reiss and Roth, *Understanding and Preventing Violence*; Mazzitelli, "Mexican Cartel Influence"; Kilmer et al., *Reducing Drug Trafficking Revenues*; "Mexican Drug Cartels: Two Wars"; *Globalization of Crime*, 27–28; "Mexican Drug Wars Update"; "Mexican Drug Cartels: Government Progress"; Burton, "Mexico"; and UNODC, *Transnational Organized Crime in Central America and the Caribbean*.

2. Reuter, "Systemic Violence in Drug Markets."

3. The book draws excerpts heavily from my dissertation throughout: Jones, "State Reaction."

4. My conception of the state is heavily influenced by the work of Tilly, who views the state as a form of organized crime providing security in exchange for taxation, albeit in a more professionalized and legitimate fashion than organized crime. See Tilly, *Coercion, Capital, and European States*; Tilly, "War Making and State Making"; Skaperdas, "Political Economy of Organized Crime"; and Skaperdas and Syropoulos, "Gangs as Primitive States."

5. For a discussion of predatory organized crime, see Lupsha, "Transnational Organized Crime." For a discussion of alternative governance, see Clunan and Trinkunas, *Ungoverned Spaces*, introduction.

6. Clunan and Trinkunas, *Ungoverned Spaces*, introduction; Andreas, *Border Games*; Andreas, "Redrawing the Line"; Olson and Salazar, *Profile of Mexico's*; Williams, "Transnational Criminal Networks"; Sullivan, "Transnational Gangs"; Buscaglia, Gonzalez-Ruiz, and Ratliff, "Undermining the Foundations"; *World Drug Report 2010*; Raab and Milward, "Dark Networks as Problems"; Konrad and Skaperdas, "Market for Protection"; Williams, "Here Be Dragons."

7. Spruyt, *Sovereign State and Its Competitors.*

8. Territorial networks are most likely to engage in what Vanda Felbab-Brown refers to as "competition in state-making." Felbab-Brown, "Conceptualizing Crime as Competition," 55.

9. For a discussion of the predatory state metaphor, see footnote 4 in Olson, "Dictatorship, Democracy, and Development."

10. "Outsmarted by Sinaloa."

11. For an excellent elaboration of illicit network alliances in the Mexican context, see Chindea, "Fear and Loathing in Mexico."

12. Moore uses the phrasing "We're the lesser of evils." Moore, "Myth of a 'Good Guy.'"

13. In another example of both the US and Mexican governments operating along these lines, e-mails between private intelligence firm Stratfor and an anonymous Mexican diplomat referred to as "MX-1" suggested that the US and Mexican governments will respond heavily to drug-related violence in an effort to get Mexican illicit networks to negotiate among themselves to minimize violence. "Outsmarted by Sinaloa"; Conroy, "US, Mexican Officials Brokering."

14. Bailey, *Politics of Crime in Mexico,* 24.

15. George and Bennett, *Case Studies and Theory Development,* chap. 3.

16. Burnett and Penalosa, "Mexico's Drug War."

17. Kenney, "From Pablo to Osama."

18. Pachico, "Re-Emergence of Splinter Criminal Group"; Pachico, "Mexico Cartels Operate," 16.

19. Larano and Cuneta, "Philippines Says Drug Raid."

20. Pachico, "Mexico Cartels Operate"; Mazzitelli, "Mexican Cartel Influence."

21. Kenney, "From Pablo to Osama"; Sadiq, *Paper Citizens*; Van Schendel and Abraham, *Illicit Flows.*

22. Sadiq, *Paper Citizens*; Andreas, "Illicit Globalization"; Friman and Andreas, *Illicit Global Economy*; Van Schendel and Abraham, *Illicit Flows.*

23. Sadiq, *Paper Citizens,* 57–58.

24. Van Schendel and Abraham, *Illicit Flows*; Van Schendel, *Bengal Borderland.*

25. Makarenko, "Crime–Terror Continuum"; Asal, Milward, and Schoon, "When Terrorists Go Bad"; Raab and Milward, "Dark Networks as Problems."

26. The term "cartel" will only be used henceforth for the popularly used names of drug networks—for example, the Sinaloa cartel. "Drug network" will be the preferred term. For excellent discussions of the misuse of "cartel," see Lacey, "Drug Wars"; Cook, *CRS Report for Congress*; Sadiq, *Paper Citizens*; and Van Schendel and Abraham, *Illicit Flows.*

27. Kenney, *From Pablo to Osama,* 26; Kenney, "From Pablo to Osama."

28. Other terms often used to describe profit-seeking illicit networks include "terrorist organizations," "transnational criminal organizations" (TCOs), "clandestine transnational actors" (CTAs), "drug-trafficking organizations" (DTOs), "illicit networks,"

"dark networks," and "organized criminal groups" (OCGs). Cook, *CRS Report for Congress*; Andreas, "Redrawing the Line"; Bakker, Raab, and Milward, "Preliminary Theory."

29. Friman and Andreas, *Illicit Global Economy*; Sadiq, *Paper Citizens*; Arquilla and Ronfeldt, *Networks and Netwars* (see chapter by Phil Williams); Naím, *Illicit*.

30. Andreas, "Illicit Globalization"; Friman and Andreas, *Illicit Global Economy*; Andreas, *Border Games*.

31. Andreas, "Illicit Globalization"; Andreas, *Border Games*; Andreas, "Redrawing the Line"; Van Schendel and Abraham, *Illicit Flows*.

32. Andreas, "Illicit Globalization"; Andreas, *Border Games*; Andreas, "Redrawing the Line"; Van Schendel and Abraham, *Illicit Flows*.

33. Bloomekatz, "Federal Marijuana Memo."

34. Gray, *Why Our Drug Laws*.

35. Bagley, *Drug Trafficking and Organized Crime*.

36. Reuter and Kleiman, "Risks and Prices," 303.

37. Bowden, *Killing Pablo*; Bagley, *Drug Trafficking and Organized Crime*.

38. Bagley, *Drug Trafficking and Organized Crime*.

39. Ibid.

40. Garzón, *Mafia & Co*; Pardo, "Colombia's Two-Front War."

41. Bagley, *Drug Trafficking and Organized Crime*.

42. Astorga and Shirk, *Drug Trafficking Organizations*; Sabet, "Confrontation, Collusion and Tolerance."

43. Arquilla and Ronfeldt, *Networks and Netwars*.

44. Raab and Milward, "Dark Networks as Problems."

45. Thompson, *Between Hierarchies and Markets*; Arquilla and Ronfeldt, *Networks and Netwars*; Arquilla and Ronfeldt, *Advent of Netwar*; Arquilla and Ronfeldt, *In Athena's Camp*.

46. Kenney, *From Pablo to Osama*, 34.

47. Ibid.

48. Thompson, *Between Hierarchies and Markets*; Arquilla and Ronfeldt, *Advent of Netwar*; Wasserman and Faust, *Social Network Analysis*; Scott, *Social Network Analysis*.

49. Arrow, *Limits of Organization*.

50. Clunan and Trinkunas, *Ungoverned Spaces*.

51. Arquilla and Ronfeldt, *Networks and Netwars*; Arrow, *Limits of Organization*; Wasserman and Faust, *Social Network Analysis*; Podolny and Page, "Network Forms of Organization."

52. Arquilla and Ronfeldt, *Networks and Netwars*; Sadiq, *Paper Citizens*.

53. Podolny and Page, "Network Forms of Organization," 59.

54. Ibid.

55. Kenney, *From Pablo to Osama*.

56. Because this and many of the works in the illicit networks literature discuss the relationship of illicit networks to the state, they do not meet the strict requirements of social network analysis insofar as they compare across different units of analysis

stretching across what Everton calls the "micro," "meso," and "macro." For Everton these analyses might better be called "link analysis" instead of social network analysis. See Everton, *Disrupting Dark Networks*, 5.

57. Weick, "Educational Organizations."

58. Ibid.

59. Chabot, "Historical Case Study"; Weick, "Educational Organizations"; anonymous scholar, interview on network structures, School of Social Sciences, University of California, Irvine, 2008.

60. Kenney, *From Pablo to Osama*; Kenney, "Architecture of Drug Trafficking."

61. Wagley, *Transnational Organized Crime*.

62. In his writing on the network structures of Al Qaeda, Kahler focuses on Al Qaeda as a network of organizations rather than individuals. Kahler, *Networked Politics*, 104.

63. Ravelo, *Los capos*; Hernandez, *Narcoland*; Buscaglia and Van Dijk, "Controlling Organized Crime and Corruption," 8.

64. Steve Duncan (law-enforcement investigator [CA Dept. of Justice] focused on the AFO), interview by the author, San Diego, 2010.

65. Arquilla and Ronfeldt, *Networks and Netwars*, introduction.

66. Arquilla and Ronfeldt, *Networks and Netwars*; Arquilla and Ronfeldt, *Advent of Netwar*.

67. Kenney, *From Pablo to Osama*, 29.

68. Kenney, *From Pablo to Osama*; Williams, "Transnational Criminal Networks."

69. Arquilla and Ronfeldt, *Networks and Netwars*.

70. Ibid.

71. Kenney, *From Pablo to Osama*, chap. 1; Bowden, *Killing Pablo*.

72. Kenney, *From Pablo to Osama*; Bailey and Chabat, *Transnational Crime and Public Security*; Bowden, *Killing Pablo*; Arquilla and Ronfeldt, *Networks and Netwars*.

73. Garzón quotes a Colombian law-enforcement official calling them "baby cartels." Garzón, *Mafia & Co.*, 9.

74. Gurney, "Colombia Takes Down."

75. Kenney, *From Pablo to Osama*, 25.

76. Kenney, *From Pablo to Osama*; Kenney, "Architecture of Drug Trafficking."

77. This drop in homicides is debated and does not extend to disappearances, kidnappings, or cases of extortion. "Mexico's Drug War."

78. Astorga and Shirk, *Drug Trafficking Organizations*; Sabet, "Confrontation, Collusion and Tolerance."

79. For "state capture," also see Bailey and Godson, *Organized Crime and Democratic Governability*; Buscaglia, Gonzalez-Ruiz, and Ratliff, "Undermining the Foundations."

80. Arias, *Drugs and Democracy*, 49.

81. Lupsha, "Transnational Organized Crime"; Bailey and Godson, *Organized Crime and Democratic Governability*; Sabet, "Confrontation, Collusion and Tolerance"; Astorga and Shirk, *Drug Trafficking Organizations*.

82. Reuter, "Systemic Violence in Drug Markets."

83. Reiss and Roth, *Understanding and Preventing Violence*; MacCoun, Kilmer, and Reuter, *Research on Drugs–Crime Linkages.*

84. Mazzitelli, *Mexican Cartel Influence*; UNODC, *Transnational Organized Crime in Central America and the Caribbean*, 18.

85. Felbab-Brown, *Focused Deterrence*; Kleiman, "Targeting Drug-Trafficking Violence"; Kleiman, "Surgical Strikes."

86. Bailey, *Politics of Crime in Mexico.*

87. Naím, *Illicit.*

88. Andreas, "Illicit Globalization."

89. Andreas, *Border Games*, chap. 1.

90. Andreas, *Smuggler Nation.*

91. Kenney, *From Pablo to Osama*, 34.

92. Arquilla and Ronfeldt, *Networks and Netwars.*

93. Jones and Eilstrup-Sangiovanni, "Assessing the Dangers."

94. For a discussion of the exaggerated nature of various drug-profit statistics, see the following excellent reports written by RAND scholars such as Beau Kilmer addressing these issues: Kilmer et al., *Reducing Drug Trafficking Revenues*, chap. 5; Kilmer et al., *What America's Users Spend*; Kilmer, "Debunking the Mythical Numbers." See also Perkins and Placido, "Drug Trafficking Violence in Mexico."

95. See Chabot, "Historical Case Study," for a discussion of the value of law-enforcement interviews.

1

The State Reaction and Illicit-Network Resilience

ILLICIT NETWORKS INCLUDE INSURGENT networks such as Al Qaeda and the Islamic State in Iraq and Syria (ISIS), Mexican drug networks such as the Arellano Félix Organization (AFO), prison gangs such as the Aryan Brotherhood, and street gangs such as Mara Salvatrucha (MS-13).[1] These "dark networks" threaten the security of states by directly challenging state governance and flouting legal norms.[2] States have expended great resources attempting to combat these networks, to little avail.[3] How do they structure themselves to be resilient? How can they be dismantled? Why do states attack some illicit networks and not others?

An extensive literature identifies dark networks and "netwar actors" as threats to security. In this literature, network structure is identified as critical to understanding why these networks survive. Arquilla and Ronfeldt argue that "flatter," "headless," or "hydra-headed structures" will be more likely to survive because these structures are minimally impacted when leadership is removed.[4] Illicit networks face incredible threats to their survival and thus operate under highly risky conditions.[5] They compete with states that have the ability to arrest or kill leadership figures as a regular feature of business, and they face rival networks that have the ability to gather intelligence against them in the underworld.[6]

Understanding why states target some illicit networks over others requires an understanding of the state. I concur with Tilly's argument that "if protection rackets represent organised crime at its smoothest, then war risking and state making—quintessential protection rackets with the advantage of legitimacy—qualify as our largest examples of organised crime."[7] This analogy of the state as organized crime helps us to understand why some drug networks touch the state in such a tender spot.[8] It is the state that is meant to provide protection in exchange for taxation. This reality is key to understanding why some drug networks engender the wrath of the state more than others. While Gambetta argues this analogy is "facile" and "must be resisted," he goes on to say that "in analytical terms the state and mafia do indeed deal in the same commodity."[9]

For Gambetta that commodity is protection, and I argue in the same vein as Tilly that for society, the state's minimal duty is to provide this protection, not just from external threat as Tilly argues but from domestic challengers as well. The problem for Mexico is that by virtue of the nature of the international system it is internationally recognized as a state, giving it international legal sovereignty as Krasner would describe, but due to its weak state capacity and inability to seal borders—due in part to free-trade policies—it lacks a monopoly on force, legitimate or otherwise, in its territory.[10]

States maintain large potential economic advantages over drug networks but can only marshal those resources when the political will of the state and civil society is "galvanized."[11] Determining precisely when and why the state reaction becomes salient requires an understanding of illicit-network business strategies.

A Typology of Illicit Networks

I posit that there are three ideal types of illicit networks: (1) insurgent, (2) "transactional" or trafficking-oriented, and (3) territorial.[12] The first is characterized by insurgency, defined as a political movement attempting to overthrow a state through the unconventional use of force. Terrorist groups such as Al Qaeda that use terrorism as "a logic of action" are included in this type but so are more traditional insurgencies that use terrorism as "a method of action" while retaining their

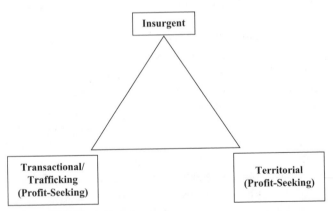

Figure 1.1   A Three-Part Illicit-Network Typology

Note: Author's figure draws on an interview with an anonymous Mexican government official (2010) and on Reuter, "Systemic Violence in Drug Markets"; MacCoun, Kilmer, and Reuter, *Research on Drugs–Crime Linkages*; Reiss and Roth, *Understanding and Preventing Violence*; "Outsmarted by Sinaloa"; and Mazzitelli, "Mexican Cartel Influence." See Mazzitelli for similar "transportista vs. territorial" concepts.

"mass base of support."[13] As Marks argues, the presence of political, religious, and ethnonationalist ideologies are useful characteristics in defining insurgent illicit networks, though ideology alone is insufficient.[14]

The relative importance of the political ideology must be evaluated in relation to the illicit network's profit-seeking activities. This can be done qualitatively and on a case-by-case basis, although quantitative metrics would be useful for an evaluation of each illicit network. The relative strength of various cells within the network—assuming it can be defined as a single network with a coherent identity—is also important to the evaluation of illicit networks as insurgent versus profit-seeking. My focus is not on insurgent networks but on profit seekers that make up the base of the triangular continuum shown in figure 1.1.

Explaining why the state reacts to insurgent networks is simple: It is directly challenged and threatened by insurgent violence. Insurgents seek to overthrow the state through violence that challenges the state's "monopoly on the legitimate use of force."[15] Insurgent networks attempt to delegitimize the state and limit the state's "domestic" sovereignty, calling into question its sovereignty.[16] Whether the state is democratic or authoritarian is irrelevant to a strong state response to an insurgency. Rather, the success of the insurgency will depend on its strength vis-à-vis the state. The state's relationship with networks primarily dealing with drugs is far more complex.

Two Profit-Seeking Drug-Network Types

The business strategy of profit-seeking drug networks can be divided into two ideal types: the trafficking-oriented and the territorial.[17] Drug networks can be viewed as being on some point on a continuum according to the proportion of their various activities in the network. No drug network perfectly embodies all of the characteristics, but some come very close. Network conceptions such as those described by Sánchez Valdéz show us how network nodes with different business models can network to distribute risk.[18]

The transactional or trafficking-oriented drug-network type focuses on the business of drug trafficking, emphasizes money laundering, uses sophisticated businessmen and college graduates, corrupts the state, minimizes violence, and maintains a low profile.[19] Its members hide their wealth behind front businesses and are the most difficult to study because they can appear entirely licit. At its extreme, a trafficking-oriented drug network is a single, "flat," trafficking or money-laundering cell with one layer of management.[20] I define trafficking-oriented in a similar vein to Reuter's "transactional" conception and Mazzitelli's conception of *transportistas* in Central America. These conceptions differentiate between criminal markets and groups that focus on the business of moving drugs over the control of territory and taxing those who pass through it via violent enforcement that they both refer to as territorial.[21]

Trafficking-oriented drug networks tend to use violence only to fend off or attack rival traffickers while avoiding the use of violence against the local population. Due to the need for specific trafficking routes, even trafficking-oriented drug networks may sometimes act territorially and maintain violent cells, but they do not typically extort the local population. When extortion is necessary, they focus instead on illicit actors or high-profile targets (wealthy individuals). They also focus on bribing higher levels of government such as the military and federal and state law enforcement. Conversely, territorial drug networks are more apt to keep local police on the payrolls. If the argument presented holds true, we should expect the arrest of illicit-network members to be more numerous among territorial drug networks that use teenagers as low-level extortionists and are unable to establish relationships with the state because of their violent territorial business strategies and limited profits. Further, trafficking-oriented drug networks or cells should be arrested at lower rates and would be more likely to bribe higher-level government officials.

A trafficking-oriented drug network may dominate a territory, but it does not make the bulk of its profit from the "predatory" "extraction" of that territory.[22] Rather, it profits from trafficking illicit narcotics through it. It may tax others for this service, but that taxation typically does not extend into the licit world. Drug networks that tax other networks for passing drugs over their territory are sometimes referred to as "toll-collector" drug networks.[23] This is an activity in between purely territorial and trafficking-oriented drug networks. Trafficking-oriented drug networks also assist licit businesses in exchange for *piso* (which translates to "the floor" and is another term referring to a tax). These are not only extortion schemes but also actual business services. These services include the provision of government permits, protection from predatory police officers, and business connections, among many other potential forms of assistance.[24]

During fieldwork I did find examples of what I could surmise were trafficking-oriented networks charging protection fees, but these could not be described as exclusively extortionist. In one interview, I spoke with a businessman who was contacted by a friend who knew "someone who could make his business grow." In exchange for a set monthly fee, the man promised useful business services such as the rapid facilitation of government permits that could take months through normal channels, the elimination of police harassment of drivers—a common problem in Tijuana—and many other services.[25] For trafficking-oriented networks, even protection fees involved real business-facilitating services and were not purely extractive. This is consistent with Gambetta's work on the subject of organized crime in Sicily and its ability to survive.[26] Trafficking-oriented networks, like traditional mafias and illicit networks, garner local support. For Gambetta this is about trust; in the case of Tijuana, this appeared to be about protecting the business from the very real predations of the state. The question then becomes, Is organized crime vested in the status quo of a predatory state for the purpose of maintaining the demand for the protection racket?

Trafficking-oriented drug networks are more likely to share territory with other trafficking networks. The research of Coscia and Rios mapping the presence of Mexican drug networks over time using large data demonstrates that drug networks often share territory. I argue that a more fine-grain analysis would likely find within this data that the drug networks that can coexist tend to be trafficking oriented or the trafficking-oriented cells within larger territorial networks. Two networks can conceivably share a road used to traffic drugs,[27] but, as we will see in the next section, the "predatory extraction" of wealth from a given territory is most profitable when combined with a monopoly on territory.[28] Thus, trafficking networks are more adept at establishing alliances with other trafficking networks and forming mutually beneficial relationships. Territorial drug networks, on the other hand, play a zero-sum game.[29] The violent externalities produced by trafficking-oriented networks occur in consumption states, but, as is a growing concern in Mexico, transit countries are becoming drug consumers as well.[30]

The Territorial Type

Territorial drug networks focus on the control of territory that can generate revenue through taxation, much like the state itself. Territorial networks may traffic drugs through their territory but may also rely on taxing other traffickers to use their *plazas* (drug-trafficking corridor) and taxing legal and quasi-illegal businesses through extortion and kidnapping. In the Mexican context, the taxing of drugs passing though the territory is sometimes referred to as "toll collecting" by scholars such as Guerrero Gutiérrez.[31] A purely toll-collecting drug network could be viewed as on the continuum between territorial and trafficking-oriented moving toward territorial as this activity increases in proportion to trafficking activities. Territorial networks diversify by engaging in activities such as kidnapping, human trafficking, firearms trafficking, extortion, taxing licit and illicit activities, prostitution, domestic distribution of drugs, and copyright piracy. Territorial drug networks tend to be more hierarchical because they must police their territories to prevent other smugglers from trafficking without paying the *cuota* (tax). Thus, they need more enforcers and managers. Their primary commodity is the control of taxable territory.[32]

Territorial drug networks are the most likely to try to establish themselves as what Olson calls "stationary bandits." A "roving bandit" plunders sporadically, but a stationary bandit establishes himself a monopoly on taxation in an area.[33] By minimizing anarchy and regularizing taxation, he can regularly plunder, improve his lot, improve the lot of the population, and even be incentivized to provide public goods.[34] Olson points out, "Even when there is a balance of power that keeps any one leader or group from assuming total control of a large area or jurisdiction, the leader of each group may be able to establish himself as an autocrat of a small domain."[35] Territorial drug networks attempt this in the context of the sovereign Mexican state, which in reality promotes anarchy and thus triggers a stronger state reaction. While Olson suggests that central powers unable to control these areas are better off making deals, I argue the legitimacy of the state in the modern democratic context would be harmed and therefore the state must focus on improving its strength and capability vis-à-vis the territorial drug network.[36]

The negative externalities of territorial drug networks are borne primarily domestically and locally through violence, extortion, weakened democratization, and eroded state capacity. Territorial drug networks also use violence to demonstrate that the state and/or rival drug networks lack control over territory and are incapable of governing. One way they do this is by arranging the bodies of their victims with *narco-mensajes* (notes left by drug traffickers) to convey messages to the local population, state agencies, and rivals.[37] Another way to signal the control of territory is through the use of what Sullivan calls "extreme violence," which may include crucifixions and other public displays of violence to send messages to rival traffickers and the local population.

A drug network's business strategy is structurally determined by its "comparative advantages in violence,"[38] number of enforcers, degree of hierarchy, local knowledge and relationships, ability to negotiate, business connections, and other characteristics of the individuals and cells that network comprises. Drug networks often cannot consciously choose business-strategy types (territorial/trafficking) because they have certain structural advantages or disadvantages that constrain their decisions. For example, the next chapter will illustrate how the El Teo network of the AFO tried to become more trafficking-oriented but, with heavy overhead and limited drug-source connections, was forced to continue kidnapping activities despite the societal backlash. The business strategy also has a "feedback loop" relationship with the degree of hierarchy in drug networks because the high number of enforcers needed to patrol territory requires more managers and therefore more degrees of hierarchy.[39]

Most large Mexican drug networks have a minimum of five layers of management and are central nodes in wheel networks, as described in the introduction.[40] Territorial drug networks tend toward higher levels of organizational hierarchy, while trafficking-oriented drug networks tend toward flatness (see figure 1.2). Although drug networks with the same level of hierarchy can be found choosing both business strategies, trafficking-oriented networks with high levels of hierarchy tend to be much larger in size relative to similarly hierarchical territorial networks. For example, the Sinaloa cartel is primarily trafficking oriented in character but uses many "go-betweens" to protect core members of the network. It could be argued to have a higher level of hierarchy. This is due to its vast size in comparison to other Mexican drug networks.[41] Trafficking-oriented illicit networks also tend to increase their degree of hierarchy in response to challenges from territorial networks, though it is a last resort necessitated by war.[42]

The most manpower-intensive need of territorial drug networks is enough enforcers, *halcones* (lookouts), and corrupted local police to control a given territory. Enforcers must be recruited and trained along disciplined, hierarchical, police, and military lines. They mimic the institutions from which they buy training—corrupted military, police, and state-trained mercenaries.[43] Trafficking-oriented drug networks increase their profits by limiting "overhead" by employing fewer but highly trained and sophisticated individuals and by using corruption to "rent" the hierarchy of the state apparatus. Where labor is needed, it can be contracted similar to Reuter's argument on "transactional" drug markets.

Most drug networks are hybrids between the territorial and the trafficking-oriented types, with varying proportions of each. The appendix presents a list of twenty-six key business-strategy characteristics of territorial versus trafficking-oriented drug networks.

Low Degree of Hierarchy "Flat"	Transactional Business Strategy
High Degree of Hierarchy	Territorial Business Strategy

Figure 1.2   Hierarchy and Business Strategy in Drug Networks

Note: Author's figure draws on MacCoun, Kilmer, and Reuter, *Research on Drugs–Crime Linkages*; Reuter, "Systemic Violence in Drug Markets"; Mazzitelli, "Transnational Organized Crime"; Kenney, *From Pablo to Osama*; Steve Duncan (law-enforcement investigator [CA Dept. of Justice] focused on the AFO), interview by the author, San Diego, 2010; and author's conversation with Prof. Tony Payan about organized crime structures in Mexico, Baker Institute, 2013.

Risk

This section defines risk and puts recent Department of Homeland Security (DHS) risk conceptions into the context of dark networks. While traditional definitions of risk have defined it simply in terms of the probability of an unwanted event and the impact of that event, the DHS and the academic literature created for it has developed a more comprehensive approach to risk. The DHS-extended definition of risk is "potential for an adverse outcome assessed as a function of threats, vulnerabilities, and consequences associated with an incident, event, or occurrence."[44] Mathematically, this translates into "risk [as] a function of threat, vulnerability, and consequence," or "$R = f(T,V,C)$."[45] This is an extended form of likelihood and consequence, as threat and vulnerability together constitute likelihood, with threat as the probability that something is tried. Vulnerability is the conditional probability that something occurs if it is tried. Threat and vulnerability combine to form the probability that something occurs—that is, likelihood. Threat, vulnerability, and consequence are often combined multiplicatively ($R = T x V x C$), but this can be problematic when the components are not independent of each other. This is a particular concern related to adaptive adversaries; the likelihood that terrorists will attack a site may depend on how much damage they can do and how likely they are to succeed. But while this generalized formula can be difficult to implement, it is conceptually sound.[46] Academics and experts at the National Academy of Sciences have evaluated the DHS risk framework as effective: "The basic risk framework of Risk = $f(T,V,C)$ used by DHS is sound and in accord with accepted practice in the risk analysis field."[47]

Scholars such as Kenney have written about risk in the context of dark networks and provide useful insights. However, to the best of my knowledge, none has yet applied new DHS conceptualizations of risk to dark networks. I intend to do so here by discussing the component risk variables of consequence, threat, and vulnerability and incorporating specific examples where the existing literature in addition to my own fieldwork has identified dark-network risk and dark-network risk-mitigation techniques. I will place special emphasis on the *threat* component because, as my state-reaction argument emphasizes, threat of state action against dark-network operations is their primary source of risk, and this is the best point at which to discuss the probability of state reaction to a dark network. Mixed throughout the discussion will be dark-network risk-mitigation techniques that will often address mitigating various risk components.

Risk must not be conflated with uncertainty, which is defined as the "degree to which a calculated, estimated, or observed value may deviate from the true value."[48] Uncertainty can refer to the estimated likelihood of an event or to the true value of consequences of a given event.[49]

Consequence

Our discussion of risk naturally begins with the consequence/risk component because avoiding the negative consequences of adverse events is the primary motivation for both governments and dark networks to minimize risk. C represents consequence of an adverse event, which in engineering conceptions corresponds to the "magnitude" of an adverse event.[50] In the context of a drug network, an adverse event can be the arrest or killing of key or nonredundant network members/nodes, the loss of major drug loads, the loss of key resources such as safe houses or weaponry, the freezing of money-laundering assets, bulk cash seizures, the loss of key territory, the loss of societal support and resources, and so forth. These consequences can be quantified financially in context (though I make no attempt to do so here) and in terms of their potential damage to the network and its "operational capacity," as Bakker, Raab, and Milward define resilience.[51]

Dark networks will sometimes use sacrificial lambs to mitigate the state response to a given activity, thereby reducing consequence and risk. Dark networks will sometimes accept a negative consequence in order to avoid a worse potential consequence. This can be viewed as similar to when a licit firm purchases costly insurance to minimize the consequences of bad outcomes and thereby reduce risk. When dark networks know a state reaction is pending, they will do everything in their power to mitigate the consequences of that reaction. Following the death of the archbishop of Guadalajara at the hands of AFO assassins, the AFO arranged payments to corrupt officials and the sacrifice of individuals involved in the crime and safe houses to placate the government reaction to the assassination.[52]

The use of "blind mules" to minimize the exposure of members to legal prosecution is also common. Blind mules are individuals who are tricked into working for drug networks, usually through an offer of lucrative pay for ostensibly legal work.[53] Drug mules do not necessarily have to be tricked, given a steady supply stemming from high wages relative to legal occupations.[54] The use of mules who are not members of the network is a common means by which to minimize risk. In some cases the loss of a successful and prolific mule can be costly and thus a source of risk, as was the case of the ninety-year-old mule for the Sinaloa cartel in the United States who was recently captured.[55] Nonetheless, as Kenney points out, mules are simply fodder and can be easily replaced.[56]

Threat

In this framework, threat is considered a component of risk, which focuses on the "probability" or "likelihood" that an adverse event is attempted or, in the case of natural disasters, occurs. While it is presented in terms of probabilities, the activities of an adversary are not actually probabilistic like a role of the dice. Instead, threat is a subjective probability of whether a hazard will manifest itself. In the homeland-security context, this can include thoughtful assessments of the likelihood of attacks, qualitative assessments of threats to critical infrastructure based on natural hazards, terrorism, and threats from dark networks more broadly.

But there is also a second meaning to threats, that of a "natural or man-made occurrence, individual, entity, or action that has or indicates the potential to harm life, information, operations, the environment, and/or property."[57] In this way, one can talk about the threat (likelihood of attack) of a threat (the bad actor). For drug networks, the greatest adversary and thus source of threat is the state both in terms of host state and foreign support states. This adversary has vast resources, which can be used to target the dark network in both a kinetic and nonkinetic fashion. Kinetic operations such as high-value targeting of key figures for death or arrest can eliminate leadership and, if the pace is sufficient, dissolve a network.[58] Nonkinetic operations can separate the dark network from the local population through psychological operations and support for the local population.[59] All of this can lead to reduced dark-network resilience.

The threat of the state to dark networks comes primarily in the form of kinetic operations and, as Sabet argues, a galvanized civil society response to specific types of crime such as kidnapping.[60] Understanding this threat and preemptively attempting to mitigate trafficking-oriented networks avoid high-risk activities. Territorial networks, being structurally unable to avoid these activities, attempt to mitigate the state response in various ways.

While this argument focuses on the threat of the state, rival drug networks may in some cases pose a great or greater threat to a drug network than the state. Trafficking-oriented drug networks have made strategic pushes into the plazas of territorial drug networks such as the Gulf cartel and Los Zetas, testing their resilience in addition to providing to the state intelligence against them. The threat of rival networks is part of the overarching high-risk environment created by the prohibition regime.

The trafficking-oriented business model has more capacity for maintaining "legitimacy," identified as an important resilience feature by Bakker, Raab, and Milward, because it does not target the local population.[61] Legitimacy can be gained by providing real business services in the context of protection of clients from the predations of corrupt state officials. It can also be purchased at the local level through the funding of churches, schools, roads, and social services and by providing employment to a large portion of the population. Further, cash give-aways are also effective in garnering local support. The pursuit of legitimacy also lends credence to the comparison of drug networks to insurgents. In this sense, the work of Bunker and Sullivan and of Sullivan and Elkus on criminal insurgency is illustrative.[62]

Authors such as Raab and Milward also identify "invisibility" as a critical feature of dark-network resilience. Invisibility also reduces the threat of state reaction because a powerful state response is impossible prior to state awareness of the existence of a dark network. They also identify "state capacity" as a critical factor in the reduction of the resilience of dark networks. This idea is similar to Kenney's discussion of the "force advantage" of the state and what I call the strength of state institutions and the state's "preponderance of power," which is similar to the international relations literature on hegemony and neorealism.[63]

Payoffs to corrupt government officials through "networks that span the state"[64] can be a mechanism for the reduction of risk via the reduction of threat and consequence. Corrupt officials can be used to minimize the threat of capture; to change the policy direction of the state, thus reducing threat to the network; or to provide information on rivals to recover seized resources and such. A specific instance where the AFO used a corrupt government official to minimize risk is documented in the Luz Verde indictment, as discussed in the next chapter. The indictment summarized wiretapped phone calls involving AFO members and the chief liaison officer of the Mexican government to the US government, Jesus Quiñones. The recordings detailed his abuse of power and protection of the AFO in exchange for payoffs.[65]

Vulnerability

Vulnerability is defined by the DHS as a "qualitative or quantitative expression of the level to which an entity, asset, system, network, or geographic area is susceptible to harm when it experiences a hazard."[66] Thus, while threat describes the probability an adverse event will occur, vulnerability conceptualizes the likelihood it will do harm if attempted. In the context of dark networks, vulnerability can refer to organizational structural vulnerabilities or features that make it susceptible to harm in the event of a disruptive event.

Hierarchy can make the network vulnerable to severe disruption if no succession mechanisms are in place.[67] I define hierarchy as Kenney does, in terms of layers of management, not necessarily in the context of social-network analysis metrics, such as various measures of centrality.[68] Further, a lack of compartmentalization—despite improving daily operational efficiency in terms of maximizing communications—can make the network vulnerable to kingpin strikes or the removal of "structural holes" or "intermediaries."[69] The use of communication devices such as cell phones and various Internet communication techniques can make a network susceptible to sophisticated signals intelligence used by states. Through security procedures, drug networks can mitigate these vulnerabilities. For example, drug lord Joaquín "El Chapo" Guzmán Loera used sophisticated network-structure procedures and multiple intermediaries to relay messages via a combination of BlackBerry messaging and retyping messages using Wi-Fi hotspots located in public cafés.[70]

As Kenney and others in the terrorist literature argue, dark networks often organize themselves in cellular structures to minimize the effects of the loss of any one cell. Cellular structures are a method of compartmentalization, which has been identified as a common dark-network and government strategy for minimizing the risk of the loss of any one individual or cell.[71] As the dark-network literature argues, there is a trade-off in the flow of information or network efficiency for security in compartmentalization. Given the high risk of the dark-network environment and the presence of powerful state adversaries, most networks are willing to make this trade but can only go so far. As Everton argues, it is the networks that find balance on this scale that appear most resilient.[72]

Drug networks will also employ strategies of cooperating with authorities against rivals to minimize their personal risk of prosecution by reducing sentences and mitigating the threat of rival traffickers. In the Mexican context they have also been known to employ strategies of pretending to cooperate with authorities by providing legitimate intelligence in an effort to secure short-term freedom and return to Mexico to continue operations.[73]

While financial risk is generally not a problem for large drug networks given the high profits created by the prohibition regime, large drug seizures or stolen drug or bulk cash loads can cause them major financial instability. Territorial drug networks such as the AFO with many enforcers have significant payroll obligations. When these are not met, enforcers may begin freelancing into activities such as kidnapping and extortion that draw state attention. Small drug networks with high levels of capitalization can reduce risk by using intermediaries—"cut-outs."[74] Those without capitalization are at much higher risk. In cooperative periods, traffickers are known to split loads and pool money for drug loads as a means by which to minimize or insure losses in the event of seizure.[75] Drug networks will also coordinate many simultaneous smuggling operations to overwhelm state capacity to respond, in a process Arquilla and Ronfeldt call "swarming."[76]

Bulk cash seizures or the targeting of money-laundering assets and properties by law enforcement and regulatory agencies such as the US Department of the Treasury can also impose significant losses (consequence) and thus increase of risk for drug networks. Drug networks launder their money through sophisticated money-laundering schemes and put assets in the names of trusted associates and family members. One example in the Mexican context concerns the assets of Juan José "El Azul" Esparragoza Moreno (considered third in command of the Sinaloa cartel, behind only Guzmán and Ismael "El Mayo" Zambada), who has likely faked his own death in an effort to avoid state attention. The Treasury Department is skeptical, as evidenced by its continued targeting of his family members' assets via Office of Foreign Assets Control (OFAC) sanctions.[77] This is what Raab and Milward would argue is a dark network attempting to reattain "invisibility." Unfortunately for El Azul, the high profile and long career of the Sinaloa drug network make this unlikely.

Resilience

Resilience is a burgeoning area of research for scholars and government agencies over the last decade. For example, the State Department's Mérida Initiative (2007), which provides funding to the Mexican government, added a fourth pillar in subsequent iterations, "building resilient communities," to what had hitherto been a security- and equipment-focused partnership. This increase in interest in resilience has likely been due to the recognition of its importance after Hurricane Katrina (2005) that the negative effects of natural disasters may not be accurately predicted for prevention or that the cost of prevention is so high that it may be prohibitive. Thus, there is a major focus on planning to be able to respond to major catastrophes. As Ross points out, resilience is often colloquially defined as the ability to "bounce back" from disruptive events.[78] Bakker, Raab, and Milward identify resilience in this way:

> We define dark network resilience as a dark network's ability to either remain operational in the midst of shocks or attacks ("robustness capacity") or to bounce back from untoward events by transforming itself over time ("rebounding capacity"). . . . We operationalize dark network resilience as a latent construct that can be observed from the network's pattern of operational activity. Operational activity refers to the extent to which a dark network is able to perform the tasks it was set up to accomplish, as demonstrated in observable activities (such as bombings, acts of sabotage, assassinations).[79]

Unfortunately, data on drug shipments—the optimal measure of resilience or "operational capacity" for a drug network—is not available, and thus I conceptualize resilience through organizational change over time in response to shocks and disruption. This is a proxy for operational capacity, which can be assessed qualitatively through expert interviews and archival research on both primary and secondary sources.

While Bakker, Raab, and Milward did apply their operational capacity variable to a dark network with heavy drug-trafficking operations (the Fuerzas

Armadas Revolucionarias de Colombia—the FARC), they focused on mea-
suring cultivation as a way to suggest that operational capacity had been unaffected. I cannot use this method here given that Mexican drug networks are not
focused on cultivation of drugs, though they do engage in some cultivation of
marijuana and opium poppy, because they are largely trafficking enterprises. It is
also interesting to note that since publication of their article, Colombia has been
surpassed by Peru as the world's largest coca producer.[80]

Resilience Definition

As Chabot argues, resilience is more than the ability to survive a disruptive
event.[81] For a drug network such as the AFO, daily operations are fraught with
the potential for disruptive events, including the arrest or death of key leaders.
Seizures of large shipments of drugs can also potentially bankrupt core nodes
of the drug network. Recognizing that disruptive events are a regular feature
of business for drug networks is insufficient. The circumstances under which
a drug network can be shown to be more or less resilient—even if only ex post
facto disruptive events—must be delineated.[82]

A significant weakness in the existing literature on resilience is that it is
treated as a simple either–or variable—the organization survived or it did not.[83]
In reality, resilience has variance. We intuitively know that there are levels of survival. An individual can survive a traumatic event but go into "shell shock," or
an individual can treat deep traumas as empowering events, as in the case of
cancer survivors who complete long chemotherapy treatments with hope and
optimism despite enduring traumatic pain and illness.[84] Resilience applies not
just to individuals but to networks and hierarchies as well.[85]

My contribution to the literature is to present a continuum-based typology of
levels of resilience. Figure 1.3 visualizes levels of resilience. A description of each
level of resilience follows.

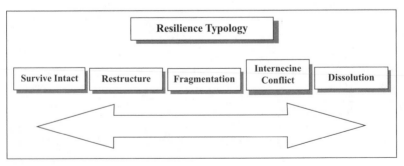

Figure 1.3   Resilience Typology

Note: Guerrero Gutiérrez has written extensively on kingpin strikes and fragmentation.
See *At the Root of the Violence.*

Survive intact. After a disruptive event, an organization can survive intact without requiring major reorganization to survive. This is the highest level of resilience and is what Bakker, Raab, and Milward would refer to as "robust." It is best characterized by *contingency theory*, which argues that organizations maintaining highly adaptive structures as a matter of standard operating procedure will be most adaptable and resilient.[86] Any reorganization following a disruptive event is thus a matter of course and does not constitute a major restructuring of the organization. Organizations with this type of amorphous design are highly adaptive but may be weaker in responding to predictable threats that a reified hierarchy could address efficiently.

Restructuring. The second-highest level of resilience is the survival of the network after a disruptive event that results in the need to restructure. This could be the drug network's internal recognition that, to prevent similar events from occurring in the future or to better withstand them, major network structural shifts must be made. Or it could be the result of a major disruption within the network. For drug networks, disruptive events can include the arrest or killing of key leaders. These events can force the rapid restructuring of drug networks or, worse, violent fragmentation.[87] This is consistent with Bakker, Raab, and Milward's definition of "rebounding."[88]

Fragmentation.[89] This is when a disruptive event leads to a splitting of the illicit network into smaller parts. This often occurs along lines of functional specialization—for example, smugglers and enforcers splitting from each other.[90] As the discussion on the split between the Gulf cartel and Los Zetas will show, fragmentation does not always immediately degenerate into conflict, which in that case took two to three years.

Internecine conflict usually results from fragmentation, though this is not always the case. These splits are usually violent as factions vie for control of the formerly unified whole. It is thus a lower level of resilience than peaceful restructuring.

Dissolution. Finally, drug networks can be *dissolved*. This can be the result of state action in which the entire node is systematically dismantled beyond recognition. "Wrapping up" entire networks can be achieved through complex, tedious, and sophisticated law-enforcement operations. As Privette points out, this has been carried out effectively against organized crime networks in the United States.[91] Dissolution is what Bakker, Raab, and Milward refer to as "nonresilient."[92]

Resilience of Drug Networks

Different drug-network structures and business strategies trigger different state responses. Territorial drug networks will be targeted by states and rival networks. Given that states continue to have "the preponderance of power in the international system"—based on economic size, moral legitimacy, and the resources of state allies, and assuming that to be true for the foreseeable future—the most critical factor for the survival of a profit-seeking illicit network is its relationship to its host state.[93]

In periods of profit drought, territorial drug networks must pay their large number of enforcers and therefore diversify criminal activities. The criminal activities they choose rely on taxing their territory through extortion and intelligence activities typically associated with mafias.[94] Territorial drug networks challenge the logic of the "territorially sovereign state" and create a societal backlash through extortion activities that prompt a strong state response. States tend to view territorial drug networks as common threats, increasing the likelihood that states will cooperate with each other and with trafficking-oriented drug networks against this challenge to the dominant unit of the international system.[95]

No illicit network is perfectly resilient, but some are more resilient than others. Mexican drug networks are highly resilient. They survive under tremendous pressure, but with the application of sufficient state resources they can crumble. The state rarely applies the necessary resources against illicit networks and is vastly limited in bringing resources to bear efficiently against them. The AFO is an example of this lukewarm reaction from the state. While the AFO has fragmented, its remnants may be more resilient than before due in part to their new business strategies that allow for a modus vivendi with other drug networks. They can also go largely ignored by the state because of their low-profile character, their low violence, and, resulting from higher profits, their ability to corrupt.[96]

The Life Cycle of Drug Networks

Figure 1.4 illustrates the inputs of the business strategies, the state's reaction to them, and the output of the level of resilience. It graphically illustrates how the state reaction is weak against trafficking-oriented networks, resulting in their

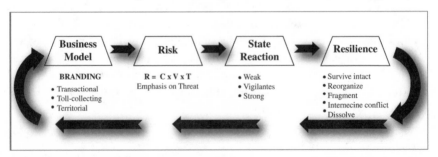

Figure 1.4   Life Cycle of Drug Networks

Note: Author's figure draws on fieldwork interviews, Canales, "Deadly Genius";
Guerrero Gutiérrez, *Security, Drugs, and Violence*; Reuter, "Systemic Violence in Drug
Markets"; and *DHS Risk Lexicon 2010 Edition.*

survival or reorganization. It also shows how the state reaction is strong against territorial drug networks, which results in fragmentation or dissolution. Whether the drug network survives intact, reorganizes, fragments, or dissolves depends upon the strength of state institutions and the strength of state reaction it triggers.

Oftentimes, large drug networks will contain both territorial and trafficking-oriented cells. When attacked by the state or rivals through "decapitation" or "kingpin strikes,"[97] they fragment along trafficking-oriented and territorial lines and the process begins anew. The surviving networks again trigger a powerful or weak state reaction based upon their new business strategies. The process continues in an evolutionary fashion, always favoring the trafficking-oriented when state institutions are strong.

The argument focuses on the host state's reaction to drug networks, though it alludes to the reaction of other affected states, such as consuming nations where the negative externalities of drug consumption occur. These states are also likely to react more aggressively toward territorial drug networks, depending upon how much territorial extortion characterizes the drug network's business strategy. Democratic transition and effective state institutions reduce the state's tolerance of drug networks. However, the absence of extortion and violence from trafficking-oriented drug networks means that even democratic and effective states will prioritize targeting territorial drug networks that focus their efforts on extortion, kidnapping, and murder. These violent activities also engender greater media and civil society responses, further galvanizing the state reaction.

In Colombia and Mexico, an expression has arisen to describe the corrupting strategies of drug networks: "*plata o plomo*," meaning "silver or lead." Will an individual be corrupted through money or killed by bullets? The expression refers to the inducing and deterrent strategies used in the coercive repertoire of drug networks. Due to the lack of high profit margins and the need to keep many enforcers or hit men on the payroll, territorial drug networks use violent threats more heavily. The more a drug network relies on extortion and threats, the more it threatens civil society and the state.[98] Those threats trigger a strong response that will reduce the resilience of the drug network if the state apparatus is strong enough to force it to restructure or dissolve it entirely by arresting or killing all of the network members. Trafficking-oriented drug networks that rely more heavily on *plata* are more resilient because they can corrupt the state or at least engender a weak response from it.

How Civil Society Galvanizes the State Reaction

Civil society can generate intense pressure and galvanize the state reaction to territorial drug networks because those networks victimize society and challenge the state's "monopoly on the use of force."[99] Even civil society agrees with Tilly's conception of the state as organized crime "with the advantage of legitimacy" when the state's "monopoly of force" is challenged.[100] The most basic function of the state is to provide security in exchange for taxation. While modern states are expected to do far more by providing social services,[101] the ability to provide the citizenry with protection is considered fundamental.[102]

The territorial business strategy directly victimizes society through the widespread application of extortion and kidnapping.[103] Territorial drug-network violence has several causes, including young and inexperienced leaders,[104] a comparative advantage in violence, and limited drug-source connections. Territorial networks have a comparative advantage in violence because they take with them low-level enforcers in their splits with larger drug networks. Their labor force, however, makes any decision to become more trafficking-oriented difficult because of payroll obligations. The networks are thus limited to the extortionist business strategy until they can establish strong money-laundering, trafficking, and political contacts.

Once territorial drug networks enter a trafficking corridor, conflict with other drug networks becomes inevitable because of their attempts to monopolize and control the territory. The violence resulting from intra- and inter-drug-network conflict creates an intolerable situation for society by increasing homicides, kidnappings, and extortion cases. Civil-society networks pressure the state to react against territorial drug networks because they perpetrate the violent "high-impact crimes" that victimize civil society. The violence is likely to be highly localized along trafficking corridors, but homicide rates and media attention force national and local governments to react. When extortion and kidnapping reach into the lower middle class, professional class, and political elite, a critical mass of civil society is achieved. It is civil society that exerts strong pressure on the state and forces it to react.

Many victims of kidnapping and extortion are state employees, officials, and leaders, as well as local businessmen and professionals. This, too, increases the state's propensity to respond to territorial drug networks. Networks that are antagonized by territorial networks may support the state and civil society and are likely to be trafficking networks, the members of which are likely to be closely socially tied to public officials and civil society in "networks of complicity" and genuine "social networks" of "trust" and "kinship."[105] Lubricating this relationship between the state and trafficking networks are the high capital reserves and incredible profit-to-membership ratios they possess. These profits allow trafficking networks to corrupt the state apparatus. Trafficking networks are incentivized to provide intelligence to the state's coercive apparatus against their territorial rivals.[106]

As territorial networks become increasingly aware that the coercive apparatus has turned against them, they are likely to become ever more desperate in their attempts to change the relationship. With limited profits and capacity to corrupt, they often turn to violence, such as terrorist bombings against the police and members of the military. This further galvanizes the state, civil society, and trafficking networks in a coercive response against territorial competitors. Having only violence in their management-skills toolbox, territorial networks rely on the threat and actuality of terrorist bombings against the police and extreme violence against the population to cow both groups into submission. With the full might of the coercive apparatus, the state, rival networks, and even foreign governments against them, territorial networks suffer from reduced resilience, resulting in fragmentation, internecine conflict, or dissolution.

The only situation in which territorial drug networks appear to be resilient is when the state is sufficiently weak and the networks are sufficiently strong to supplant the state. This is rare but possible, as in Central America, where the small states of the region must combat drug networks that developed in much larger states. If, hypothetically, a state is so weak that it verges on failure or is failed, then a territorial drug network might serve as a viable "alternative governance structure."[107]

The strength of state institutions and the level of democratic consolidation are critical to understanding the state reaction. Effective state institutions and increased democratization have ameliorative effects on the state's ability to control organized crime, though sometimes democratic transition can pose difficulties in the state-organized crime relationship. Effective states, especially effective democracies, have less tolerance for illicit networks of any kind and are also more likely to reach across state borders to target drug-network leadership. This is politically feasible because the public in consolidated democracies supports strong anticrime efforts and is particularly willing to act aggressively and violate other states' sovereignty when national security is threatened through acts such as the killing of their law-enforcement agents.[108] State bureaucrats in all states are also more likely to increase and institutionalize cooperation with foreign-state counterparts when threatened by violent traffickers, thus increasing the diffusion of democratic values at the bureaucratic level.[109]

It is important to understand interstate cooperation against drug networks because it explains why states maintain the preponderance of power in the international system despite threats from illicit networks. States such as Mexico have large GDPs and potential tax bases to fund their own coercive apparatuses to mitigate drug networks.[110] Unfortunately for the modern state in its competition with illicit networks, it also has multiple, competing obligations, such as providing education, infrastructure, and basic social services.[111] This results in a situation where drug networks have greater resources to direct toward intelligence and combating government efforts than states have to combat them. This situation changes, however, when the state reaction is galvanized to fight drug networks.

Rival Illicit Networks as an Alternative Explanation

A counterargument to my state-reaction argument of drug-network resilience is that rival drug networks may be more effective at destroying other drug networks than states are. This is certainly relevant to Mexico, where levels of violence correlate strongly with inter-drug-network warfare. Inter-drug-network conflict has also been high where there is a strong state military presence in Mexico. This could be explained by the fact that governments are likely to send the military to areas that have high levels of violence already. It could also be explained by the fact that the military and police target drug-network leadership figures, which creates power vacuums and exacerbates violence as rival drug networks vie for power.[112] Drug networks often defeat their rivals by successfully allying themselves with the state. We observe trafficking-oriented drug networks corrupting the state and directing the state's wrath toward territorial rivals.[113] Thus, my state-reaction argument addresses rival illicit networks' effect on resilience through the inclusion of trafficking-oriented drug network corruption and provision of underworld intelligence to the state as factors that magnify the efficacy of the state's reaction against territorial networks.[114]

Conceptual Implications of the State Reaction to Illicit Networks

If territorial drug networks are less resilient because of the state's reaction to them, then trafficking-oriented drug networks will tend to survive and will be lacking in political agenda other than what is necessary to meet their business needs. The surviving trafficking-oriented drug networks will have grafted themselves into the state apparatus and created areas of "dual sovereignty" within the state, largely in areas related to law enforcement, trafficking routes, and money laundering.[115] Where the size and strength of these networks is sufficient and the ability to accumulate resources in core nodes of wheel networks is sufficient, drug networks will influence national, as well as local, politics. The ability to combat these illicit networks will have less to do with military capability than it will have to do with improved judicial and penal institutions and other aspects of the legal system associated with consolidated democracies. The profit concentrations of trafficking-oriented illicit networks allow them to fund political campaigns and insert themselves into the political system.[116]

To recapitulate, states and territorial drug networks are enemies because they are so much alike. They are territorial, hierarchical, resilient, prone to violence, and funded by taxation. Thus, states will target territorial drug networks first, thereby reducing their resilience. Territoriality leads to the "diversification of criminal activities," such as extortion, kidnapping, oil theft, and retail drug sales, all of which increase societal pressure on democratic states to eliminate the threat.[117] A societal backlash reduces territorial drug-network intelligence-gathering capabilities and weakens them vis-à-vis the state and other illicit networks.

Periods of fragmentation and confrontations with the state speed up the process of "natural selection" between trafficking-oriented and territorial drug networks. When illicit networks fragment along their lines of functional specialization, the result is warring territorial and trafficking-oriented factions.[118] Young, inexperienced leadership will often choose to meet violence with violence and will face an ever-increasing threat from the state.[119] If territorial networks are strong enough, they will be able to withstand the onslaught of the state and provide a viable "alternate governance structure" if the state is weak.[120] Generally, this will not be the case, given that states such as Mexico can bring impressive resources to bear against territorial networks when properly motivated.

Trafficking-oriented drug networks will not emerge from these conflicts unscathed but will have increased cooperation with the state through corruption and new tactics focused on "lying low."[121] The surviving trafficking-oriented drug networks may even have increased profits, as they have reduced their enforcer-squad ranks and renewed their focus on the trafficking of illicit commodities and money laundering. They are more resilient than territorial drug networks particularly when state institutions are strong because they challenge the state less and are more capable of corrupting state institutions to carve out a modus vivendi with the state and other drug networks.[122] On the other hand, territorial drug networks are typically larger, more hierarchical networks that are more capable of directly challenging the state's "monopoly on the legitimate use of force."[123] They are thus the most threatening to the state and are least resilient when state institutions are strong. Unfortunately for states, institutions are often weak in developing nations and during democratic transitions. However, vulnerable states are often assisted in their efforts to police borders and combat illicit networks by stronger states.[124]

It must also be understood that the territorial and trafficking-oriented strategies are ideal types, and most profit-seeking illicit networks contain varying elements of the two models. Thus, understanding these illicit networks must be achieved by assessing the available data on their behaviors and structures and by assessing how strongly they correlate to these typological models. The next

chapter assesses the AFO as a historical case study, tracing its business strategies, risk-mitigation techniques, and resilience to illustrate the state-reaction
argument.

Notes

1. Chabot, "Historical Case Study"; Andreas, "Redrawing the Line"; Raab and
Milward, "Dark Networks as Problems."
2. Naím, *Illicit*; Raab and Milward, "Dark Networks as Problems"; Bakker, Raab,
and Milward, "Preliminary Theory"; Kenney, *From Pablo to Osama*; Asal, Milward, and
Schoon, "When Terrorists Go Bad"; Roberts and Everton, "Strategies for Combating";
Everton, *Disrupting Dark Networks*.
3. Manwaring, *Contemporary Challenge*; Manwaring, *Street Gangs*; Manwaring,
"New" Dynamic.
4. Arquilla and Ronfeldt, *Networks and Netwars*; Arquilla and Ronfeldt, *Advent of
Netwar*.
5. Kenney, *From Pablo to Osama*; Bakker, Raab, and Milward, "Preliminary Theory";
Raab and Milward, "Dark Networks as Problems."
6. Kenney, *From Pablo to Osama*; Kenney, "Architecture of Drug Trafficking"; Bailey
and Chabat, *Transnational Crime and Public Security*.
7. Tilly, "War Making and State Making."
8. I am indebted to Prof. Tony Payan for the use of the "tenderspot" metaphor. Conversation with Prof. Tony Payan on organized crime structures in Mexico at the Baker
Institute for Public Policy, Houston, Texas, 2013.
9. Gambetta, *Sicilian Mafia*, 2.
10. Krasner, *Sovereignty*, 3–4.
11. Sabet, "Confrontation, Collusion and Tolerance."
12. "Outsmarted by Sinaloa"; Creechan, "Cartels, Gangs"; Reuter, "Systemic Violence in Drug Markets"; Mazzitelli, "Mexican Cartel Influence." I look forward to the
further theoretical development of business-model and organizational structure as it
relates to Mexican organized crime from Prof. James Creechan based on his 2014 Latin
American Studies Association presentation.
13. Tom Marks, interview by the author at the Center for Hemispheric Defense
Studies, 2007, National Defense University; Marks, "Counterinsurgency."
14. Marks, interview, 2007.
15. Weber, *From Max Weber*.
16. Krasner, *Sovereignty*, 3–4.
17. The observation of the different business strategies is attributed to an unnamed
Mexican government source in a recent *Economist* article, "Outsmarted by Sinaloa";
Reuter, "Systemic Violence in Drug Markets."
18. Sanchez Valdéz, *Criminal Networks and Security Policies*.

19. Ideal types are a staple of political science. The most famous example in political science is Weber's use of typologies to describe where legitimacy is derived. He argued that all authority was provided by some combination of three types—"charismatic," "legal," and "traditional." No individual case would perfectly fit this model, as they were "ideal types" like Plato's "forms." Ideal types are nonetheless useful for understanding sources of authority or, in this case, business strategies and their different implications for governance. Weber, *From Max Weber*; "Outsmarted by Sinaloa."

20. Kenney, *From Pablo to Osama*.

21. Reuter, "Systemic Violence in Drug Markets"; Mazzitelli, "Mexican Cartel Influence"; UNODC, *Transnational Organized Crime in Central America and the Caribbean*.

22. For theoretical discussions of predation and extraction by organized-crime groups, see Lupsha, cited in Bailey, *Politics of Crime in Mexico*, and in Bunker and Sullivan, "Cartel Evolution Revisited."

23. Guerrero Gutiérrez, *Security, Drugs, and Violence*.

24. Tijuana businessman, interview by the author, Tijuana, 2011; Gambetta, *Sicilian Mafia*, 28 and 277.

25. Ibid.

26. Gambetta, *Sicilian Mafia*.

27. Coscia and Rios conducted impressive organized crime research using data mining techniques and mapping. Coscia and Rios, *Knowing Where and How*.

28. Olson, "Dictatorship, Democracy, and Development."

29. Jones, "Monopoly of Force"; Chindea, "Fear and Loathing in Mexico."

30. "Growing Drug Abuse in Mexico."

31. Guerrero Gutiérrez, *Security, Drugs, and Violence*.

32. Tilly, *Coercion, Capital, and European States*; Tilly, "War Making and State Making."

33. Olson, "Dictatorship, Democracy, and Development."

34. Olson, *Power and Prosperity*, 7–8; Olson, "Dictatorship, Democracy, and Development."

35. Olson, "Dictatorship, Democracy, and Development," 573.

36. Olson, "Dictatorship, Democracy, and Development."

37. Booth and Fainaru, "Widespread Oil Theft."

38. Konrad and Skaperdas, "Market for Protection."

39. Easton, *Framework for Political Analysis*; Klotz and Lynch, *Strategies for Research*.

40. US law-enforcement official, telephone interview by the author, 2010; Steve Duncan (law-enforcement investigator [CA Dept. of Justice] focused on the AFO), interview by the author, San Diego, 2010.

41. Marosi, "Flying High"; Marosi and Ellingwood, "Mexico Drug War."

42. For example, the Sinaloa cartel recruited very heavily from local gangs and significantly increased its size to battle the Juarez cartel and its armed wing La Linea for control of the Juarez plaza. "Mexico Security Memo November 10, 2008"; Associated Press, "Mexico Says."

43. For a discussion of institutional isomorphism, see Peters, *Institutional Theory*.

44. *DHS Risk Lexicon 2010 Edition*, 27.

45. National Research Council of the National Academies, *Review of Approach to Risk Analysis*, 2.

46. I am indebted to my colleague Dr. Russell Lundberg for his edits and suggestions in this section on risk and dark networks. *DHS Risk Lexicon 2010 Edition*.

47. National Research Council of the National Academies, *Review of Approach to Risk Analysis*, 11.

48. *DHS Risk Lexicon 2010 Edition*, 38.

49. Following the logic of my argument, as territorial business models increase the likelihood that the state will attack a dark network, uncertainty about such attacks goes down while risk of such attacks increases. *DHS Risk Lexicon 2010 Edition*.

50. I am indebted to my panel chair Karl Sorenson at the International Studies Association and the American Political Science Association's ISAC–ISSS joint conference in Austin in November 2014 for his observation on this point and provision of engineering conceptualization of risk. Jones, "Resilience and Destruction."

51. Bakker, Raab, and Milward, "Preliminary Theory."

52. I am indebted to my colleague Dr. Russell Lundberg for his advice on the risk section. Chabot, "Historical Case Study"; Caldwell, "Cartel Secrets"; Caldwell, "Cold-Blooded Killers"; Caldwell, "Captured."

53. Mason, "Blind Mules"; Smith, "'Blind Mules' Unknowingly Ferry."

54. Kenney, *From Pablo to Osama*.

55. Dolnick, "90-Year-Old Drug Mule."

56. Kenney, *From Pablo to Osama*.

57. *DHS Risk Lexicon 2010 Edition*, 36.

58. Everton, *Disrupting Dark Networks*.

59. Ibid.

60. Sabet, "Confrontation, Collusion and Tolerance."

61. Bakker, Raab, and Milward, "Preliminary Theory."

62. Gambetta, *Sicilian Mafia*, 28 and 277; Bunker and Sullivan, "Cartel Evolution Revisited"; Sullivan and Elkus, "State of Siege."

63. Waltz, *Man, the State, and War*, x; Waltz, *Theory of International Politics*; Mearsheimer, *Tragedy of Great Power Politics*; Keohane, *After Hegemony*.

64. See Sadiq, *Paper Citizens*, for the concept of networks that span the state.

65. "Indictment: United States vs. Armando Villareal Heredia et al."

66. *DHS Risk Lexicon 2010 Edition*, 38.

67. Privette has a discussion of the importance of hierarchy and succession mechanisms. Privette, "Organized Crime in the United States."

68. Everton, *Disrupting Dark Networks*; Kenney, *From Pablo to Osama*.

69. Burt, *Structural Holes*; Everton, *Disrupting Dark Networks*.

70. Keefe, "Hunt for El Chapo."

71. Kenney, *From Pablo to Osama*; Arquilla and Ronfeldt, *Networks and Netwars*.

72. Everton, *Disrupting Dark Networks*; Kenney, *From Pablo to Osama*; Arquilla and Ronfeldt, *Networks and Netwars*.

73. Duncan, interview.

74. Dorn, Oette, and White, "Drugs Importation."

75. Duncan, interview.

76. Arquilla and Ronfeldt, *Networks and Netwars*, introduction.

77. "'Treasury Sanctions Mother-in-Law.'"

78. Ross, *Local Disaster Resilience*, 6.

79. Bakker, Raab, and Milward, "Preliminary Theory," 35.

80. Bakker, Raab, and Milward, "Preliminary Theory"; Corchado, "Mexican Drug Cartels"; Romero, "Coca Production Makes a Comeback"; McDermott, "4 Reasons Why Peru Became."

81. Chabot, "Historical Case Study."

82. Ibid.

83. Ibid.

84. Ibid., 35–37.

85. Chabot, "Historical Case Study."

86. For a discussion of contingency theory, see Rothstein, *Afghanistan and the Troubled Future*, chap. 3.

87. Arquilla and Ronfeldt, *Networks and Netwars*.

88. Bakker, Raab, and Milward, "Preliminary Theory," 36.

89. Williams and Guerrero Gutiérrez separately discuss fragmentation and its role in increasing violence. I define it slightly differently here as a division that may not immediately lead to conflict, while their definitions of fragmentation are more akin to the internecine conflict in the next section. Williams, "Illicit Markets"; Guerrero Gutiérrez, *At the Root*.

90. I am indebted to Prof. Raúl Benítez Manaut for an early conversation about this point of the split along functional lines of specialization, during which he confirmed some of my own thoughts on the matter. Splintering or fragmentation can lead to an increase in violence in multiple ways. First, rival members vie for power. Second, rival networks perceive weakness and attack. Third, new networks cannot operate based on the "reputation for violence" once maintained by the original networks. The original network—for example, Cosa Nostra in the United States—oftentimes does not actually have to kill because the threat of violence is credible. This requires the reestablishment of a reputation for violence, which can increase violence. Further, violence may be advertised in more shocking and dramatic ways in an effort to establish the reputation. Central nodes of trafficking wheel networks are often characterized more as protection rackets than smugglers. Pablo Escobar was not a clever entrepreneur adapting new trafficking and smuggling methods. Rather, he coerced other entrepreneurs into his network as they discovered new routes and methods. He can be credited with providing new resources to empower these smuggling cells by offering access to his airstrips, etc., but

he was not the originator of smuggling techniques. See Schelling, *Arms and Influence*, for credible threats. See Reuter, "Systemic Violence," page 279, for reputation enhancement. See Williams, "Illicit Markets," page 324, for reputation for violence.

Privette, "Organized Crime in the United States"; Sabet, "Confrontation, Collusion and Tolerance"; Bowden, *Killing Pablo*.

91. Privette, "Organized Crime in the United States."

92. Bakker, Raab, and Milward, "Preliminary Theory," 36.

93. Waltz, *Man, the State, and War*; Waltz, *Theory of International Politics*.

94. Resa Nestares, "Los Zetas."

95. Spruyt, *Sovereign State*.

96. Duncan, interview.

97. Kingpin strikes or decapitation strikes are defined as the removal of leadership figures through arrest or killing by the state. Kingpin strategies migrated to counternarcotics from military special operations, where it was referred to as high-value targeting (HVT) in the late 1980s. Dudley, "Bin Laden"; Orama, "U.S. Military Evolution," 20–21.

98. Bowden, *Killing Pablo*.

99. Weber, *From Max Weber*; Sabet, "Confrontation, Collusion and Tolerance." My argument and findings in fieldwork are consistent with the work of Sabet, which also identified civil society as playing a role in galvanizing the local response to the El Teo faction. Numerous interviews with municipal police officers and civil society leaders in my research confirmed this finding. Sabet, "Confrontation, Collusion and Tolerance"; Bailey, *Politics of Crime in Mexico*; Jones, "Unintended Consequences."

100. Tilly, "War Making and State Making."

101. Benson, "Review of *The Sicilian Mafia*," 218.

102. Tilly, "War Making and State Making."

103. Sabet, "Confrontation, Collusion and Tolerance"; Bailey, *Politics of Crime in Mexico*, chap. 4.

104. Felbab-Brown, "Stemming the Violence."

105. Scott, *Social Network Analysis*, introduction; Sadiq, *Paper Citizens*; Everton, *Disrupting Dark Networks*; Krebs, "Uncloaking Terrorist Networks."

106. Sadiq, *Paper Citizens*.

107. Clunan and Trinkunas, *Ungoverned Spaces*.

108. One example of a drug network killing a state law-enforcement official is the 1985 killing of Enrique Camarena, which triggered a powerful response. That US reaction resulted in the dismantlement of the Guadalajara cartel or the loose federation that had dominated Mexican trafficking. Shannon, *Desperados*.

109. Allison, *Essence of Decision*.

110. Jones, "Applying Lessons"; Gonzalez-Ruiz, "Public Safety in Mexico."

111. Buscaglia, Gonzalez-Ruiz, and Ratliff, "Undermining the Foundations."

112. Escalante Gonzalbo, "Homicidios 2008–2009"; Guerrero Gutiérrez, *At the Root*.

113. We also observed the Cali cartel's coordination with the Colombian government against the Medellín cartel in 1993. I am indebted to Prof. John Bailey for pointing out this important point. Bowden, *Killing Pablo*.

114. Burnett and Penalosa, "Mexico's Drug War"; Burnett and Montagne, "On the Trail "; "Sinaloa Drug Cartel Said."

115. Clunan and Trinkunas, *Ungoverned Spaces*, sec. Desmond Arias; Grayson, *Mexico: Narco-Violence*.

116. Interestingly, corruption can actually provide a check against trafficker's ability to buy elections. Government contracts in Mexico are typically much larger than the actual cost of the contract. A portion of the markup is then used to fund political campaigns in an effort to garner more contracts. In this fashion, it is government money that funds elections and mitigates the effects of drug money on the political process by decentralizing the sources of corruption. Tijuana businessman, interview by the author, Tijuana, 2011; Arias, *Drugs and Democracy*.

117. Kidnappings in Mexico became so widespread that they included "virtual kidnappings" in which territorial drug networks or independent kidnapping cells/networks that had not kidnapped anyone called victims and claimed to be holding a friend or family member. They attempt to extort a smaller ransom as rapidly as possible, sometimes in as little as fifteen minutes. Kidnapping of doctors and engineers (middle-class professionals) in Tijuana became so rampant by 2008 that the city's doctors threatened a strike. Lacey, "At Least 6 People Abducted"; Conery, "Mexican Drug Cartels."

118. Prof. Raúl Benítez Manaut, conversation with the author, Tijuana, 2009.

119. Vanda Felbab-Brown, interview by the author on Mexican drug cartels, Washington, DC, 2010.

120. Clunan and Trinkunas, *Ungoverned Spaces*.

121. Duncan, interview.

122. Astorga and Shirk, *Drug Trafficking Organizations*; Felbab-Brown, "Violent Drug Market"; Felbab-Brown, *Shooting Up*.

123. Weber, *From Max Weber*.

124. "Al Día: Merida Initiative"; Danelo, "New Approach "; "Cable Viewer"; Cook, Rush, and Seelke, *Merida Initiative*; Lacey, "Report Says U.S. Fails"; Johnson, "Merida Initiative."

2

The Arellano Félix Organization's Resilience

THE ARELLANO FÉLIX ORGANIZATION (AFO) was considered one of the most powerful illicit networks in Mexico in the late 1990s.[1] In the first decade of the twenty-first century, it lost nearly all of its first-generation, top-level leadership figures to arrest or death. It fragmented into a short but bloody internecine conflict that challenged the Mexican state at a time of high narco-violence.[2] The historical context of the AFO is critical to understanding its business strategies and resilience over time. I will apply here the conceptual framework developed in the previous chapter to the empirical case study of the AFO to demonstrate how it changed its business strategy toward the transactional drug-network type and how the territorial splinter network was dissolved by the reaction of the state.[3] Throughout I will discuss how the territorial business model increased risk and state attention while the transactional or trafficking-oriented model reduced it. [4] To give the case study structure, I will identify four distinct phases in the AFO's history: the Pax Padrino phase, the territorialization phase, the dismantlement phase, and the restructuring phase.[5]

The First Phase: Pax Padrino

The Arellano Félix family consisted of seven sons and four daughters in the Mexican cities of Badirguato and Culiacán—the capital of the state of Sinaloa and widely considered the heart of Mexican drug trafficking.[6] According to Grayson, "five of [the sons] (Francisco Rafael, . . . , Benjamín, Ramón Eduardo, and Francisco Javier) dedicated themselves to smuggling clothing and electronics before entering the drug trade."[7]

Drug trafficking in Mexico in the 1980s was a highly transactional, "loosely coupled federation,"[8] led by Miguel Ángel Félix Gallardo, who was known as "El Padrino" (the Godfather) and was the head of the Guadalajara cartel. In the 1980s, the Arellanos were small traffickers operating under the Guadalajara cartel umbrella in Tijuana. Gallardo was adept at managing volatile personalities such as Rafael Caro Quintero, who had developed a marijuana empire in Sinaloa and Sonora. With high-quality sinsemilla marijuana, Caro had created vast, productive, and profitable fields in the deserts and mountains of Mexico.[9] The Arellano Félix brothers have incorrectly been rumored to be the nephews of Miguel Angel Félix Gallardo, the most important Mexican trafficker of the 1980s. According to my US law-enforcement interviews and an interview of Gallardo himself conducted by a journalist in Mexico, Gallardo is not uncle to the Arellanos and is from another region altogether, as many academics such as Grayson and journalists have argued.[10]

The relationship among Mexican traffickers was cooperative during the 1980s and can be described as a Pax Padrino, or "Peace of the Godfather."[11] Three primary factors contributed to this peaceful period among traffickers: (1) a corrupt Dirección Federal de Seguridad (DFS)[12]; (2) an authoritarian ruling party, Partido Revolucionario Institucional (PRI), capable of making credible long-term promises to traffickers; and (3) the managerial capabilities of Miguel Ángel Félix Gallardo.[13]

First, high-level Mexican government officials were corrupted, thus making the Mexican state and security services highly complicit in the drug-trafficking business. The DFS was notoriously corrupt. This allowed it to mediate conflict among traffickers and thereby have a pacifying effect on levels of violence in Mexican drug trafficking.[14] This high-level state protection made the drug trade extremely lucrative and, for the most part, peaceful. In reality, it was the DFS that controlled traffickers. The DFS divided trafficking in Mexico among territories and appointed the traffickers that would control the various regions.[15]

Second, the PRI and the DFS, as institutions of the one-party state, could make credible, long-term reciprocal promises to traffickers because they were not subject to losing power in democratic elections. This period represented a "Pax Mafiosi" between the state and drug networks in Mexico.[16]

During this period, the Arellanos did not possess a monopoly on the Tijuana plaza but were considered major traffickers working with Jesús "El Chuy" Labra Avilés, who would become their chief adviser. The Arellanos arrived in the Tijuana area in the 1980s and were immediately accepted by Tijuana high society. They created a mystique around trafficking that lured the children of Tijuana's wealthy elite into their employ as "narco-juniors." They recruited attractive, affluent youths with dual citizenship because they could cross the border with minimal inspection, thus minimizing risk. Even if they were arrested, the risks and consequences were minimal. If the narco-juniors were arrested with a limited amount of cocaine, prosecutors strapped for resources simply would not prosecute, and their parents were in denial. They wanted to believe their children's front businesses were legitimate.[17] Young people in the 1980s in Tijuana remember seeing the Arellano brothers Ramón and Benjamín in the most upscale night clubs where they would buy young patrons drinks and recruit them into trafficking and enforcing for the organization.[18] Many joined not out of economic desperation but for the excitement and glamour of the criminal lifestyle.[19]

Mexican trafficking in this phase was small in terms of the number of individuals involved and did not require heavy firepower or large enforcement apparatuses because it could rely on the state for protection and the mediation of intercartel disputes. Traffickers such as Félix Gallardo of Guadalajara, Amado Carrillo Fuentes of Ciudad Juárez, Chapo Guzmán of Sinaloa, the Arellano Félix family of Tijuana, and Caro Quintero of Sonora were so cooperative in this period that they would pool money to buy large loads of cocaine and share in the profits.[20] In this period the federal government, through its relationship with Miguel Ángel Félix Gallardo, controlled traffickers in a hierarchical fashion.[21]

The ability of Gallardo to manage personalities and maintain a Pax Mafiosi meant that while the Mexican trafficking superstructure aligned under him was "hierarchical" and "centralized,"[22] the individual organizations were internally flat.[23] The business strategy in this period was almost entirely transactional, given the cooperative nature of the business and the collusion and controls of state authorities.[24] Traffickers did not need to employ many enforcers in this period because they contracted the security services of the state.[25] Fewer enforcers meant fewer managers, and thus drug trafficking in this era was a fairly nonhierarchical affair.

The Death of Enrique Camarena

The brutal torture and killing of the US Drug Enforcement Agency (DEA) agent Enrique "Kiki" Camarena in 1985 put incredible pressure upon the Mexican government. The killing of a US law-enforcement agent was an exception to Gallardo's transactional business strategy, which tried to minimize violence and attention from the state. The DEA lobbied the White House and other US government agencies such as Customs to take a hardline position with the Mexican government on Camarena's death. It also pressured the Mexican government to actively and genuinely cooperate in the investigation. As it became apparent that Camarena was unlikely to be found alive, pressure was applied to the Mexican government to find his body.[26]

The US government began car-by-car searches of vehicles from Mexico at the US border with the stated desire of finding Camarena. In reality, the intent was not to find Camarena but to shut down the border by slowing traffic to a grinding halt. This put incredible pressure on American and Mexican businesses along the border. This policy could not be maintained indefinitely on either side of the border due to domestic political demands in the United States and pressure from the Mexican government, which viewed the shutdown as punitive. It did, however, send an important message to Mexican traffickers. Shutting down the US border would hurt the pocketbooks of Mexican traffickers who would be unable to piggyback their illicit cargo through the border's legal channels. Targeting US law enforcement operating inside Mexico would be met with a strong state reprisal on multiple fronts. The political and economic ramifications for traffickers and the Mexican government would be too great and too disruptive.[27]

The Second Phase: The Territorializing of the AFO

The territorializing phase of the AFO was marked by its independence from other Mexican drug networks and its increase in numbers of "enforcers" to meet new challenges. It moved from a transactional and "loosely coupled" coalition with other Mexican drug networks to an independent, violent, mixed transactional–territorial and internally hierarchical model.[28] The rise in territoriality would be driven by conflict with rival networks and the increased importance of "toll collecting" in the business model.[29] The territorializing phase ended when US–Mexican joint law-enforcement efforts began to effectively dismantle the first generation of AFO leadership in the 2000s.

The Fall of the Godfather (First Critical Juncture)

In 1989, Miguel Ángel Félix Gallardo was arrested, tried, and placed in a maximum-security prison for his complicity in Camarena's death. By 1991, he had been moved to La Palma prison, where he could no longer continue to run his operations via cell phone.[30] This "critical juncture"[31] marks the end of the Pax Padrino period and the beginning of the "territorializing" period for the AFO. Varying accounts suggest that Gallardo called a meeting of major traffickers in Acapulco and divided the territories among his lieutenants.[32] He instructed them not to fight among each other and to continue cooperating. Recent prison interviews with Gallardo contradict this claim.[33] He and others suggest the lieutenants divided the territories into plazas themselves. My interviews with Mexican law-enforcement officials indicated that the most likely explanation is that the DFS had already divided the territories and that the AFO's increased territoriality was a natural result of the removal of Gallardo as leader and the dismantlement of the DFS following US demands.[34] Under the new arrangement, traffickers would pay each other a cuota to traffic through each other's plaza.[35] This would serve as the beginning of the increase in hierarchy, territoriality, and violence among the Mexican drug networks.[36]

The Tijuana territory was supposedly given to Jesús "El Chuy" Labra Avilés.[37] In reality, Benjamín Arellano Félix was the strategic head of the organization, with El Chuy as his chief adviser and Ramón Arellano Félix as the enforcer of the family.[38] Joaquín "El Chapo" Guzmán Loera received the nearby Mexicali trafficking corridor in addition to Sinaloa, his traditional area of control.[39] This would later become a source of tension between Guzmán and the Arellanos.[40]

Conflict with Héctor "El Güero" Palma

While the epoch under Gallardo was largely cooperative, this transitional period planted the seeds for later conflict. Héctor Luis Palma Salazar, called "El Güero" for his fair skin and light eyes, was a major trafficker from Sinaloa working under Gallardo. In 1989, likely after Gallardo's arrest, he decided to strike out on his own to maximize profits with Chapo Guzmán, another Gallardo lieutenant. Gallardo, likely in coordination with the Arellanos, sent a Venezuelan trafficker named Clavel to infiltrate Palma's organization.[41] Clavel seduced Palma's wife, then forced her to remove $7 million from bank accounts before cutting off her head and sending it to Palma. He also threw two of Palma's children off a bridge in Venezuela. Palma aligned himself with Guzmán, who would later form the Sinaloa cartel.[42] As we will see, the conflict between the Arellanos and Guzmán and his allies would become one of the dominant factors contributing to the territorialization and paramilitarization of Mexican drug networks following the loss of state support.

Conflict with Joaquín "El Chapo" Guzmán Loera

Almost immediately upon the AFO taking control of the territory, there was conflict between the Arellanos and Chapo Guzmán. There are varying accounts as to what precipitated it. They include the Arellanos charging too much tax to pass through their territory, the discovery of a secret Guzmán tunnel in Arellano territory for which taxes had not been paid, one of Guzmán's lieutenants running off with Benjamín's sister Enedina Arellano Félix (which brothers considered a statutory-rape situation), the killing of a drunken Guzmán lieutenant who tried to enter an Arellano family party and was shot by one of the Arellano brothers, and others. Regardless of the source of the conflict, by 1991 there were tit-for-tat killings between Guzmán and the AFO.[43]

The Arellanos and Guzmán attempted to reconcile their differences at a meeting in Puerto Vallarta in November of 1992. Following the meeting, Ramón Arellano Félix, Francisco-Javier Arellano Félix, David Barron Corona, and Ismael "El Mayel" Higuera Guerrero went to Christine's Disco, where they came under attack from Guzmán's enforcers in the early morning hours. Benjamín Arellano Félix was not there because he was at a hotel with his wife and family. Fortunately for the AFO leadership present, they were in the bathroom when the attack began. Logan Street Gang member and AFO bodyguard Barron Corona protected the brothers with suppression fire while they escaped through an air-conditioning duct. Francisco Javier Arellano Félix went one direction while Ramón, Barron, and El Mayel went another. From the roof, the three returned fire and jumped to the ground, where they encountered a rival assassin armed with an AK-47. The three had only one bullet left between them. Barron Corona killed the assassin with it, and the three escaped.[44]

The critical juncture of the imprisonment of Gallardo was the "precondition" for a new, increasingly territorial AFO business strategy in the newly anarchic environment of Mexican drug trafficking. However Guzmán's attempted assassination of the Arellanos at Christine's Disco was the precipitant for change.[45] Following this event, Benjamín and Ramón decided to actively increase their enforcement squads, realizing they would have to prepare for war against all other drug networks in Mexico. They were now in conflict with traffickers based in Sonora, Juárez, and Sinaloa. They needed more enforcers, more bodyguards, and the ability to defend their lucrative territory against encroachment.[46]

They also needed an extremely good intelligence system to be able to find clandestine traffickers and force them to pay cuota. Failure to pay this shipping tax would result in death and/or torture. The Arellanos killed in ways designed to terrorize other networks and signal a reputation for violence.[47] By doing this in select and brutal ways, they increased profits by forcing traffickers moving through their territory to pay them. They continued to emphasize transactional business-strategy elements. They trafficked large amounts of cocaine and marijuana into the United States and developed sophisticated money-laundering fronts. In this period, both transactional and territorial business strategies coexisted, with the transactional largely controlling the territorial, though the territorial was gaining in importance.

In David Barron Corona, the Arellanos had an important link to two major US criminal networks that served as important recruitment sources for enforcers. Barron grew up in the Logan Street Gang in San Diego and was also a member of the prison gang known as the Mexican Mafia or La Eme. He served a three-year prison term in the Federal Correctional Institution (FCI) Arizona following his 1987 arrest for burglary and possession of an M-16. He was also convicted of drunk driving in 1990. He maintained positive relations with the prison gang by sending money orders to his fellow gang members and was also a highly prized member of La Eme because of his links to the AFO, which were viewed as a lucrative source of revenue for the gang.[48] When asked by Ramón and Benjamín Arellano Félix to find enforcers, he recruited heavily from his street and prison-gang affiliations, using a family member as an intermediary because he could no longer pass back and forth across the border because of US law-enforcement surveillance and his immigration status.[49]

The men Barron recruited were trained as enforcers for the AFO by foreign mercenaries, including one from Syria referred to as "El Iraqui," and by corrupted members of the Mexican military and police in camps in the mountains outside of Tijuana. The new AFO enforcers were paid $500 per week and told to be ready to kill on a moment's notice. They were paid significantly more for successful missions.[50] These enforcers became the territorial wing of the AFO in Tijuana in the 1990s.[51]

Many have attributed the arms buildup in Mexican drug trafficking to the Gulf cartel's recruitment of Los Zetas from a former military special operations

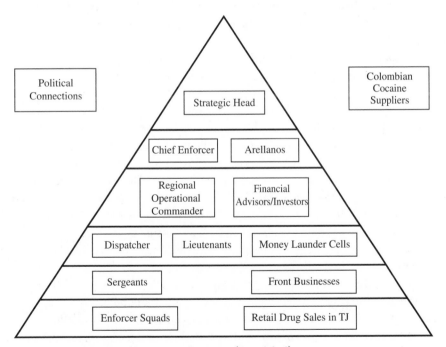

Figure 2.1   The AFO's Structure after 1991 (Simplified)

Note: Author's figure based on extensive in-depth interviews and archival research. Duncan, interview; *Harrod, Scharf and Ziegler*; Bergman, "Drug Wars: Interviews"; Blancornelas, *El cártel.*

unit in the late 1990s.[52] In reality, this trend occurred in every major Mexican drug network by the mid-1990s due to the competition for lucrative plazas. The trend was especially pronounced within the AFO because of its early conflict with El Chapo Guzmán of Sinaloa and other drug networks.

The AFO's increase in enforcer squads required the training of such person-nel by corrupted military, police, and foreign mercenaries and the creation of a system to manage a large compartmentalized network. The AFO is a powerful case of mimicking the state.[53] Mexican drug networks learned their territorial-ity from the state. The DFS organized them along territorial lines in the 1980s, and when it could no longer mediate between them, drug networks purchased training from the state through mercenaries and corrupted state military and law-enforcement officers.[54] In this fashion, the AFO adopted policies, standard operating procedures, and tactics from the Mexican state and even from other states, through its use of foreign mercenaries.

The mimicry of police structures by the AFO is logical, given the peculiar nature of drug trafficking in Mexico and, in particular, the northern bor-der states of Mexico. Mexico's comparative advantage in drug trafficking is intrinsically linked to the control of plazas. The AFO controlled the most lucrative plaza on the southern US border—the San Ysidro crossing into San Diego.[55]

Mexican drug networks, particularly in the border region, increasingly became territorial entities. For the AFO following the Pax Padrino phase, the most important functions of the drug network became the ability to defend and police the lucrative plaza from the external threats of rival traffickers, especially Chapo Guzmán. "Toll collecting" can mean taxing the commodity as it moves through the plaza, or it can also involve the purchasing of transportation ser-vices.[56] Further, an array of services can be purchased, including transportation, trafficking, safe houses for the product, and so forth. The plaza also had to be policed to control low-level smugglers who might traffic on behalf of other drug networks or independent freelancers. The inability to prevent small smugglers from operating without paying a tax to the AFO would encourage others to do the same and erode the AFO's profits and the legitimacy of its control over the illicit market in its territory.[57]

A reputation for violence and brutality would bring to the network a certain number of smugglers who are willing to pay taxes without being captured. Thus, brutal public killings are a highly effective and "rational" short-term, "low-cost" strategy to cow the population and low-level smugglers into cooperation.[58] However, a reputation for violence is irrelevant if the drug network cannot also establish a reputation for catching freelance smugglers and make rapid decisions on how they should be treated.[59]

The Dispatcher

To prevent freelance smuggling, the AFO developed enforcer squads with access to rapid communications and exceptional intelligence. It established a radio system, replete with a centralized dispatcher, and structured its network in an ingenious fashion to maintain security yet guarantee the flow of needed information. Lack of coordination was a fundamental difficulty in patrolling a territory with a compartmentalized network. If a smuggler is captured with drugs freelancing in AFO territory, he might truthfully claim he is trafficking on behalf of another cell of the AFO. The AFO enforcer squad that has discovered him has no way of knowing whether or not the other enforcer squad actually exists, unless they happen to know the squad sergeant personally.[60] Further, they don't know if an agreement has been made between the smuggler and the enforcer cell or if the smuggler is lying to them.[61] This was a classic "information vs. security" problem, in which the functioning of the network could come into conflict with the risk of network damage due to attack from rivals and the state.[62]

To address this problem, the AFO used radio communications on rotating frequencies to a central dispatcher, who could call the rest of the drug network cells. If the smuggler was "vouched for" by someone in the drug network and was determined to be paying taxes already, it would have been a bad business decision to execute him. If he was not vouched for, a decision had to be made whether to execute him for trafficking through AFO territory or to annex him into a taxable smuggling cell of the organization. These decisions could be made in twenty minutes or less. In this fashion, the AFO blended compartmentalization with centralized command-and-control through advanced technology. This structure remained stable in the 2000s when US law enforcement, through the radio surveillance of Operation United Eagles (fall of 2003 to August 14, 2006), counted fifteen hundred names called over AFO frequencies. Most of the people whose names were heard over the radios simply disappeared, implying that they were killed.[63]

Nowhere is the AFO's learning from the state more powerfully demonstrated than in the use of police codes over their radio-communication frequencies. The AFO used standard police radio codes for their communications, and also had orders to kill.[64] All their communications were coded, in that all persons and locations had nicknames or cartel codes. These codes were not particularly sophisticated in that they did not necessarily rotate frequently and were understood over time by law enforcement. However, the limited coding of proper nouns would at least slow and confuse Mexican and American law-enforcement surveillance over the short term, without making communication among network members so cumbersome that business could not be conducted.[65]

Figure 2.1 demonstrates the AFO's increase in hierarchy to five or six layers of management with the addition of the territorial business practice of patrolling territory. It also illustrates the central role that enforcer squads and the dispatcher played in the drug network. The level of compartmentalization found in terrorist networks such as Al Qaeda would be problematic in a drug network such as the AFO that must patrol a plaza with independent enforcer-squad cells.[66]

The above description of the AFO territorial structure is based largely on US law enforcement specializing in prosecuting the AFO. Anonymous interviews of Mexican law-enforcement officials described the structure very differently: a flat AFO with only three layers of management, which was based on the *capitalismo* (capitalist profit motivation) of transactional trafficking.[67] My interpretation of the varying results is that both US and Mexican law enforcement are correct in their assessments of the AFO in this period—they were simply focused on different portions of the same network. The Mexican prosecutors were targeting high-level Mexican traffickers: the Arellano family and close associates. US law enforcement, having more contact with US street gangs with AFO connections, built many of their cases against high-level traffickers based on intelligence from the territorial cells of the AFO. Because transactional cells dominated the territorial cells of the AFO in this period, violence was minimized, and the Mexican state was not as threatened by the AFO as it would be a decade later.

The AFO's business strategy was focused on drug trafficking and used interesting risk-mitigation strategies. Some of those who trafficked through their territory described the Arellanos as reasonable businessmen, though it should also be noted that their use of random violence in social settings was problematic for them and engendered many enemies.[68] For those trafficking through their territory, protection services and fees were established. If one trafficked through their territory and a load was lost, it was possible that the Arellanos would give people chances to make up for lost loads.[69] Allowing individuals to work off lost loads increased the likelihood of cooperation, trust, and getting their money back. It also reduced the likelihood that traffickers would try to cheat them and sneak loads through their territory. Failure to work off the load was, however, punished severely, and as the discussion of the territorial patrol apparatus described, getting caught smuggling in the Arellanos' territory without their permission was also punishable by death. There was an expectation that if a load was lost to state authorities, legal documents showing the police had taken the drug shipment should be produced.[70] This mitigated the likelihood of an individual stealing from the network. With the help of the Arellanos and other traffickers, it was also possible to buy back seized drug loads from authorities. The Arellanos were successful in corrupting state authorities. Even when federal authorities were rotated through an area regularly, the Arellanos would make sure they were introduced to the incoming commander, usually by the existing commander who was likely to be on their payroll. This allowed them to penetrate the state apparatus and was made possible by high profits from drug trafficking.[71]

Traffickers in this region regularly minimized risk by maintaining surveillance on the state security apparatus where it could not be corrupted, particularly in relation to US law enforcement. They broke large drug loads into smaller packages to minimize the consequence of losing any single load to seizure. They used decoys to divert state law-enforcement attention from real drug loads. It is even reported that they purchased insurance that would pay out in the event of a lost load.[72]

In some ways, as the United Nations Office on Drugs and Crime (UNODC) report *Transnational Organized Crime in Central America and the Caribbean: Threat Assessment* argues, territorial networks face lower risk because they can subcontract risky drug trafficking to other groups.[73] This may mitigate the risk of capture, but given the Arellanos typically also financed drug trafficking due to the high capital requirements, they were never free of financial risk because of their territoriality. Further, it was this territoriality and the disputes it led to that would lead them into conflict with the state, their greatest risk.

The Assassination of Archbishop Posadas

While it may have been structurally determined, the conflict between Chapo Guzmán and the Arellanos was also deeply personal. The Arellanos were reported to have given rousing speeches to their *sicarios* (hit men) who were hunting Guzmán about how he "was bad for Mexico" and "evil."[74] The hunt for Guzmán and his allies Ismael "El Mayo" Zambada García, "El Güero" Palma, and the Carrillo Fuentes family ranged throughout Mexico and included an attempted car bombing of a hotel in Guadalajara where a Juárez cartel meeting was being held.[75]

The most significant event in the history of the AFO occurred on May 24, 1993, when AFO hit men assassinated Cardinal Juan Jesús Posadas Ocampo, the archbishop of Guadalajara, at the Guadalajara airport. They had received word that Guzmán would be in Guadalajara, so Logan Heights enforcer squads were sent to meet up with Los Mochis (an enforcement squad from Los Mochis, a city in the Mexican state of Sinaloa) and kill him. As they were preparing to leave Guadalajara after not having found Guzmán there, they received intelligence that he would be arriving at the airport in a white Grand Marquis. When such a car arrived, they riddled it with bullets, and the assassins left believing they had killed Guzmán.[76] Only later would they learn from news reports that Guzmán had not been the victim but rather Cardinal Posadas. The killing of a cardinal and archbishop of the Catholic Church, the most respected institution in Mexico, forced the government to crack down on the AFO. The AFO leadership immediately understood the significance of the error and knew it could destroy the AFO if not handled properly.[77]

The AFO Response

The AFO response to the crisis was largely "transactional," focusing on bribes and avoiding state attention and thereby minimizing risk. According to Everardo Arturo "Kitty" Páez Martinez, a high-ranking AFO lieutenant, the AFO leadership immediately began bribing high-level Mexican government officials to minimize the government response. This effort included a $10 million bribe to the head of the Federal Judicial Police, Rodolfo Leon Aragón. Benjamín Arellano Félix arranged for AFO safe houses to be sacrificed after incriminating documents were removed. He also arranged for the AFO enforcers involved in the killing of the cardinal to be arrested. All of this was designed to provide a public appearance of a strong crackdown by the Mexican government.[78] This was a conscious strategy of mitigating the consequences of the state reaction and thereby minimizing the risk to the organization as a whole. The AFO leadership went into hiding following the assassination. Ramón Arellano traveled throughout Mexico hunting El Chapo and El Mayo and enforcing for the AFO. Benjamín Arellano, the strategic head of the organization, went into hiding in the United States.[79]

The AFO was starved for profits in the immediate aftermath of the killing of Cardinal Posadas and could not pay its enforcers. It made calculated top-down (or core to periphery) decisions to engage in kidnapping, typically "on an as-needed basis" and for high-profile targets, to restore revenue.[80] Kidnapping is generally associated with territorial drug networks, but this is an example of how the territorial network cells of largely transactional networks may engage in kidnapping when profit-starved, with the consent or tolerance of the transactional leadership. Prior to 1993, the AFO rarely engaged in kidnapping, instead deriving nearly all of its profits from drug trafficking and smuggling activities.[81]

These high-profile kidnappings required intelligence on the target's habits, surveillance of the target, safe houses, and the capability to hold the victim for long periods of time. Typically, the AFO had inside information about the target and a corrupted official within the Mexican antikidnapping unit. Usually someone on the target's security detail would make a commission from the ransom for providing information. Thus, the intelligence often came to the AFO based upon their "reputation for violence" and their reputation for paying commissions to those who provided intelligence.[82]

The AFO had "offices" where enforcers were expected to be ready to work each morning. No advance warning would be given to those participating in a kidnapping. A lieutenant of the drug network would arrive at the office on the morning of a kidnapping operation and give minimal instructions to the partici- pating enforcers. Typically these were instructions on what to wear, what arms to carry, and what type of vehicle to drive. This is an example of information compartmentalization through procedures within the drug network. It is also an example of "the need for security" coming into conflict with "the need for infor- mation" flows within an illicit network. The AFO failed in some of their attempts to kidnap high-profile targets during this period, likely due to the compartmen- talization of information. Because of its compartmentalization, however, it also likely survived this period intact without large numbers of major arrests.[83]

Rule by Proxy: El Mayel

The AFO could be structurally characterized as under "rule by proxy" from 1993 to roughly 1995 when Benjamín and Ramón Arellano Félix were outside Tijuana lying low. The operation of the organization was left to Ismael "El Mayel" Higuera Guerrero, a top-level lieutenant personally responsible for brutal tortures and kill- ings on behalf of the AFO. Higuera became the node through which all informa- tion from the top-level leadership passed.[84] In social network analysis terms, he was "a structural hole"—a nonredundant node, the removal of which would cause significant damage to the drug network's functioning. Benjamín Arellano Félix was still the symbolic and strategic head of the organization, but operations were controlled by Higuera, who had significant independent decision-making capa- bilities in this period.[85] His brother Gilberto also controlled Mexicali on behalf of the drug network, increasing both of their relative importance.[86]

The role of Higuera during this period demonstrates the limits of the AFO's emphasis on consanguinity. Being a member of the Arellano family is extremely important symbolically for heading the network but is not a prerequisite for holding an important operational position. Trust through social-network ties is attained not simply through blood relations but can be earned over an extended period of time through personal loyalty and performance within the AFO.

The Arrest of "Kitty" Páez

The first major arrest of an AFO lieutenant occurred in 1997. The arrest of Eve- rardo Arturo "Kitty" Páez Martínez at his favorite Japanese restaurant in Tijuana was a blow to the AFO. Páez had been an important narco-junior and lieutenant for the AFO. He was arrested three weeks prior to the death of David Barron Corona and played a key role in the events leading up to it.[87]

In 1997, Barron was killed in his attempt to kill famous *Zeta* editor Jesús Blancornelas in response to stories Blancornelas had written about Barron in the magazine.[88] In his assassination attempt, Barron was killed by friendly fire. A ricocheted AK-47 round struck him in the eye and resulted in an iconic photo of Barron slumped over dead, propped up by his shotgun. Miraculously, Blancornelas survived the attack, but his bodyguard was killed defending him.[89] For the AFO, Barron's death represented the loss of a skilled, well-connected enforcer. He was so respected that the AFO enforcer who accidentally killed him was executed. By this point, however, the AFO ties to La Eme and street gangs in San Diego had been institutionalized, and his death did not in itself represent a loss of connections to these recruitment sources.[90]

The Third Phase: AFO Dismantlement (2000–8)

The year 2000 represented the beginning of the success of US–Mexican law-enforcement kingpin/decapitation strategies and the beginning of a severe weakening of the strength of the AFO.[91] Operation United Eagles represented unprecedented cooperation between US and Mexican law enforcement and included the electronic surveillance of the AFO and the training of elite Mexican police forces.[92] The details of this operation will be described at length in the next chapter, but the effects of the state reaction on the AFO will be described here.

The dismantlement period began in 2000 in earnest with the arrest of El Chuy and El Mayel, two of the cartel's most important leaders. These events constituted the "critical juncture,"[93] marking the end of the territorialization phase and the beginning of the dismantlement phase. The two lieutenants were important to the functioning of the transactional side of the business as first-generation leaders. Unlike previous extradition subjects, they were full Mexican nationals who would eventually be extradited to US prisons, thereby eliminating their ability to conduct business from behind bars.[94] While the arrests of the year 2000 were a blow to the AFO, 2002 would prove to be far worse. That year, chief enforcer Ramón Arellano Félix was killed in Mazatlán by a Mexican police officer, and shortly thereafter his brother, AFO strategic head Benjamín, was arrested in Puebla.[95] The death of Ramón and the arrest of Benjamín represented the loss of the most important and experienced first-generation of the AFO leadership.

With the death of Ramón in 2002, Kitty Páez, who had been extradited to the United States in 2001, began to cooperate with authorities because his fear of retribution from the AFO leadership dissipated. His cooperation would prove critical to the further dismantlement of the network. Páez had been extradited shortly after Mexico's 2001 Supreme Court ruling that Mexican citizens without dual citizenship could be extradited to the United States. Two weeks after this decision, Chapo Guzmán escaped from La Puente maximum-security prison.[96] This event would prove of critical importance to the future of the AFO.

While the AFO was largely resilient following disruptive events in 2002, a spin-off cell did emerge. The cell was known as Los Pallilos ("The Toothpicks"), which had broken from the AFO following a personal dispute with a high-ranking AFO member. They used their knowledge of the drug network to target San Diego AFO members for kidnapping and large ransoms. US law enforcement captured the network after many violent kidnappings. This could be considered a minor fragmentation over a personal dispute. The state-reaction argument still holds if we consider that this lapse in ability to enforce discipline followed the arrest/death at state hands of Benjamín and Ramón Arellano Félix and later the capture of "El Tigrillo."[97]

The AFO under El Tigrillo (2002–6)

Following the arrest of Benjamín and the death of Ramón, the natural successor to head the AFO was their youngest brother, Francisco Javier Arellano Félix— "El Tigrillo." He had been in charge of daily operations since 2000, presumably following the arrest of El Mayel.[98]

During this period of decapitation and loss of key leaders, the AFO network structure did not change, despite the loss of major Colombian cocaine connections, which dramatically reduced its profits.[99] The drug network continued to employ large enforcer squads that entailed high overhead costs. To compensate for the loss of cocaine profits, AFO cells were forced to diversify their criminal activities. While this included the expansion of marijuana cultivation and trafficking, kidnapping also became a major source of revenue for the cells associated with Eduardo Teodoro "El Teo / Tres Letras" García Simental, leader of the El Teo network, and his brother, Marco Antonio "El Cris" García Simental.[100] El Tigrillo held this increasingly territorial network together under transactional leaders for four years.[101]

When his fishing boat, the *Dock Holiday*, ventured into international waters on August 14, 2006, El Tigrillo was arrested as part of a joint DEA–Coast Guard operation, Shadow Game. He was brought to the United States, where he was charged with drug trafficking and racketeering. A more detailed account of the arrest from the perspective of the state and its law enforcement leading the operation is provided in the next chapter. After his arrest, control of the AFO fell to Luis Fernando "El Ingeniero" Sánchez Arellano, a nephew of the Arellano Félix brothers. Eduardo Arellano Félix—"El Doctor"—the last of the original AFO brothers alive and unjailed, acted as a mentor and adviser to El Ingeniero. He had long had a peripheral role in the illicit network and was known as a recluse.[102]

The Fourth Phase: The Restructuring of the AFO

The death and arrests of key AFO leaders throughout the first decade of the twenty-first century forced a fragmentation of the network, reducing its resilience according to the resilience typology established in the conceptual framework. The primary structural change came in the form of an internecine conflict and the dividing of the plaza that once included Tijuana, Tecate, and Mexicali into smaller plazas.[103]

The rise of El Ingeniero, the son of Norma Isabel Arellano, between 2006 and 2008 represented a new generation of leadership for the AFO and a fundamental restructuring of the drug network.[104]

El Ingeniero's rise demonstrated that top-level leadership would remain in the Arellano family and that this leadership is based on consanguinity. It would have been impossible for a non-Arellano to become the symbolic head of the AFO. This may have been equally as important to non-Arellanos as it was to Arellano family members, as keeping leadership within the family may provide a sense of stability and identity for the drug network because it prevents the usurpation of power by hungry and aggressive younger lieutenants. It did not, however, prevent the split with El Teo, which, as I will describe, fragmented the AFO and led to internecine conflict.[105]

Internecine Conflict (April 2008–January 2010)

The onset of an internecine conflict between El Teo and El Ingeniero within the AFO represents another critical juncture that fragmented the network and reduced its resilience. In the early 2000s, the AFO suffered major arrests, while at the same time the 9/11 terrorist attacks resulted in increased US border enforcement. Together these made it more difficult to traffic drugs across the border and forced some AFO cells to diversify activities into retail drug sales and kidnapping. In the early to mid-2000s, El Cris, an AFO lieutenant and the brother of El Teo, began kidnapping more individuals for smaller and smaller ransoms. El Cris was arrested in 2004 in a shootout involving a mounted .50-caliber machine gun, but El Teo continued the practice with his enforcer cells. This would lead to one of the most important splits within the AFO.[106]

The El Teo network of the AFO relied heavily on kidnapping as a revenue source, a fact universally recognized by Tijuana citizens, scholars, businessmen, journalists, civic leaders, and law-enforcement officials.[107] As it was implemented in Tijuana in 2007, kidnapping was a highly territorial activity and was the means of enforcing extortion payments for El Teo.[108]

The kidnapping operations were not sophisticated, though they did include a large number of people, cell phones, and safe houses. Most of the people operating these kidnapping cells were *mugrosos*—drug-using teenagers doing the dirty work of the El Teo network.[109] There was little previously collected intelligence on the victims being kidnapped, and they were typically not held for very long periods (usually four or five days). The victims were often killed. An illicit network relying on mugrosos is highly resilient because they can be readily recruited and replaced due to a large number of severely impoverished young people in Mexico.[110]

Holding the victims for short periods allowed an increase in the number of kidnappings that could be undertaken. Once the El Teo network began kidnapping small business owners, they were kidnapping for much smaller amounts—usually only $5,000 to $10,000—than when the AFO kidnapped in the 1990s. This dramatically increased the number of potential victims that could be harvested and the number of people in Tijuana touched by the kidnapping wave. What the El Teo network lost in profit margin, it made up in volume. The psychological impact upon the victims was devastating. Female victims were raped repeatedly and "would never be the same."[111] The sense of security of all of the victims, their family, and friends was shattered.[112]

El Teo Kidnapping Procedures

According to multiple Tijuana citizens and confirmed by anonymous government officials, kidnapping victims (usually business owners) would be abducted and held for ransom. They often negotiated their own ransom and were asked for exorbitant amounts. The victims would offer a lower amount that they could produce. The kidnapping cell would accept the lower amount but on the provision that the victim provide ten names of people who could pay the same amount. In this fashion, the kidnappings occurred along the lines of social networks. For example, an auto mechanic knows other auto mechanics and would give their names. Eventually kidnappings got to the professionally educated classes, such as doctors, engineers, and lawyers, and triggered a societal backlash.[113]

To avoid being kidnapped, an illicit or licit business owner was usually given an opportunity to pay cuota regularly. Again, anecdotally, the pattern appeared to be that the business owner had a "protector" to whom he could contact to arrange payments. Sometimes payments would become dramatically larger when, for example, "the boss has a birthday coming."[114] If a business owner wanted to shut down his business, he had to arrange a final payment, usually larger than his regular payments. This was not uncommon in the period between 2008 and 2010, in which the AFO, led by El Ingeniero, and the El Teo drug network were at war. One business owner lamented being told by police that it was "not a good time to be in business," fatalistically acknowledging that they could not keep the business safe."[115] Business people paying piso were also given an opportunity to provide ten names of people that would not be kidnapped based on this arrangement. This usually included immediate family and employees.[116]

After the experience of narco-juniors in the 1990s, Tijuana society wanted a separation between "polite society"—the elites of the licit world—and the criminal underworld, although there were those who may have blurred the line. [117] The criminal world was allowed to function, largely ignored, provided that polite society went unmolested.[118]

Kidnappings of those who were uninvolved in illicit businesses were shocking to Tijuana society. Doctors installed panic rooms in their offices and even talked of going on strike, threatening to refuse to treat police officers and the public until the kidnappings of doctors ended.[119] The abduction of Dr. Fernando Guzmán, the general surgeon of a leading Tijuana hospital and the ensuing civil society reaction, was a turning point. Approximately twenty doctors had been kidnapped and even more had received ransom demands of up to $50,000. In response to the kidnapping, civil society groups representing doctors mobilized and threatened a strike. Shortly thereafter, Dr. Guzmán was released.[120]

Kidnapping was at the center of the split between the El Teo network and the El Ingeniero–led AFO in April of 2008. The El Ingeniero network believed that the El Teo cells were "*calentando la plaza*," or heating up the trafficking corridor, with too many kidnappings and drawing negative attention that hurt the trafficking business. The desire to cool the plaza demonstrates a conscious awareness of trafficking networks to minimize the risk of state attention. The AFO was all too aware of the dangers of a hot plaza because representatives of Zambada García of the Sinaloa cartel had actively tried to heat up the Tijuana plaza by sending cells to increase violence in the late 1990s and early 2000s. El Teo believed that El Ingeniero was a weak leader, a spoiled child not from the Tijuana streets and unworthy of leadership of the drug network. He also needed the profits that kidnapping brought to his network, while El Ingeniero needed a calm plaza to traffic drugs and operate money-laundering front businesses. Neither El Teo nor El Ingeniero was present for the violent April 2008 gun battle on the streets of Tijuana that marked their split.[121]

El Teo had many advantages in the internecine conflict with El Ingeniero. First, he and his brother were Tijuana natives. They had grown up in the city and had operated as enforcers there for most of their lives. It is reported that El Teo and his brother began in the criminal world as teenagers, taking undocumented aliens across the border on foot. Second, El Teo was able to establish a short-lived alliance with the Sinaloa cartel, led by Chapo Guzmán and Mayo Zambada. The Sinaloa cartel is widely considered the most powerful drug network in Mexico, and this alliance provided El Teo with the drug connections he lacked. The Sinaloa cartel had already taken control of the nearby Mexicali plaza in 2004, giving it resources in the area to facilitate cooperation. Third, El Teo had extensive contacts within the local police force.[122] Fourth, as the leader of a territorial drug network, El Teo's use of extreme violence was high—a key prediction of my state-reaction argument.[123] Two other factors may have contributed to El Teo's extremely violent behavior. He was rumored to have had a drug-use problem with *cristal* (methamphetamine) and was an inexperienced leader.[124] Because El Teo's network was territorial and relied on extorting the local population, it needed a strong reputation for violence to get compliance from extortion victims. An efficient way to establish a reputation for violence is to use public or communicative acts of violence.[125] He was known for leaving the heads of victims on top of vats of acid where their bodies had been dissolved. This defeated the purpose of having a *pozolero* (soup maker) to hide the carnage but had a strong psychological impact upon rival cartels and the local population.[126] He was also known for having many local police on his payroll and for killing police who did not cooperate.[127] This violence was a double-edged sword for his network.[128] It terrorized and cowed the population into submission but also led to a societal backlash.

Sandra Dibble of the *San Diego Union-Tribune* provides the following account of the break between El Teo and El Ingeniero: "Officials say the differences were long-simmering, though the final split took place with a confrontation April 26 [2008] in eastern Tijuana that left at least 14 dead. Law enforcement officials say that Sánchez [El Ingniero] had called a meeting to rein in García [El Teo] and his crewmembers, who were conducting abductions outside their designated zone. But the meeting disintegrated into a gunbattle."[129] Following the gun battle, El Teo retreated to Sinaloa, only to return in September 2008 to restart his conflict with El Ingeniero.[130] The time between 2008 and 2010 was a chaotic period filled with fear for the citizens of Tijuana.

El Teo's arrest on January 12, 2010, in La Paz, Baja California Sur, while loading drugs for shipment to the United States, marked a major public relations victory for the Calderón administration.[131] One of El Teo's top lieutenants, Raydel López Uriarte, also known as "El Muletas," and El Teo's younger brother Manuel García Simental were arrested in February of 2010, dealing another blow to this territorial drug network.[132] Many have speculated that the information that led to El Teo's arrest was provided by elements of the Sinaloa cartel that had switched to an alliance with El Ingeniero's transactional drug network.[133] This is a plausible, if unconfirmed, scenario that confirms the state-reaction argument's expectation that transactional drug networks prefer alliances with other transactional networks because they employ low-profile business strategies that do not trigger harsh state responses.

Through a powerful state and rival drug-network reaction, the territorial drug network led by El Teo was dissolved, and subsequent iterations of the AFO have used low-profile strategies that minimize violence to reorganize and prove themselves resilient. This case study demonstrates the evolutionary process that eliminated one drug network for its emphasis on territorial extortion and allowed another to survive because of its transactional character and its ability to form alliances with the state and other powerful transactional drug networks. The next chapter will explain my state-reaction argument of drug-network resilience from the perspective of the state and detail the strategies used by the Mexican and US governments to fight these drug networks.

Since the destruction of the El Teo network, the AFO continued under the leadership of El Ingeniero. The precise relationship between the Sinaloa cartel and the AFO in the aftermath of 2010 is impossible to determine with certainty. Some speculated that the Sinaloa cartel charged a tax to the AFO to operate in the region and that the AFO effectively became a subsidiary of the Sinaloa cartel. The arrest and interrogation of Juan Francisco "El Ruedas" Sillas Rocha in November 2011 countered that the AFO and the Sinaloa cartel have established a truce in Tijuana and operate side by side.[134] All analysts, media, and law enforcement agree that the Sinaloa cartel had become more important in the plaza since 2008, and all noticed that violence levels reduced dramatically between 2010 and 2012.

Another disruptive event in this period would contribute to increased violence and internecine conflict in 2013. Amando "El Gordo" Villareal Heredia, who reported directly to El Ingeniero, was arrested in 2011 in Guadalajara.[135] The arrest was a major blow following the Luz Verde (which translates to Green Light and refers to an organized-crime authorization to kill an individual) indictment in 2010 of forty-three AFO members. By 2013, there was fragmentation and internecine conflict, as some cells such as Los Pelones left to work with the Sinaloa cartel.[136]

In 2013, violence attributed to retail drug-dealer conflicts, primarily among Sinaloa cartel–affiliated dealers, began to raise homicide levels in the Tijuana area.[137] The El Ingeniero–led AFO suffered some significant arrests in this period. The most notable was the arrest of Melvin "El Melvin" Gutiérrez Quiroz in March 2013.[138] El Melvin had been a lieutenant and important connection to the San Diego Logan Street gang. The most significant arrest, which has forced a reorganization of the network, was the arrest of El Ingeniero himself in June 2014.[139]

A number of other significant events have occurred since then. According to the secretary of public security in Tijuana, Alejandro Lares Valledares, in February of 2015, the AFO is restructuring under the leadership of Juan Lorenzo "El Chan" Vargas Gallardo. Interestingly, the "resurgence" of the AFO has been fueled by judicial reforms, which forced the release of those arrested improperly by the military.[140]

In March 2015, *Zeta* magazine reported small clashes between the AFO and the Sinaloa cartel in various areas of Tijuana. There continue to be AFO loyalists lying low in Guadalajara.[141] The AFO's restructuring is a reduced level of resilience, according to my resilience proxy typology. Law enforcement and the media repeated the phrase "a shadow of its former self" to describe the AFO in this period.[142] Nonetheless, it outlasted the more territorial El Teo network by using a trafficking-oriented and low-profile strategy. In competition with the larger, more trafficking-oriented Sinaloa cartel and its representatives José Antonio "El Tigre" Soto Gastélum, Alfonzo "El Aquiles" Arzate García, and his brother René "La Rana" Arzate García in Tijuana, it has suffered significant arrests and state attention, which has forced it into a new reorganization period. It is interesting to note that the unintended consequences of state action have led to the AFO resurgence described by officials in the region. This is reminiscent of Varese's argument about unintended consequences of state actions leading to the territorial expansion of mafias.[143] While many think it likely that the remaining AFO loyalists may jettison the AFO name, only time will tell if it will dissolve in competition with the larger, trafficking-oriented Sinaloa cartel.

Notes

1. Blancornelas, *El cártel*; Jones, "Unintended Consequences."
2. Shirk and Rios, *Drug Violence in Mexico*.
3. Kenney, *From Pablo to Osama*.
4. Reuter, "Systemic Violence in Drug Markets."
5. See my previous work cited in the late George Grayson's recent book, *The Cartels*. He refers to the dismantlement phase as the "embattled phase."
6. Grayson, *Mexico*, 81.
7. Ibid.
8. Steve Duncan (law-enforcement investigator [CA Dept. of Justice] focused on the AFO), interview by the author, San Diego, 2010; Weick, "Educational Organizations."
9. Shannon, *Desperados*.
10. For a reference to the myth of the Arellanos as nephews of El Padrino, see Grayson's *Mexico: Narco Violence*, page 81. Again, law enforcement interviews refuted this point. Duncan, interview; Enrique Osorno, *El Cartel de Sinaloa*, 213; Hernandez, *Narcoland*.

11. Duncan, interview.

12. Flores Pérez, "Organized Crime."

13. Duran-Martinez and Snyder, "Does Illegality Breed Violence?"

14. Shannon, *Desperados*; Flores Pérez, "Organized Crime."

15. Duran-Martinez and Snyder, "Does Illegality Breed Violence?"; Hernandez, *Narcoland*.

16. Duran-Martinez and Snyder, "Does Illegality Breed Violence?"; Astorga and Shirk, *Drug Trafficking Organizations*.

17. Former high-ranking Mexican law-enforcement official, interview by the author, Mexico City, November 2010.

18. Tijuana resident, interview by the author, Tijuana, July, 2010.

19. "Steve," former AFO trafficker, interview; Bergman, "Drug Wars: 'Steve.'"

20. Duncan, interview.

21. Duncan, interview; Flores Pérez, "Organized Crime," 91; Flores Pérez, *El estado en crisis*; Astorga and Shirk, *Drug Trafficking Organizations*.

22. Flores Pérez, "Organized Crime," 91; Flores Pérez, *El estado en crisis*.

23. The Arellanos, being from Sinaloa, also enjoyed extensive social networks that spanned trafficking networks, which, though they would come into conflict, ultimately served to alleviate conflict and assist in the creation of alliances and nonaggression pacts with members of the Sinaloa cartel. Duncan, interview.

24. Sabet, "Confrontation, Collusion and Tolerance."

25. Former Mexican law-enforcement official, interview.

26. Shannon, *Desperados*; Astorga, "Organized Crime," 76.

27. Shannon, *Desperados*.

28. Weick, "Educational Organizations."

29. Guerrero Gutiérrez, *Security, Drugs, and Violence*, 28.

30. Shannon, *Desperados*.

31. Thelen, "Historical Institutionalism."

32. Blancornelas, *El cártel*.

33. Enrique Osorno, *El Cartel de Sinaloa*, 213; Rios Contreras, "How Government Structure."

34. Mexican official, interview by the author, Tijuana, 2011.

35. Blancornelas, *El cártel*; Flores Pérez, "Organized Crime," 97–98.

36. Duncan, interview.

37. Blancornelas, *El cártel*.

38. Bergman, "Drug Wars."

39. Blancornelas, *El cártel*.

40. Dillon, "Mexican Traffickers Recruiting."

41. Rotella, "Mexico's Cartels Sow Seeds."

42. DePalma, "Mexico Reports Troops."

43. Duncan, interview; Blancornelas, *El cártel*; Caldwell, "Cartel Secrets."

44. *Harrod, Scharf and Ziegler;* Dillon, "Mexican Traffickers Recruiting"; Duncan, interview; Rotella, "Mexico's Cartels Sow Seeds."

45. In his analysis in "On the Etiology of Internal Wars," Eckstein argued that "preconditions" are the underlying causes of war but often require a "precipitant" to begin an internal war. In this case I have identified critical junctures as laying the preconditions for change and also identified precipitating events like the attack at Christine's Disco.

46. Duncan, interview.

47. See Reuter, "Systemic Violence in Drug Markets," 279, for violent "reputation enhancement." For descriptions of the violence of the AFO, see Chabot, "Historical Case Study." My interviews with Duncan also indicated violent killings and use of torture in ways designed to frighten others into compliance.

48. Dillon, "Mexican Traffickers Recruiting."

49. Ibid.; Duncan, interview.

50. Duncan, interview.

51. The term "enforcer" refers to members of a DTO who specialize in providing violence on behalf of the organization. A common term for enforcer in Latin America is *sicario* (hit man).

Marks, "Counterinsurgency"; United States Department of the Army and United States Marine Corps, *U.S. Army / Marine Corps Counterinsurgency Field Manual*; Felbab-Brown, *Shooting Up*; Downie, *Learning from Conflict*.

52. Brands, "Los Zetas"; Grayson, "Los Zetas."

53. This could also be viewed as institutional isomorphism. See Peters, *Institutional Theory*; Powell and DiMaggio, *New Institutionalism*, 63.

54. Peters, *Institutional Theory*.

55. Duncan, interview.

56. Guerrero Gutiérrez, *Security, Drugs, and Violence*; Bergman, "Drug Wars: Interviews."

57. Duncan, interview; Skaperdas, "Cooperation, Conflict, and Power"; Skaperdas, "Political Economy of Organized Crime"; Skaperdas and Syropoulos, "Gangs as Primitive States."

58. Hampson, "Extreme Violence"; Hampson, "Rationalizing the Profane."

59. Skaperdas, "Cooperation, Conflict, and Power"; Skaperdas and Syropoulos, "Gangs as Primitive States"; Skaperdas, "Political Economy of Organized Crime."

60. Duncan, interview.

61. Ibid.; Kenney, *From Pablo to Osama*.

62. Kenney, *From Pablo to Osama*.

63. *Harrod, Scharf and Ziegler*.

64. Here I use learning from the state in lieu of institutional isomorphism as described by Peters. Duncan, interview; Peters, *Institutional Theory*.

65. Duncan, interview.

66. In a compartmentalized network, in which not every node in the networks is aware of each other's operations, there must be some centralization of information. Drug

trafficking is distinct from terrorism in that terrorist networks such as Al Qaeda do not need to coordinate their operations to the same degree. Drug trafficking requires regular communication to secure drug loads and coordinate shipments, making communication more important. After 9/11, most experts agree that Al Qaeda flattened its organizational structure and relied on local social movements and insurgent groups to launch their own small attacks against the United States and Western allies. This is evidenced by the amateurish attempted attacks of the "shoe bomber" and "underwear bomber" and even the successful train attacks in Spain. These attacks are launched by cells with plausibly no connection to or communication with the central Al Qaeda leadership. Rather, Al Qaeda provided the strategic vision and inspiration for the attacks and encouraged these groups to act independently. In the underwear bomber's attempted attack, Bin Laden claimed credit ex post facto but was unlikely to have had advance knowledge of it. This reduced the likelihood of being discovered and having the attack thwarted by law enforcement or US intelligence. The Islamic State in Iraq and Syria (ISIS) follows a similar model in which it inspires lone wolf attacks in the West through social media calls to sympathizers. Kahler, *Networked Politics*; Kenney, *From Pablo to Osama*, 27; Kean et al., *9/11 Commission Report*.

67. Former high-ranking Mexican law-enforcement official, interview.

68. Bergman, "Drug Wars: Interviews"; Duncan, interview.

69. Bergman, "Drug Wars: Interviews."

70. Ibid.

71. Caldwell, "Cartel Secrets"; Caldwell, "Cold-Blooded Killers"; Caldwell, "Captured."

72. Bergman, "Drug Wars: Interviews"; Keefe, "How a Mexican Drug Cartel."

73. UNODC, *Transnational Organized Crime in Central America and the Caribbean*, 20.

74. Former high-ranking Mexican law-enforcement official, interview by the author, Mexico City, November 2010.

75. Ibid.

76. According to a Mexican military recording of its interview with Hodoyan, a former AFO member, the Logan Heights assassins were incompetent and possibly high when this occurred. Bergman, "Drug Wars."

77. Duncan, interview; Caldwell, "Cartel Secrets."

78. Caldwell, "Cartel Secrets."

79. Duncan, interview.

80. Ibid.

81. Ibid.

82. Ibid.

83. Ibid.; Kenney, "From Pablo to Osama"; Kenney, "Architecture of Drug Trafficking."

84. Duncan, interview.

85. Burt, "Structural Holes versus Network Closure"; Burt, *Structural Holes*.

86. "Cae 'El Tigrillo'"; Caldwell, "Cartel Secrets"; Caldwell, "Captured"; "Major Cartel Lieutenants Arrested"; "Members of Arellano-Felix Organization."

87. Caldwell, "Cartel Secrets"; Caldwell, "Captured"; Caldwell, "Cold-Blooded Killers."

88. Dillon, "Mexican Traffickers Recruiting."

89. Duncan, interview.

90. Ibid.; "FBI Informant Details."

91. The embodiment of "kingpin" or "decapitation" strategies is the designation of "consolidated priority organization targets" (CPOTs) by the DEA. Dudley, "Bin Laden, the Drug War."

92. Operation United Eagles will be discussed in more detail in the following chapter. "Major Cartel Lieutenants Arrested"; "Members of Arellano-Felix Organization"; Bergman, "Drug Wars."

93. Thelen, "Historical Institutionalism."

94. "Leaders of Arellano-Felix"; Caldwell, "Cartel Secrets"; "40 años de cárcel"; "Suspected Tijuana Drug Kingpin"; "Members of Arellano-Felix"; "Major Cartel Lieutenants Arrested in Mexico."

95. Sullivan, "Tijuana Gang Figure"; Kraul, "Weakened Tijuana Drug Cartel"; "Suspected Tijuana Drug Kingpin"; "Juez falla a favor."

96. Caldwell, "Cartel Secrets"; Walser, "U.S. Strategy"; Grayson, "Mexico and the Drug Cartels."

97. Longmire, *Cartel*, 85–86; Jones, "Unintended Consequences "; Grayson, *Mexico*; Chivis, "Trial Begins"; Duncan, interview.

98. Duncan, interview; Moore, "War without Borders"; "Cae 'El Tigrillo.'"

99. Duncan, interview.

100. Kidnapping has long been a problem in Latin America. However, the victims of kidnappings were typically wealthy and returned alive after ransoms were paid. As drug networks such as El Teo's of the AFO began targeting middle-class professionals such as doctors and engineers, the practice began to terrorize the mass population and impact every facet of Mexican life. Tijuana professionals began living on the US side of the border and minimizing their time in Mexico. A backlash against the drug networks was triggered from society at large. This led to the split between El Ingeniero and El Teo. El Ingeniero viewed the kidnappings as bad for business, while El Teo wanted to continue. Ibid.

101. This paragraph contains excerpts from Jones, "Unintended Consequences."

102. Marosi, "Mystery Man Blamed"; Duncan, interview.

103. Blancornelas, *El cártel.*

104. Conflicting media reports have led to serious debate among academics who specialize in Mexican drug-trafficking organizations on the accuracy of nicknames for narco-bosses. Some have even suggested that the confusion may be an intended consequence and part of an AFO strategy. Grayson, *Mexico.*

105. Dibble, "Split within Arellano Félix Cartel."

106. This paragraph was excerpted from Jones, "Unintended Consequences." The next eight paragraphs are also excerpted from this article with permission. "'El Chapo' y

'El Mayo'"; "'Los Teos' rentan sicarios"; Ojeda, "Ruffo y Franco Ríos"; Reza Gonzalez, "'Cae' narco miembros."

107. Mexican official, interview by the author; family member of Tijuana doctor, interview by the author; Tijuana businessman, interview by the author, Tijuana, 2011; Tijuana municipal police officer, interview by the author, Tijuana, February 2011; Tijuana journalist, interview by the author, Tijuana, February 2011; Tijuana business leader, interview by the author, Tijuana, February 15, 2011; Tijuana resident, interview by the author, Tijuana, July, 2010.

108. Family member of Tijuana doctor, interview by the author; Tijuana municipal police officer, interview by the author, Tijuana, February 2011; Tijuana journalist, interview by the author, Tijuana, February 2011; Tijuana business leader, interview by the author, Tijuana, February 15, 2011.

109. Tijuana municipal police officer, interview by the author, Tijuana, February 2011.

110. Tijuana business leader, interview by the author, Tijuana, February 15, 2011.

111. Duncan, interview.

112. Ibid.; Tijuana resident, interview by the author, Tijuana.

113. Tijuana business leader, interview by the author, Tijuana, February 15, 2011; Tijuana resident, interview by author, Tijuana, July, 2010.

114. Tijuana businessman, interview by author, Tijuana, 2011.

115. Ibid.

116. Ibid.

117. Bergman, "Murder, Money, and Mexico"; Jones, "Arrest of Tijuana Ex-Mayor"; Cearley, "Many Ignore Official's Alleged Link."

118. Tijuana businessman, interview by author, Tijuana, 2011; Tijuana resident, interview by author, Tijuana, July 2010.

119. Family member of Tijuana doctor, interview by author; Marosi, "Diagnosis: Irony."

120. Marosi, "Diagnosis: Irony."

121. Marosi, "Tijuana Blood Bath"; "Massive Gunbattles Break Out."

122. Tijuana municipal police officer, interview by author, Tijuana, February 2011.

123. Ellingwood, "Actually Violence Is Down"; Marosi, "Tijuana Blood Bath"; Jones, "Report Tracks How"; Carroll, "US Has Lost Faith."

124. Marosi, "Mystery Man Blamed."

125. Hampson, "Rationalizing the Profane"; Hampson, "Extreme Violence of Uganda's Militant LRA."

126. De Mauleon, "Tijuana"; Dudley, "Tijuana Cartel"; Marosi, "Mystery Man Blamed."

127. Before El Teo's arrest, I visited Tijuana in 2009 and noticed that municipal police traveled in groups of two trucks, with at least two men each sitting in the truck bed with automatic weapons. Motorcycle police, which typically enforce traffic violations individually, rode in groups of three. Seven months after El Teo's January 2010 arrest,

police appeared to be calmer and rode in their trucks with one partner in the cab with them and no one in the truck bed. This is an example of the impact that his arrest had on the Tijuana psyche. It calmed municipal police by reducing the daily threat of police assassination. Tijuana businessman, interview by the author, Tijuana, 2011; Tijuana municipal police officer, interview by the author, Tijuana, February 2011.

128. Kenney, *From Pablo to Osama*, 209.

129. Dibble, "Tijuana's Bloodiest Year."

130. "Mexican Drug Cartels: Government Progress"; Marosi, "Tijuana's Security Chief"; Dibble, "Tijuana Violence Slows"; Spagat, "Reputed Mexican Drug Lord."

131. Spagat, "Reputed Mexican Drug Lord."

132. Marosi, "Reputed Drug Cartel Leader."

133. Anonymous scholar in Mexico, conversation with the author, March 2011.

134. Jones, "Captured Tijuana Cartel Boss."

135. Jones, "Cartel Lieutenant's Capture."

136. "Los asesinos de la mafia."

137. Ibid.

138. Chivis, "Mexican Army Captures 'El Melvin'"; Dibble, "Soldiers Arrest."

139. Bargent, "Tijuana Cartel Leader Arrest."

140. "Balaceras, 'se reorganiza el CAF'"; Gagne, "Tijuana Cartel Resurgent"; Rios Contreras, *Mexico's* Petite Révolution.

141. Steve Duncan (law-enforcement investigator [California Department of Justice] focused on the AFO), correspondence with the author, March 31, 2015.

142. Perkins and Placido, "Drug Trafficking Violence in Mexico."

143. Duncan, correspondence; Varese, *Mafias on the Move.*

3

The State Reaction

THE SUCCESSFUL DESTRUCTION of the territorial drug network led by Eduardo Teodoro "El Teo" García Simental in Tijuana in 2010 represented an important victory of the state over a violent extortionist network. To understand the victory that led to an enviable reduction in violence in a once violent plaza, we must comprehend the historical preconditions that made the state reaction possible. In reality, it was not one state reaction but the reaction of two states, the United States and Mexico, and many levels of government in two federal systems. Interestingly, state responses via kingpin strikes against the AFO directly led to the territorial drug network's splitting from the broader trafficking-oriented network, a process this chapter will trace. Later, the state reaction dissolved that territorial network but allowed a trafficking-oriented network to survive though with reduced resilience.[1] The preconditions for the successful state reaction include the broader history of US–Mexico cooperation on counternarcotics, the transfer of technology between states, the resources and prior capacity building in the local police, the quality of the military units in the region, and, most important, civil society's role in galvanizing the state response. All of these factors played a major role in Tijuana's response to the El Teo drug network, as well as the lesser/delayed response to other transactional drug networks in the region.

While I argue that states react more strongly to territorial networks than to transactional networks, thus reducing network resilience, the strength of state institutions and democratic transition also strengthen or weaken the state reaction's impact on a drug network's resilience. This chapter will assess the state reactions to the AFO, moving from the broad to the specific, from the national to the local. I will begin with a discussion of the role of democratic transition in mitigating or magnifying the state reaction to drug networks through the lens of the broader US–Mexican counternarcotic policies. I will then assess the US and Mexican federal responses to the AFO in the 1990s and 2000s, continue with a discussion of the visceral local state reactions to the El Teo network, and conclude with a discussion of the state reaction to the current situation in which two trafficking-oriented drug networks operate in the city in a low profile and diffuse fashion.

The US–Mexican relationship on drug trafficking can be characterized as cooperative and tempered by Mexican sovereignty concerns. For Mexican elites, the fear of US invasion is not abstract. It stems from the loss of territory called for in 1848 by the Treaty of Guadalupe Hidalgo after the Mexican–American War and from the punitive raid of Brig. Gen. John J. Pershing's troops against the forces of Pancho Villa during the Mexican Revolution. The power differential between the United States and Mexico is tremendous.[2] Despite the differences in economic development and military size, the two countries are natural trading partners and have codified the relationship with the 1994 North American Free Trade Agreement (NAFTA), which increased economic interdependence between the two nations.[3] Drug networks have taken advantage of the increased flow of goods between the United States and Mexico. As Mexico's struggle with organized crime has become more violent, US assistance in the form of equipment, training, and embedding of law-enforcement agents in Mexico has been offered and quietly accepted by the Mexican government. The Felipe Calderón administration also negotiated unprecedented levels of cooperation between US and Mexican law enforcement in the fight against Mexican drug networks.[4] While these levels of cooperation may be cooling with the new administration of Enrique Peña Nieto, "drug wars" have become a source of mutual interest and cooperation between the two nations. This pattern is also noticeable in other regions, such as South and Central America.[5]

Democratization and the State Reaction

As a consolidated democracy, the United States had a confrontational policy with drug networks in the late twentieth century, while Mexico shifted from a "collusive" to a "confrontational" policy during its long, democratic transition period.[6] Official Mexican state policy on drug traffickers has long been confrontational, but the deeply corrupt internal security service DFS colluded with traffickers through much of the 1980s.[7] While others have pointed to the decentralization of the Mexican state to explain the shifting relationships with traffickers,[8] I, like Flores Pérez, view democratization as an encapsulating process that explains much of Mexico's change in policy toward confrontation with drug networks over the past thirty years.[9]

Higher levels of democratization lower the state's tolerance for organized crime, particularly if that crime results in violence. Democratic transition, defined as the movement from authoritarian to liberal democratic rule, results in a short-term weakening of institutions that can hinder the state's response to organized crime. Over the long run, however, the state is better served against organized crime under well-established, liberal, democratic regimes because of the institutions they have established to maintain the rule of law.[10] Democracy is not a panacea for organized crime, but its characteristics, including the rule of law, transparency, accountability, decentralization of power, and checks and balances, are the most effective means by which to combat organized crime.[11]

Criminal activity threatens the foundations of liberal democracies and engenders resentment from the population, as well as political demands to reduce crime and violence. Populations in democracies are rarely willing to allow the state to engage in "dirty deals" or "pacts" with organized crime in exchange for peace. When they do, it is usually a short-term response to extreme events. The fact that political leaders want to survive politically explains democratic democratization's movement toward confrontational relationships with traffickers.[12] Even in societies with a high degree of organized-crime penetration, public acknowledgments of connections between organized crime and political elites can mean politicians become subject to electoral losses. Democratic societies tend to punish corruption. For example, a Sinaloa gubernatorial candidate whose son had been kidnapped by others and returned by Sinaloa cartel leader Ismael "El Mayo" Zambada did not fare well in the election when he refused to renounce the trafficker.[13] Traffickers threaten the state by threatening the position of traditional political elites. Political survival thus explains the ways in which democratization moves states toward confrontational relationships with traffickers. Traffickers also threaten rule-of-law norms and institutions through their impunity, further triggering a societal backlash.[14]

Democratic transition can be a long and winding road. It may include demands for peace and accommodation with illicit networks in the short term.[15] Nowhere is this clearer than in Mexico. Under the seventy years of one-party rule (by the Partido Revolucionario Institucional, or PRI), Mexico developed an ever-increasing drug-trafficking problem fueled by US and, increasingly, international demand. Under the PRI, however, drug trafficking was tolerated so long as it occurred nonviolently and made significant payments to corrupt state officials in the DFS and military. It was only in situations where the interests of the United States were harmed that the Mexican government arrested major drug network figures and restructured its security apparatus to combat traffickers.[16]

When the Guadalajara cartel killed American DEA agent Enrique Camarena, severe pressure was brought to bear on the Mexican government. Thus, democracy did force a change in Mexico's drug policy; however, it was a foreign democracy.[17] The Mexican government would later increase the strength of its reaction against the AFO following the killing in 1993 of Juan Jesús Posadas Ocampo, an archbishop of Mexico's most respected institution, the Catholic Church. The killing of the respected archbishop put incredible pressure upon the state to combat the drug networks responsible for this act.[18]

Democratization has weakened Mexico's ability to negotiate with drug traffickers.[19] The movement away from the single-party rule and the dismantlement of the DFS security agency has made long-term "credible commitments" to traffickers on behalf of the Mexican government difficult.[20] Baja California was the first state to break the PRI's unified grip on power in Mexico. It was also the first place where the local trafficking network (the AFO) built up its enforcer apparatus. Multiple factors came together to create this situation. First, the AFO had difficulty engaging the security services of the state due to competition with other traffickers and the assassination of Posadas Ocampo. Second, due to democratization, the state was no longer a unified actor in its negotiations with other traffickers, which led to increasing conflicts between traffickers.[21] As a result, this was the period when Mexican drug networks came into conflict with each other and needed to raise their own independent paramilitary apparatuses.

The more progressively democratic Mexico has become, the stronger the state response to drug networks has been. Carlos Salinas de Gortari, president from 1988 to 1994, was considered corrupt and in collusion with the Gulf cartel and the drug networks from Sinaloa at various times.[22] President Ernesto Zedillo (1994–2000) began a slow fight against drug networks that resulted in the arrest of numerous major traffickers, including the head of the Gulf cartel. While some argue that Zedillo was in the pocket of corrupt narcos, I agree with Grillo's assessment that Zedillo wanted to target narcos but had corrupt agents in his administration. Zedillo's "drug czar," Gen. José de Jesús Gutiérrez Rebollo, was discovered to be colluding with the Juárez cartel, which explained his successes against the AFO. Zedillo made sure his drug czar was prosecuted and "coaxed the PRI to loosen its grip on power before it gave up the presidency."[23]

The election of Vicente Fox (of the National Action Party, or PAN) to the Mexican presidency in 2000 represented the first democratic presidency in Mexico in a hundred years. Fox began the use of the military against drug networks, although at a much lower level than his successor Calderón would. Some of the most important arrests of drug network leaders occurred during the Fox administration, including the 2002 arrest of Benjamín Arellano Félix, head of the AFO; the 2003 arrest of Osiel Cárdenas Guillén, head of the Gulf cartel; and the 2006 arrest of Francisco Javier "El Tigrillo" Arellano Félix, head of the AFO.[24]

President Calderón ramped up the use of the military in the drug war and also dramatically deepened cooperation with the United States. His administration sent more than sixty thousand federal soldiers and more than five thousand federal police to cartel hot spots throughout the country.[25] The resulting arrests were impressive, with twenty-five of thirty-seven kingpins captured.[26] But as kingpins were captured, violence only increased.[27]

The Mérida Initiative

Upon taking office, the Calderón administration realized it would need the support of the United States in its fight against organized crime. The conception of the idea for the Mérida Initiative occurred in 2007 when President Calderón first mentioned a cooperation agreement to President George W. Bush in Mérida. The ongoing sovereignty-sensitive initiative is a US–Mexican "partnership" in which Mexico receives $2.5 billion in US military equipment and aid from fiscal year 2008 to fiscal year 2015 for its fight against drug networks. The equipment was slow to arrive in the time after the agreement was reached, and Mexican officials told American diplomats they had come to the conclusion that it should have included more training and personnel capacity building early on.[28]

Capacity building and training in the early Mérida Initiative were minimized and subcontracted to private security firms due to Mexican sovereignty sensitivities.[29] According to leaked State Department cables available from WikiLeaks, Calderón administration officials have acknowledged that the de-emphasis of capacity building in the early Mérida Initiative was problematic for its success. The equipment provided would be useful they argued, but training and capacity building would have been more useful and were emphasized in later iterations.[30]

ATF Project Gunrunner

Both the Bush and Barack Obama administrations have acknowledged the US responsibility to stop the flow of guns into Mexico from the United States. Seventy percent of guns recovered in crimes in Mexico that are entered into the ETRACE system of the Bureau of Alcohol, Tobacco, Firearms and Explosives (ATF) came from the United States.[31] Guns are purchased through straw buyers and modified by illegal gunsmiths in the United States or Mexico before or after being trafficked into Mexico. The US response has been to send more ATF agents to border areas where guns are most likely to be trafficked to Mexico.[32] The ATF received criticism for Operation Fast and Furious, which, it was argued, allowed "gun walking" into Mexico in an attempt to track the weapons to high-ranking cartel figures. The ATF lost track of the guns, one of which may have been used to kill Border Patrol agent Brian Terry.[33] The nature of this gun walking has been debated. There have been two narratives on Operation Fast and the Furious. The dominant one argues that the ATF engaged in intentional gun walking by allowing straw purchasers under surveillance to smuggle the guns into Mexico, in the hope of finding high-value cartel figures. Another narrative reported in *Fortune* magazine suggested that the ATF had no intention of gun walking in the operation but was stymied by prosecutors whose worldview prevented the seizure of the guns.[34] My intent is not to weigh in on this debate but simply to acknowledge that it exists.

US–Mexican Cooperation against the AFO in the 1990s

Following the breakup of the Guadalajara cartel in the 1980s, Mexican drug networks took control of their various territories and began building paramilitary apparatuses to police them.[35] As they slowly became more territorial, US and Mexican informal bureaucratic cooperation increased for a number of reasons. As US law-enforcement interviews indicated, the appropriation of increased funds and resources in the late 1980s and early 1990s in the border region—part of the US government's High Intensity Drug Trafficking Area (HIDTA) program, established in 1988—significantly increased opportunities to collaborate with Mexican law-enforcement counterparts.[36]

The HIDTA program designated resources for areas that were considered high-intensity drug-trafficking regions because of their geographic and strategic positions in the illicit narcotics supply chain. Cities such as San Diego and Houston received increased law-enforcement resources to address drug trafficking.[37] Those resources meant more opportunities for cooperation.

Binational cooperation occurred in interesting and unexpected ways, including the development of informal personal relationships between US and Mexican lawmen, informal training sessions for Mexican law enforcement, and the provision of surplus US equipment to Mexican law-enforcement agencies.[38] The informal interpersonal connections between US and Mexican law enforcement developed in this period laid the foundation for a later formal collaboration between US and Mexican law enforcement known as Operation United Eagles, which would target AFO kingpins beginning in 2003.

The Mexican and US government strategy to fight the AFO has focused on arresting key AFO leadership figures—better known as the kingpin strategy. This strategy is operationally referred to as "decapitation" strikes, "fugitive apprehension," or the targeting of "high value targets" (HVTs). It is argued by Lieutenant Colonel Orama that the HVT strategy migrated from counterterrorism operations sometime in the late 1980s and early 1990s.[39] In reality, the DEA had always had an HVT strategy but lacked the air resources (helicopters) to target individuals and coca-processing labs nationally.[40] One of the earliest documented cases of the approach being used in US drug operations was Operation Snow Cap, in which DEA agents working with their Bolivian counterparts sought US Army Special Forces training on how to capture HVTs and the air resources to achieve it on a large scale.[41] Kingpin strategies would earn fame in the fight against Pablo

Escobar of the Medellín cartel in Colombia when he was killed in 1993.[42] This kingpin strategy became a staple of counternarcotics operations and is embodied by DEA's consolidated priority organization target (CPOT) lists that focus on prominent drug networks and their leadership figures. The goal of decapitation strikes is the dismantlement of drug networks. Sometimes the best that can be hoped for is the disruption or fragmentation of the illicit networks, resulting in smaller networks that do not threaten the state. This is the dominant narrative of what occurred in Colombia following the dismantlement of the Medellín and Cali cartels.[43]

The actual targeting of CPOTs in the United States is overseen by the Department of Justice's Organized Crime Drug Enforcement Task Forces (OCDETF) Program, through which interagency task forces are placed in major cities throughout the United States.[44] The task force created to target the AFO includes agencies such as the DEA, the California Department of Justice, US Customs and Border Protection, the FBI, the ATF, and the US attorneys' offices. Following the assassination attempt at Christine's Disco in Puerto Vallarta in 1992, the AFO recruited heavily from gang members in San Diego. Law-enforcement agencies that would eventually join the task force saw upticks in violence in San Diego in the early 1990s, such as assassinations involving "triple taps to the head" (when an individual is shot three times in the head to assure an effective execution). These behaviors indicated a professionalization of violence that was worrisome.[45]

Capturing AFO figures was a challenge. Finding out where they were was not an issue, given the sophisticated wiretaps at the AFO task force's disposal. Despite important arrests in the late 1990s and early 2000s, however, there was a tendency for good intelligence on the whereabouts of AFO figures to be passed to the Mexican side and not be acted upon or for the target to be tipped off to an impending raid. The perception on the US side was that there were corrupt leakers in Mexican law enforcement and a lack of political will to capture major traffickers in the mid-1990s.[46] DEA agent David Herrod described a scene in 1996:

And to this day one of my most vivid memories is Chuck Labella the acting US attorney in San Diego at the time at one of these meetings, getting very angry with the government of Mexico, with the people at that . . . table. Daring them, telling them, in a very, very angry way, that the government of Mexico does not want to go after these guys, they don't have the political will to do it. I remember him pounding the table with his fist and I'm thinking to myself, when seeing this, I'm like . . . wow that's going to do well for relations. But you know what, it was tough love and lo and behold our first big break in the case, within a short period of time the government of Mexico arrested Kiki Piaz [sic: Kitty Páez] on November 8th, 1997.[47]

The US government had to push the Mexican government to act to counter drug networks during Mexico's slow democratic transition, and the two nations continue to cooperate to strengthen institutions.[48] The process that played out in the 1990s in Baja California would be a harbinger of the broader binational cooperation that would occur under the Calderón administration a decade later.

The response to the leak problem was Operation United Eagles in 2003, which represented a model for successful cooperation between US and Mexican law enforcement. Under Operation United Eagles, US law enforcement brought sixty-seven vetted Mexican agents of the Agencia Federal de Investigación (AFI) into the United States for counternarcotics training. Being located on the US side provided them with a safe and secure environment from which to train.[49] They were also cut off from communication with their families to prevent them from being threatened by drug networks. After they returned to Mexico, they were given intelligence from US wiretaps on the whereabouts of AFO leaders and served as an effective fugitive apprehension team.[50] Operation United Eagles formalized the previously informal cooperation that had developed in the 1990s between US and Mexico law-enforcement agencies responsible for prosecuting the AFO and the Mexican attorney general's office, Procuraduría General de República (PGR). The largest hindrance in the interdiction and fugitive-apprehension strategies of the 1990s was the US perception of corruption of Mexican officials that prevented the sharing of accurate intelligence. Operation United Eagles solved that problem to great effect.[51] According to a State Department report in 2005, in the first year and a half of operations, "United Eagles has resulted in the arrest of 19 members of the AFO, including 5 'Tier I' members: Efran PEREZ, Jorge Aureliano-Félix, Gilberto HIGUERA-Guerrero, Giberto [sic] Camacho Valle, and Marco Antonio SIMENTAL-Garcia."[52]

It was these arrests that led to the profit starvation of the AFO and the rise of the territorial drug network led by El Teo and his brother Marco Antonio "El Cris" García Simental.[53] Despite the arrest, El Teo continued a new kidnapping-based, territorial business strategy. While El Teo was increasing kidnappings, he would not dare engage in open revolt until the arrest of El Tigrillo, the last of the respected first-generation AFO leaders who led the cartel.

Operation United Eagles led directly to Operation Shadow Game and the downfall in the late summer of 2006 of El Tigrillo, the leader of the AFO. The AFO OCDETF task force had received intelligence that the way to get to El Tigrillo was to follow Edgardo "El 24" Leyva Escandón, a valuable procurer and personal secretary to El Tigrillo. El 24 had also filled this role for Ramón Arellano Félix, the chief AFO enforcer before he was killed in 2002.[54] El 24 had a yacht, the *Dock Holiday*, that El Tigrillo enjoyed. Realizing a golden opportunity to arrest a top leader of the AFO in international waters, the task force decided to follow it. DEA and other task force agents went to the US Coast Guard office in Alameda, California, to request it keep a ship ready to apprehend El Tigrillo whenever he made the mistake of moving into international waters. The ship was available for a month, but soon the DEA's window was closing. The Coast Guard needed its asset back. As the ship was giving up on its mission, El Tigrillo moved into international waters while chasing a marlin on El 24's yacht.[55] The Coast Guard ship was called back, and El Tigrillo was arrested. The iconic photo of him wearing a bulletproof vest, handcuffs, pink shirt, shorts, and flip-flops while flanked by DEA agents made international news.[56]

As described in the previous chapter, the mantle of leadership of the AFO fell to El Tigrillo's nephew Luis Fernando "El Ingeniero" Sánchez Arellano, who, with the support of his uncle Eduardo "El Doctor" Arellano Félix, took over the Tijuana plaza. But El Teo wasn't sure about the new leader and expanded his kidnapping business model. By April of 2008, the two groups would split in violent gun battle over the issue of El Teo's use of kidnapping. Tijuana civil society realized there was a problem and, after the kidnapping of several high-profile civil society leaders, demanded a stronger state reaction.

The Tijuana Federal and Local Response, 2007–10

Realizing kidnapping, extortion, and homicides were on the rise in Tijuana, the Calderón administration announced Operativo Tijuana in January of 2007. When the 3,300 soldiers of the Secretaría de Defensa Nacional (SEDENA) arrived, they stripped the municipal police of their weapons to conduct ballistics tests and find out which cops were in league with traffickers. In protest, many municipal police officers walked off the job, but some patrolled with slingshots to make their point.[57] The results of the tests were never revealed, and eventually the police returned to work with their weapons.[58] The military-only strategy had failed, but the military would play a critical role in the later successful iterations of the policy.

While Mexico's national counternarcotics strategy in 2006 under the Calderón administration overemphasized the military in its battles with drug traffickers, it had a successful model in Tijuana.[59] Tijuana has not made public the details of Operativo Tijuana, but they can be understood through interviews, media reporting, official statements, and statistics.[60]

Following the kidnapping of the president of the COPARMEX on September 2, 2007, Operativo Tijuana was completely revised to have local and state participation.[61] The strategy was completed by December 2007 after a series of meetings between the military, the federal government, state and local authorities, US law enforcement, and civil society groups. Leaders of business and professional associations were especially important, according to interviews conducted during my fieldwork.[62]

The strategy was premised on Los Angeles countergang strategies of the 1990s, according to anonymous interviews of those present.[63] It included both social and security programs, with an emphasis on the security. As Sabet and Felbab-Brown have pointed out, it focused on a hot-spot strategy, which attempted to concentrate resources on key areas.[64] My research indicated that the choice of the first areas was not based on high crime but the presence of the middle class. Thus, the response began in the El Centro and Playas de Tijuana areas. The social prong of the strategy included Educacíon para Rechazar el Uso y Abuso de Drogas (Education for the Rejection of the Use and Abuse of Drugs, much like the US program DARE), a program designed to educate young people to reject drug use. The army also worked extensively with local human rights groups, business leaders, and civil society groups in the planning and implementation of the strategy. This increased local buy-in and intelligence.[65] The local state reaction could be characterized as being led by a single charismatic leader in military commander Gen. Alfonso Duarte Mújica, who coordinated closely with his municipal police chief, Julián Leyzaola.[66]

General Duarte stated overtly that he prioritized targeting the El Teo network. A Los Angeles Times article quoted him as saying that "this was [El Teo's] most active kidnapping cell. . . . And we caught almost all of them. . . . We've been keeping the pressure on. . . . He's constantly moving around, changing houses. . . . He's worried."[67] The reporter went on to point out that the general "sharpened his sights" on El Teo following a shootout with the trafficker's men that left one of his special operations soldiers dead.[68] As I have argued, territorial drug networks such as the El Teo network are more likely to directly challenge the state through force of arms rather than relying on bribery and corruption. While some may see Duarte's response as personal, it is structurally predictable. Lacking bribery money and engaging in a predatory kidnapping-based business strategy, El Teo's drug network came into conflict with the state. The network killed elite soldiers and police officers—twelve in Rosarito alone—and was in turn targeted by the coercive apparatus of the state.[69]

Julián Leyzaola became chief of Tijuana's police force in 2007 and was named secretary of public security in December 2008 to expand his authority.[70] Known as a tough army colonel, he is credited with taking the narcos head on in Tijuana but also for alleged human-rights abuses.[71] Leyzaola became famous for directly participating in shootouts with drug traffickers, punching the face of a dead trafficker, personally signing criminal complaints, using cops he thought were dirty as human shields during bomb threats from El Teo, and "cleaning" up the municipal police force in an allegedly brutal fashion.[72]

"Chemotherapy" for the Municipal Police

The Tijuana strategy focused on capacity building in the municipal police force. A major element of the strategy was the elimination of corrupt police elements, which, like chemotherapy, would be a long, painful, and necessary process. These corrupt officers provided much of the logistical support and intelligence for illicit criminal networks throughout the city, especially for the El Teo network. The police had been deeply corrupted by the AFO over the previous thirty years, and the embedded officers had to be removed.[73]

The tactics for eliminating internal police corruption included regular polygraphs, background checks, drug tests, and training sessions.[74] According to media reports, torture also appears to have been used to gain intelligence and remove corrupt officers. When officers were suspected of corruption, torture in the form of beatings and electrocutions was allegedly used to garner intelligence on other officers suspected of corruption. Allegedly corrupt officers gave up the names of other allegedly corrupt officers, creating "networks" of corrupt police officers to be removed like a cancer. Former police commander Leyzaola denies these charges, but there are media reports and witnesses to support the accusation that torture was used.[75] Many corrupt officers linked to the El Teo network were arrested in this period, though many innocent police officers were no doubt implicated as well. In this sense the strategy may have succeeded in spite of the alleged torture used. There is scant evidence that officers tied to the El Ingeniero–led AFO were successfully removed in this period.[76] Without judging torture's moral implications, we can say that Leyzaola appears to have been effective to the extent that there is more public confidence in the municipal police and that El Teo and all his top lieutenants had been arrested or killed by early 2010.

Police Reform

Through the creation of a stronger, vetted, better-equipped police force and military coordination, Tijuana scored impressive successes against organized crime. The emphasis on municipal police assisted the gathering of intelligence that, when given to the military on incidents related to federal crimes, was effectively acted upon.[77] For example, cases involving assault weapons and large quantities of drugs, which were not under municipal jurisdiction, were referred to the

SEDENA. Interviews within Tijuana indicated a high level of distrust of federal police due to potential corruption. Thus, while the military was less embedded in the society and had less law-enforcement experience, it was more trusted then the federal police. One interviewee stated, *"Mejor un novato que un corrompido"*— better a rookie than a dirty cop.[78]

There were preconditions for the successful reform of the municipal police in Tijuana. Police pay had been increased under the former mayor, Jorge Hank Rhon, to the highest levels in Mexico. Despite the increases, the average police officer made only about $1,100 a month, which is still a small sum in one of the most expensive Mexican cities. Those pay increases were accompanied by other infrastructural improvements, such as new police office buildings and surveillance cameras to prevent crime throughout the city.[79]

The Tijuana "Alliance"

Civil society groups had created the demand that necessitated the strong state reaction in Tijuana. As the victims of kidnappings and extortion, businessmen became ready allies in the fight against territorial drug networks.[80] Human rights groups also participated but continued to accuse the military and police of human rights violations. José Guadalupe Osuna Millán, governor of Baja California, and President Calderón were both PANistas and committed to improving security. The federal government thus provided many of the resources necessary, including the best-trained and most competent components of the Mexican Army (SEDENA).[81]

There was one final "ally" of note in the galvanized state reaction to the El Teo network—rival drug networks. The El Ingeniero faction of the AFO provided the police and military with valuable intelligence about the El Teo network and its key leaders after their split in 2008. We can surmise that this information may have been taken unwittingly by the state through a hotline that the military had established to garner intelligence and tips on narco-traffickers operating in the area or through networks of corrupt police officers on the AFO payroll.[82] The remnants of the AFO are a transactional drug network with extensive money-laundering and trafficking operations that did not want to "heat up the plaza." El Ingeniero was at war with the El Teo territorial drug network from April 2008 to early 2010.[83] When the El Teo territorial drug network broke from the AFO, it increased kidnappings and homicides in the city and issued quotas on the number of police its hit men had to kill for refusing to cooperate. Also, it threatened Chief Leyzaola with bombings of police buildings. The El Teo network had many corrupt police, but some remained loyal to the AFO still led by El Ingeniero. Thus, the AFO internecine conflict was also felt within the municipal police.[84] The El Teo network was territorial, hierarchical, and unable to corrupt or threaten the police and military as thoroughly as some suspect the network led by El Ingeniero did.[85]

"Incompetent Enemies"

The success of the government effort can in part be attributed to "incompetent enemies."[86] The El Teo network was not particularly sophisticated in its methods of kidnapping or intelligence. The victims of kidnapping in this period were not high-level, wealthy individuals in Tijuana society but small business owners, middle-class engineers, restaurateurs, mechanics, and others. This created a strong societal backlash that put tremendous pressure on the state apparatus and made El Teo's soldiers visible to the local population.[87] Intelligence fed to the government by the El Ingeniero–led AFO also certainly played a role.[88] Its ability to create a de facto "alliance" with local authorities and the Sinaloa cartel made it better able to survive the onslaught and redirect the state's energies toward the El Teo network. The state reaction culminated in El Teo's January 2010 arrest. Over the next three months, all of his top lieutenants would also be arrested, marking the successful dissolution of the territorial network.[89] The El Teo territorial network did not have the sophisticated training of the Zetas, who were founded initially by Mexican GAFES (special operations troops). This may explain why the Zetas have outlasted the El Teo network but also why they are drawing so much state attention and suffering so many arrests.[90]

The Mexican government response had many advantages. US law enforcement had specialized task forces eavesdropping on cartel radios and telephone systems and may have fed intelligence to the Mexican state on the El Teo network, as WikiLeaks cables demonstrate the DEA did in the case of the Mexican marines' killing of Arturo Beltrán Leyva in Cuernavaca in December 2009. Mexican law enforcement also benefitted from the training and cooperation of US law enforcement.[91]

The Resilience of the Transactional Drug Network

The transactional remnants of the AFO proved more resilient, though US prosecutors call it by a new name, the Fernando Sánchez Organization (FSO), after having forced its reorganization. The AFO was severely weakened and after 2010 had to share the Tijuana plaza with the formidable Sinaloa cartel, now considered the most powerful cartel in Mexico. The two transactional networks achieved some kind of agreement to keep violence low and focus their efforts on drug trafficking. Many speculate that the Sinaloa cartel pays the AFO a cuota in an agreement the nature of which no one outside the illicit networks understands. Tijuana was considered such a success that President Calderón took Baja California leader Francisco Blake Mora as his new interior minister—a position equivalent in importance to the US vice presidency.[92]

Tijuana has not eliminated its organized crime, but the municipal police have strengthened themselves sufficiently such that illicit networks have taken a lower profile.[93] Organized crime, at least the El Teo network, could not rely on corrupt police officers to provide logistical support and was quickly dissolved by early 2010. Tijuana itself has become too secure for most high-level traffickers to reside in. Most have moved to Baja California Sur; the arrest of El Teo was in La Paz. Murders and the settling of scores between criminal groups, *narcomenudistas* (retail drug dealers) and buyers, continue to occur, but not in broad daylight. Extortion cases and kidnappings, referred to as "high impact" crimes, are also down in the city, as figure 3.1 demonstrates.[94]

Figure 3.1 illustrates that the homicides, kidnappings, and extortion cases surged in Tijuana during the internecine conflict between the territorial drug network led by El Teo and the transactional AFO network led by El Ingeniero. Later, all three violence metrics went down following the dissolution of the El Teo network, suggesting that while the transactional AFO network survived, violence has been reduced in Tijuana. Most important, the sense of security of the average Tijuana citizen has improved. Cartels no longer battle in broad daylight in shiny SUVs. Kidnappings and extortion of people uninvolved in drug trafficking are no longer common. The general sense of fear in Tijuana has abated. The leaders of the state reaction were hailed as heroes. General Duarte

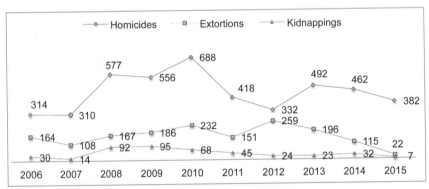

Figure 3.1   Tijuana Homicides, Kidnappings, and Extortions, 2006–15

Source: Data from the state of Baja California. "SEGURIDAD BC," Secretaria de Seguridad Publica de Baja California, September 2015, http://www.seguridadbc.gob.mx/Estadisticas/2015/inci_Tijuana.pdf?id=1899448383. Figures for 2015 based on first eight months.

Mújica received a standing ovation from a business association for his work to improve security. In the ultimate endorsement, Chief Leyzaola was transferred to Ciudad Juárez by the Mexican government in the hope that he could give the Tijuana treatment to that embattled city.[95]

The destruction of the El Teo network brought two years of peace to Tijuana, but some fear a return to violence. Data for 2013 suggest there was an uptick in violence in Tijuana, though it was due to local retail drug dealers competing for territory and not necessarily high-level organized crime battles.[96] Numbers for 2014 indicate a decline from the previous year, and, as seen in figure 3.1, 2015 is on track to be slightly lower than 2014.

Fortunately, the perception of violence was low for society in the two years after El Teo was arrested. Tijuana did not fear a return to the pitched open-street battles between drug networks vying for control of the lucrative plaza. There was more faith in local law enforcement, and it appeared that the Sinaloa cartel and the AFO achieved a more peaceful equilibrium for the city.

As of mid-2015 the situation is different. The trafficking-oriented Sinaloa cartel has entered the Tijuana plaza, and its primary lieutenants operating there are José Antonio "El Tigre" Soto Gastélum and Rene "La Rana" Arzate García, with his brother Alfonso "El Aquiles" Arzate García. The DEA wanted poster for the Tijuana plaza released in 2013 focused on the Sinaloa cartel operatives in Tijuana, demonstrating their importance in the area.[97]

As described in the previous chapter, El Ingeniero was arrested June 2014, which seemed to augur the dissolution of the AFO. Due to the Mexican government's shift from a Napoleonic judicial system to a centralized and uniform oral-trial accusatory system beginning with the Calderón and continuing with the Peña Nieto administration, many military arrests of traffickers from the previous five years have not held up to the scrutiny of the new system.[98] The release of many AFO-affiliated traffickers has led to a "resurgent" AFO, according to Secretary of Public Safety Alejandro Lares Valledares.[99] This situation calls into question the Tijuana model, which relied heavily on local police and military cooperation.

The resurgence of these AFO loyalists has already led to what the weekly magazine *Zeta* calls "small wars" with their Sinaloa counterparts.[100] While this is disconcerting from the perspective of the state, the local police are a stronger institution and are likely more capable of deterring large battles between these organized armed groups. Furthermore, an improved judiciary is a necessary prerequisite for a democratic and effective state to combat organized crime. Over the long term we can expect the state reaction to be better served, with more effective and accurate judicial outcomes.[101] Unfortunately, *Zeta* reporting as recently as January 2015 suggests more than 150 municipal police officers currently on the job have been corrupted by organized crime or are otherwise unfit for duty.[102] Firing potentially corrupt agents poses serious dilemmas. On the one

hand, cleaning up the force is important; on the other hand, these corrupt officers could join forces with organized crime and swell their ranks.

The Tijuana municipal police under the leadership of Lares Valledares have
recently begun implementation of a police body-camera program to minimize society's ability to encourage corruption through the payment of small bribes to avoid
fines.[103] This could be an effective strategy for eliminating the culture of accepting
small bribes, an activity in which officers are sometimes referred to as "grass-eaters."
However, it will likely have no deterrent effect on "meat-eaters"—officers who
actively seek larger payments for more corrupt work.[104]

The recent arrest of ten AFO kidnappers suggests that in competition with
the more trafficking-oriented Sinaloa cartel, the AFO has been forced to resort
to kidnapping and is prompting a greater state reaction. Kidnapping in the
post-internecine-conflict period has appeared much more limited than that
practiced by El Teo. According to statements from the kidnappers, victims were
to be middle-class—not famous or well known—and their numbers were to
be limited.[105] This was a clear risk-mitigation strategy designed to minimize the
threat and consequences of state reaction.

In the final analysis, the municipal police have improved their capacity, while
drug networks in the city have been significantly weakened. No single drug network maintains dominance in Tijuana. Indeed, the one group most likely capable
of achieving that dominance is the Sinaloa cartel, and it has chosen a diffuse, cellular strategy in which its own cells compete with each other to avoid any group
gaining sufficient control to fragment from the main Sinaloa network. While the
2007–10 period for the municipal police could be characterized by a strong and
visceral state reaction led by Leyzaola in coordination with Duarte and backed by
civil society, the future will likely be characterized by the mundane but important
tasks of removing corrupt officers, coordinating with civil society, acquiring body
cameras, and dealing with the retail drug markets in problem areas in the city.
Drug networks in the region appear to have learned the importance of minimizing
the risk of state attention. This could be called into question, however, if recently
released AFO remnants choose to openly confront the Sinaloa cartel in the region.
Even if they do, these are likely to remain small confrontations. Another possibility
is that the AFO has been so fragmented that its cells will jettison the AFO banner
and reform under a new name. In this case, the AFO network would be considered
dissolved to the lowest level of resilience in the state-reaction typology.

Notes

1. My fieldwork and findings on this point are also consistent with the findings
of Sabet. My fieldwork being later, in 2011, it had the advantage of hindsight on the

destruction of the El Teo network, though remnants of it led by the Uriarte brothers continue to operate independently and are referred to as Los Teos. Sabet, "Confrontation, Collusion and Tolerance"; "Guerritas del CAF y Sinaloa."

2. Camp, *Mexico's Military*; Díez and Nicholls, *Mexican Armed Forces.*

3. Central Intelligence Agency, "Mexico"; Diaz, "Before the Subcommittee"; Camp, *Mexico's Military*; Díez and Nicholls, *Mexican Armed Forces.*

4. "Al Día: Merida Initiative"; Jones, "Arrest of Tijuana Ex-Mayor"; Danelo, "New Approach Is Needed."

5. Thompson, "U.S. Widens Its Role"; Thompson and Mazetti, "U.S. Sends Drones."

6. Astorga and Shirk, *Drug Trafficking Organizations*; Sabet, "Confrontation, Collusion and Tolerance."

7. Shannon, *Desperados*; Flores Pérez, "Organized Crime and Official Corruption"; Flores Pérez, *El estado en crisis.*

8. Duran-Martinez and Snyder, "Does Illegality Breed Violence?"; Rios Contreras, "How Government Structure Encourages"; Flores Pérez, "Organized Crime and Official Corruption."

9. Duran-Martinez and Snyder, "Does Illegality Breed Violence?"; Flores Pérez, "Organized Crime and Official Corruption," 105.

10. For a discussion of liberal democracy, see Zakaria, *Future of Freedom*. For a discussion of democracy's negative correlation with organized crime, see Buscaglia and Van Dijk, "Controlling Organized Crime," 8.

11. Democratic consolidation must be careful to include legal reforms to prevent the funding of political campaigns by organized crime, as many fear has been the case in Mexico. Buscaglia and Van Dijk, "Controlling Organized Crime"; Buscaglia, *Judicial Corruption.*

12. Kenney also discusses the "survival imperative," while Solingen discusses political survival. See Bailey and Godson and Sabet on "confrontation." Solingen, *Regional Orders*; Solingen, "Domestic Sources"; Solingen, "Political Economy"; Solingen, *Nuclear Logics*, 292; Kenney, *From Pablo to Osama*, 118.

13. Hernandez, *Narcoland*, 182–84.

14. "Al Día: Merida Initiative"; Jones, "Applying Lessons"; Marosi, "Tijuana Blood Bath"; Edmonds-Poli and Shirk, *Contemporary Mexican Politics*; Solingen, *Nuclear Logics*; Solingen, *Regional Orders*; Solingen, "Domestic Sources"; Sabet, "Confrontation, Collusion and Tolerance."

15. This occurred in Colombia under the administration of Andrés Pastrana Arango in the late 1990s. The Colombian government provided a demilitarized zone to the FARC to facilitate negotiations. The demilitarized zone resulted in a de facto state for the FARC, which engaged in extensive drug trafficking and criminal activities such as car theft in the region they dubbed "FARC-landia." The FARC used the demilitarized zone to rearm and prepare for a continued struggle against the Colombian state. Negotiation was widely considered a failure. See Pardo, "Colombia's Two-Front War."

16. Shannon, *Desperados.*

17. Ibid.

18. Caldwell, "Cartel Secrets"; Hernandez, *Narcoland*; Steve Duncan (law-enforcement investigator [CA Dept. of Justice] focused on the AFO), interview by the author, San Diego, 2010; Caldwell, "Captured"; Caldwell, "Cold-Blooded Killers."

19. Duran-Martinez and Snyder, "Does Illegality Breed Violence?"; Flores Pérez, "Organized Crime and Official Corruption."

20. Duran-Martinez and Snyder, "Does Illegality Breed Violence?"

21. This was not the sole factor at play. With the removal of the DFS, other cartels were threatening to infringe upon the lucrative territory, further forcing the AFO to purchase weaponry and increase their enforcer squads recruited from San Diego gangs (see chapter 2). On the decentralization of the state and its impact on drug-related violence, see Rios Contreras, "How Government Structure Encourages."

22. Hernandez, *Narcoland*, 19.

23. Grillo, *El Narco*, 91.

24. Shirk, "Democratization and Party Organization"; Velasco, *Insurgency, Authoritarianism*; Shirk, *Mexico's New Politics*; Bailey and Godson, *Organized Crime*.

25. Wilkinson and Ellingwood, "Drug Cartels' New Weaponry"; "Mexico's Drug War: Stories."

26. Archibold, "Mexican Navy Believes."

27. Escalante Gonzalbo, "Homicidios 2008–2009."

28. Cook, Rush, and Seelke, *Merida Initiative*; Johnson, "Merida Initiative"; Ribando Seelke and Finklea, *U.S.-Mexican Security Cooperation.*

29. "Al Día: Merida Initiative"; Cook, Rush, and Seelke, *Merida Initiative*; Neher, "Mexico Cleared"; Lacey, "Report Says U.S. Fails"; Johnson, " Merida Initiative."

30. "Cable 09MEXICO2882."

31. Valdez, "ATF."

32. Jones, "Appendix A."

33. Serrano, "Family of U.S. Agent Slain"; Thompson, "Justice Department Accused"; "Brian Terry Family Sues."

34. Eban, "Truth about Fast and Furious."

35. Ravelo, *Los capos*; Blancornelas, *El cártel.*

36. US law-enforcement official, interview by the author by phone, 2014; Chabot, "Historical Case Study ," 111.

37. Former high-ranking Mexican law-enforcement official, interview by the author, Mexico City, November 2010; US law-enforcement official, interview by the author by phone, 2014.

38. US law-enforcement official, interview by the author by phone, 2014.

39. Orama, "U.S. Military Evolution."

40. I am indebted to former Houston DEA intelligence chief Gary Hale on this point. Hale, "Targeting Criminals, Not Crimes."

41. Orama, "U.S. Military Evolution," 20–21.

42. Bowden, *Killing Pablo.*

43. Garzón, *Mafia & Co*; *DEA History 2003–2008.*

44. "Organized Crime Drug Enforcement Task Forces (OCDETF)"; "DEA Programs, Organized Crime Drug Enforcement Task Force (OCDETF)."

45. Duncan, interview.

46. DEA agent David Harrod in *Harrod, Scharf and Ziegler*; Duncan, interview.

47. Quoting David Harrod in *Harrod, Scharf and Ziegler*.

48. Shannon, *Desperados*.

49. US law enforcement official, interview by the author by phone, 2014.

50. *USG Assistance*.

51. "Indictment: United States vs. Armando Villareal Heredia et al."; *DEA History 2003–2008*.

52. *USG Assistance*, 48–49.

53. Duncan, interview.

54. *Harrod, Scharf and Ziegler*, 19.

55. Ibid., 31.

56. *Harrod, Scharf and Ziegler*; Steinhauer and McKinley, "U.S. Officials Arrest"; Stout, "D.E.A. Arrests."

57. Zeller, "Tijuana's Police Take Up Arms."

58. "Tijuana Police Get Guns Back."

59. "US Embassy Cables"; Clark Alfaro, "El 'modelo' Tijuana."

60. Public statements on the plan were limited and came primarily at the federal level from the military in January 2007. Details on the actual strategy were also limited, and the public address announcing it primarily provided the numbers on forces and equipment to be sent to Baja California. It should be noted that Municipal Police Chief Leyzaola took office in September of 2008 and could not have been present for a planning session in or before January 2007. The plan underwent a major revision in December 2007 when Leyzaola arrived. There is no clear strategic statement of the operation or publicly available statistics from the government assessing it. Merlos and La Luz Gonzalez, "Pone gobierno federal"; Ortiz Aguilera, "Operativo Tijuana."

61. "Imparables Comandos de 'El Teo.'"

62. Alvarado, "Leyzaola"; Tijuana businessman, interview by the author, Tijuana, 2011; Tijuana municipal police officer, interview by the author, Tijuana, February 2011; Tijuana journalist, interview by the author, Tijuana, February 2011; Tijuana businessman, interview by the author, Tijuana, 2011.

63. Tijuana municipal police officer, interview by the author, Tijuana, February 2011.

64. I am indebted to an anonymous scholar in Tijuana in 2011 on this point. See also Felbab-Brown, who cogently analogizes the hotspot strategy to the "ink-spot" counterinsurgency concept. Felbab-Brown, *Calderón's Caldron*; Sabet, "Confrontation, Collusion and Tolerance."

65. Tijuana businessman, interview by the author, Tijuana, 2011; Tijuana municipal police officer, interview by the author, Tijuana, February 2011; Tijuana resident, interview by the author, Tijuana in Tijuana, 2011.

66. Marosi, "Tijuana's Security Chief Needs"; Marosi, "Tijuana Reels."

67. Marosi, "Mexico General Battles."

68. Ibid.

69. Ibid.

70. As Sabet points out, Leyzaola replaced Capella, an important civil society representative, whose appointment demonstrated the importance of civil society in the response. Following Leyzaola's departure for Juárez, Capella's reappointment further demonstrated the importance of civil society. Sabet, "Confrontation, Collusion and Tolerance."

71. Marosi, "Tijuana's Security Chief Needs."

72. Finnegan, "In the Name of the Law"; Marosi, "Tijuana's Security Chief Needs."

73. Tijuana municipal police officer, interview by the author, Tijuana, February 2011.

74. Ibid.

75. Associated Press, "¡Porqué se fue Leyzaola!"; Walker, "Tijuana Police Chief Leyzaola"; Finnegan, "In the Name of the Law."

76. "Sinaloa Drug Cartel Said."

77. This would later prove problematic because the arrests conducted by the military would not hold up to the scrutiny of new judicial standards following reforms. This in turn led to the release of many traffickers. Tijuana municipal police officer, interview by the author, Tijuana, February 2011.

78. Ibid.

79. Shirk, "Judicial Reform in Mexico"; Shirk, "Law Enforcement Challenges and 'Smart Borders'"; Tijuana municipal police officer, interview by the author, Tijuana, February 2011.

80. James Ackerman, president of the Tijuana Employers Confederation (COPARMEX), was kidnapped on September 2, 2007, and released shortly thereafter. Ackerman's kidnapping by the El Teo network added to a strong societal backlash against it within the AFO at this time. Tijuana business leader, interview by the author, Tijuana, February 15, 2011.

81. "Reconocen al General Alfonso Duarte Mújica"; Anonymous scholar in Mexico, conversation with the author, March 2011.

82. Felbab-Brown's interviews indicated local law enforcement believed the Sinaloa cartel manipulated the hotline tips, while my interviews suggested the El Ingeniero–led AFO did as well. Felbab-Brown, *Calderón's Caldron*; Tijuana municipal police officer, interview by the author, Tijuana, February 2011.

83. Marosi, "Diagnosis: Irony"; Marosi, "Tijuana Blood Bath"; Marosi, "Mystery Man Blamed"; Marosi, "Tijuana Drug Cartels"; Marosi, "Tijuana Reels."

84. Sabet, "Confrontation, Collusion and Tolerance," 21; Bailey, *Politics of Crime*, chap. 4; Sabet, *Police Reform in Mexico*, chap. 4; Tijuana municipal police officer, interview by the author, Tijuana, February 2011.

85. Betanzos, "Leyzaola 'pactó.'"

86. Tijuana business leader, interview by the author, Tijuana, February 15, 2011.

87. Tijuana businessman, interview by the author, Tijuana, 2011; Mexican official, interview by the author, Tijuana, 2011; Tijuana resident, interview by the author, Tijuana, July 2010.

88. Tijuana municipal police officer, interview by the author, Tijuana, February 2011.

89. Spagat, "Reputed Mexican Drug Lord."

90. *Los Zetas Factsheet*; Brands, "Los Zetas"; Grayson, *Mexico*.

91. "Cable 09MEXICO3573"; Booth and Miroff, "DEA Intelligence Aids."

92. In December 2007 there were 6,076 crimes, and in December 2010 there were 4,304, representing a 33 percent decline in general crime during the implementation of Tijuana's strategy. Mexican official, interview by the author, Tijuana, 2011.

93. Duncan, interview.

94. Mexican official, interview by the author, Tijuana, 2011.

95. Alvarado, "Leyzaola"; ibid.; Marosi, "Tijuana's Security Chief Needs"; Marosi, "Mexico General Battles."

96. For a more detailed description of the state of the underworld in mid-2013 Tijuana, see Jones, *Explaining the Slight Uptick*; Replogle, "Street Dealers Fuel."

97. Duncan, correspondence with the author, 2015.

98. Rios, *Mexico's* Petite Révolution.

99. Gagne, "Tijuana Cartel Resurgent."

100. "Guerritas del CAF y Sinaloa."

101. Rios, *Mexico's* Petite Révolution.

102. "Tortura y corrupción."

103. Dibble, "Tijuana Police to Use."

104. Here Sabet references the terms used by the Mollen commission related to different types of officer corruption. Sabet, *Police Reform in Mexico*, 103.

105. "Activos secuestradores del CAF."

4

The Sinaloa Cartel, Los Zetas, and Los Caballeros Templarios

THIS CHAPTER WILL APPLY the state-reaction theoretical framework to three minicases: the Sinaloa cartel, the Gulf cartel and its offshoot Los Zetas, and Los Caballeros Templarios (CT), an offshoot of La Familia Michoacána (LFM). The comparison will use George and Bennett's method of "structured focused comparison" and is an example of what they call "plausibility probing."[1] By developing these three mini historical case studies and comparing them to the main historical case study, I gain analytical leverage for the state-reaction argument and also show where the argument falls short, though, as I will argue in the conclusion, the cases are ongoing.

Each case was selected because of its important and representative role in Mexican drug-trafficking networks. Los Zetas are highly "territorial" but have increased transactional activities over time. The Sinaloa cartel is known for its emphasis on trafficking activities and contracting of services to smaller groups in a "transactional" manner, as Reuter might argue. The CT, having risen out of the remains of the LFM network, has continued to justify itself ideologically with a religious rationalization coupled with regional protection "branding."[2] The cases will examine the state-reaction framework by assessing the four variables—business model, risk, strength of state reaction, and resilience over time—using Thelen's historical institutionalism framework to organize the analysis.[3]

Case Study 1: The Sinaloa Cartel Resilience

As outlined in chapter 2, like the Arellano Félix Organization, the Sinaloa cartel was born of the dissolution of the Guadalajara cartel following the transfer of Miguel Angel Félix Gallardo to a new maximum-security prison. One of the first disruptive events was the conflict between Joaquin "El Chapo" Guzmán Loera, who would become one of the leaders of the Sinaloa cartel, and the Arellanos. In

many ways this event marked a fragmentation within the federation of traffickers that had inherited the Guadalajara cartel business. Up to this point, they had
largely maintained their cooperative agreements, agreeing to pay each other a
cuota to pass through each other's territories, but the conflict with the Arellanos
was one of the first events to test this new territorial arrangement among Mexican trafficking networks.[4]

After the Christine's Disco assassination attempt by Chapo Guzmán against
the Arellanos described in chapter 2, the Arellanos hunted him and his partners
Ismael "El Mayo" Zambada García and Héctor Luis "El Güero" Palma Salazar,
with whom they were already in conflict. This led to the assassination of the archbishop of Guadalajara in 1993 by AFO gunmen.[5] Guzmán narrowly escaped but
was arrested in Guatemala in 1993. El Güero, also part of the blood feud with
the Arellanos, was arrested in 1995. Guzmán was able to continue functioning
as a trafficker from behind bars in his maximum-security prison.[6] During this
period, Guzmán followed a highly trafficking-oriented and transactional business model.[7] He emphasized corruption, beginning with the prison itself, where
it has been well documented that he took full control and effectively ran the
institution and his trafficking network.[8]

The arrest of Guzmán did not have an impact upon the resilience of his group
of traffickers, who at this time were still in alliance with Amado Carrillo Fuentes,
leader of the Carrillo Fuentes Organization (CFO), also known as the Juárez cartel. As the lore goes, Carrillo Fuentes died in 1997 in a botched plastic-surgery
operation. Guzmán's importance as a trafficker increased while he was behind
bars, further mitigating the impact of his arrest on the resilience of the network.
Guillermo Valdés Castellanos, the former head of Center for Investigation and
National Security (CISEN), Mexico's premier intelligence agency, has argued
that Guzmán was one of the few traffickers for whom prison was no impediment
to running operations, which he attributed to personal characteristics, such as
"his great ability to seduce people, and great imagination and entrepreneurial
creativity."[9] In 2001, Guzmán escaped from federal maximum-security prison
roughly a week after the Mexican Supreme Court ruled that extradition of Mexicans without dual US citizenship was now permissible.[10] This escape can be
viewed as a mechanism to avoid the potentially high risk of extradition to the
United States prison system, which would have prevented him from running his
operations from behind bars. What had been a risk-mitigation strategy—running
operations from behind bars—suddenly became highly risky due to the possibility of US extradition.

As Hernandez argues, a review of documents shows a high level of complicity
between Guzmán and high-ranking federal government officials that made his
escape possible.[11] Regardless of the specifics, this is an example of high-level corruption, which is consistent with the strategies employed by trafficking-oriented

networks that use their high profits to buy the services of the state and mitigate its reaction to them.

Upon leaving prison in 2001, Guzmán moved aggressively. After the arrest of Osiel Cárdenas Guillén (2003), he viewed the Gulf cartel as weak and attempted to take the important Nuevo Laredo trafficking plaza. In coordination with the Beltrán Leyvas, Guzmán sent his lieutenant Edgar "La Barbie" Valdez Villarreal to take military control of Nuevo Laredo for trafficking purposes.[12] While the majority of Guzmán's business was trafficking oriented, this aggressive attempt to wrest control of a new territory from its existing owners is an example of strategically territorial behavior. The argument here is not that the Sinaloa cartel engaged in no territorial behavior but that it is predominantly a trafficking-oriented group, less interested in the control of territory than the flow of drugs. When it attempts strategic territorial pushes, it is to minimize the amount of money paid in taxes to rival networks in control of trafficking corridors. The bitter attempt to capture Nuevo Laredo failed by 2007, and the Gulf cartel and its armed wing Los Zetas emerged victorious and exacted a tax for passing drugs through the territory.[13]

Following the failure in Nuevo Laredo, Guzmán then set his sights on another important trafficking corridor, Ciudad Juárez. The conflict between Guzmán and the Juárez cartel became very brutal and turned Ciudad Juárez into "murder city."[14] Here the Sinaloa cartel allied with local territorial street gangs, such as the Artistas Asesinas, to fight the Juárez cartel, which contracted its own longtime allies, the corrupted local police that La Línea and the Barrio Azteca street gang comprised.[15] The transactional Sinaloa cartel also contracted the Gente Nueva hit men, who had previously been used in Veracruz against its rivals. Moore argues this weakens the transactional argument regarding the Sinaloa cartel, but the Gente Nueva appear to be used in conflict with Los Zetas and allied drug networks, not for extorting the local population.[16]

La Línea is composed of current and former corrupted police who had served as the security and bodyguard force for Vicente Carrillo Fuentes, head of the CFO. As Sullivan argues, La Línea "appears to act as a specialized variant of a third-generation gang essentially serving as mercenaries."[17] It further has links to other street gangs, such as the Barrio Azteca, common rivalries with gangs opposed to the CFO, and sophisticated tactics, including the use of improvised explosive devices. La Línea's protection of drug smuggling can be viewed as a transactional service, but its collection of extortion or war taxes and violent confrontation with authorities are highly territorial and even "insurgent" activities.[18] The Barrio Azteca gang is a violent hybrid street and prison gang that straddles both sides of the Texas border. As Sullivan argues, its "hierarchy is designed to seek profit for territorial control."[19] It engages in heavy extortion of retail drug dealers to fund its operations, and during the CFO–Sinaloa cartel, war was allied to La Línea. The CFO's increased reliance on La Línea and Barrio Azteca demonstrates a movement toward the territorial, yet, because this was a contracted service, the CFO remains transactional in the analysis. This is a place where the identification of business model becomes murky as networked actors with long-standing relationships complicate analysis.

While the Sinaloa cartel was generally considered to have emerged as the dominant force in Ciudad Juárez, the CFO persisted, finding resilience in alliances with the Gulf cartel and Los Zetas and later the Beltrán Leyva Organization (BLO).[20] The intelligence firm Stratfor has argued that as of 2014, the Sinaloa cartel was losing ground in Juárez to the CFO in alliance with Los Zetas, fitting Chindea's argument on the importance of alliances.[21]

Fragmentation and Reduced Resilience

In 2008, the Sinaloa cartel saw a reduced level of resilience as its federation fragmented into internecine conflict. The Beltrán Leyva brothers split from Guzmán and his partners El Mayo and Juan José "El Azul" Esparragoza Moreno after the arrest of Alfredo "El Mochomo" Beltrán Leyva, which his brothers viewed as Guzmán's personal handiwork, and declared war on Guzmán.[22] This is one of the difficulties in the study of organized crime. The true nature and motivations of arrests are difficult to understand and prove. On the one hand, we can view the arrest of one of the Beltrán Leyva brothers as a successful state strike against the Sinaloa drug network (a disruptive event), while it can also be viewed as an individual power play in which Guzmán—who is known for using tips to state authorities against his enemies—maintains control and power in his network by using corrupt state officials. Regardless, the internecine conflict between the Sinaloa drug network and the breakaway BLO increased violence in their home state of Sinaloa and reduced the Sinaloa drug network's resilience.[23]

The BLO was responsible for high-level bribes and was the intelligence apparatus for the Sinaloa cartel. This was evidenced by the thirty-five investigators of the anti-organized-crime unit of the Mexican attorney general's office (PGR-SIEDO) that the BLO had on its payroll in 2008.[24] It, too, was highly trafficking oriented, though as an intelligence apparatus was likely more territorial than Guzmán and his partners. This may have been an instance of two transactional networks coming into conflict over their ability to corrupt the state.[25] Hernandez argues that it may also have been about personal conflicts between Guzmán and the Beltrán Leyvas, in which case it may have boiled down to the petty rivalries and jealousies that can turn into violent conflict in illicit markets that lack dispute-resolution mechanisms.[26]

The BLO clearly emerged with reduced levels of resilience during this split. It appeared to suffer the most fragmentation, and many spin-off networks emerged from the BLO carcass in this period, including local territorial networks such as Guerreros Unidos and the South Pacific cartel among others, which played a role in increasing violence levels in the city of Cuernavaca, south of Mexico City.[27] The Guerreros Unidos, operating as local territorial group, would later be implicated in the massacre of forty-three students in Iguala.[28] These spin-off drug networks are another example of the tendency to split along functional lines of specialization.

The partnership of Guzmán, El Azul, Ignacio "Nacho" Coronel Villarreal, and El Mayo is what most once considered "the Sinaloa cartel." It is widely considered to have emerged victorious from the struggle with the BLO, leading some to even claim the BLO was dead in the 2012 period following the famous killing by Mexican marines of Arturo Beltrán Leyva in Cuernavaca in 2009.[29] Later, remnants of the fractured BLO (still calling themselves the BLO) emerged, putting those claims to rest. Government officials in the United States and Mexico also admitted that the BLO appeared to be resurgent in the subsequent years. The recent arrest of Héctor "El H" Beltrán Leyva suggests that the BLO may still continue to function. The business model of the BLO as led by El H was clearly highly trafficking oriented. At his recent arrest, he was captured with a politico/business associate who assisted with the transactional business of drug trafficking.[30]

The Sinaloa cartel smelled weakness in 2008 and attempted to capitalize on the internecine conflict between the AFO and its breakaway territorial faction led by Eduardo Teodoro "El Teo" García Simental.[31] This Sinaloa cartel alliance with El Teo was short-lived and was likely jettisoned by the Sinaloa cartel because of the violence of the El Teo network and the negative state attention it engendered. The ability to put profits and drug trafficking over conflict and territorial business models further supports the state-reaction argument by demonstrating a conscious effort to reduce risk of state intervention that would disrupt drug profits.[32]

In 2010, the Sinaloa cartel lost a major player in its federation. Nacho Coronel, who was known for methamphetamine production and cocaine trafficking in the states of Nayarit, Jalisco, and parts of Michoacán, was killed when authorities attempted to arrest him. Coronel had maintained a low profile in the years before his death—fitting the transactional model—and was close to Guzmán, who had married his niece. The remnants of Coronel's network fragmented from the Sinaloa cartel to form the Cartel Jalisco Nueva Generación (CJNG), which would eventually rejoin and function as an armed wing of the Sinaloa cartel against Los Zetas. Until an attack on April 6, 2015, in which the CJNG killed fifteen police officers, the CJNG was considered one of Mexico's fastest-growing drug networks. As Gagne argues, it will likely be weakened and fragmented following the state reaction it will likely endure.[33]

The arrest of José Rodrigo "El Chino Ántrax" Aréchiga Gamboa, in January 2014 in Amsterdam constitutes a disruptive event.[34] He was head of Los Ántrax, an elite group of hit men working for the Sinaloa cartel in a networked fashion.[35] His arrest is an example of the focus of state reactions, in this case the US government and Interpol focusing on the most violent actors in the various cartels. Analysts such as Stratfor have argued his arrest has in part limited the Sinaloa cartel's ability to push into outside territories, but it has not appeared to engender a massive fragmentation or restructuring of the group.[36]

Arrest of Chapo Guzmán

The arrest of Chapo Guzmán in early 2014 came as a shock to many who believed his ability to corrupt the highest levels of government would keep him protected. It appears the Sinaloa cartel was unaffected, because the mantle of leadership passed easily on to El Mayo, the obvious second in command. Guzmán's arrest serves as evidence that the stronger Mexican state institutions are capable of engaging in decapitation strikes against drug network leaders. However, it is also evidence of the resilience of the network. At best, the arrest could be considered to have led to a reorganization of the network, which is a reduced level of resilience in my typology. However, there has been little publicly available evidence—other than DEA official statements—that there has been a transition of Guzmán's personnel to El Mayo's in the Arizona area or that the arrest has disrupted or forced a painful reorganization of the network.[37] It is also possible Guzmán played a role in mitigating conflict from behind bars before his escape.[38]

The arrest and subsequent reporting did illustrate the sophisticated security measures Guzmán used to reduce his vulnerability to arrest through network structures and compartmentalization. He reportedly used a complex communication system, replete with intermediaries who received messages on BlackBerry smartphones and were required to write them down before relaying them via public Wi-Fi connections.[39] Guzmán's arrest must be viewed in the context of the careful case building by US and Mexican authorities. The arrest and interrogations of Mayo Zambada's sons Vicente "El Mayito" Zambada Niebla in 2009 and Serafín Zambada Ortiz in 2013 likely played a role in garnering the intelligence needed to apprehend Guzmán.[40]

Release of Caro Quintero

The release of Rafael Caro Quintero in 2013 shocked the American Drug Enforcement Administration (DEA). Quintero's role in the killing of DEA agent Enrique Camarena was a seminal event for the DEA and the Mexican government.[41] It is unknown what role Caro Quintero plays in drug trafficking in Mexico. American law enforcement officials have speculated that his release from prison was part of a settlement negotiated with the Mexican government, and some, such as Sullivan, have questioned whether Guzmán may have been able to run his business from the relative safety of a jail cell. Running operations from behind bars confers certain advantages, including "safety and refuge from rivals."[42] It was speculated that Caro Quintero is highly involved in drug trafficking and filled any void left by Guzmán's arrest. Since Guzmán's escape, Caro Quintero appears to continue to play a major role in drug trafficking and there have been no reports of conflict between the two.[43]

Escape of Chapo Guzmán

Apprehending Guzmán and incarcerating him are two different things. Guzmán's July 2015 escape from a maximum-security prison via a tunnel was a major embarrassment to the Mexican government. His arrest had been one of the great successes of the Peña Nieto administration and had allowed it to argue that it favored no drug networks.[44] For the state-reaction argument, Guzmán's arrest was a difficult data point to explain. His escape is far easier, though I don't take the simple strategy of arguing that it was purely top-level corruption that allowed him to escape, although that may yet prove to have been the case.

The state-reaction argument posits twenty-six characteristics (see appendix) that make transactional networks resilient. Many of them are present in, and may have contributed to, the escape. They include trafficking networks' focus on high profits, which facilitate corruption payments and allow for state co-option. Further, the tunnel was obviously constructed using the same expertise used to construct Guzmán's drug tunnels under the US–Mexican border.[45] There has been a general consensus that Guzmán must have had assistance from inside the prison, and numerous guards and prison leaders have been arrested on charges for suspected collusion.[46]

The administration-level collusion argument, while possible, has not had specific evidence to support it. This escape was such an embarrassment to the Peña Nieto administration during a politically difficult period (the disappearance of forty-three students has led to calls for the administration to resign) that it is hard to believe that the administration would sanction the escape.[47] In hindsight, we know the Mexican government had just weeks prior to the escape received a US government request to extradite Guzmán, which had gone unheeded. Just as the news of extradition prompted Guzmán's earlier escape (2001), rumors of extradition may too have sped up his plans.[48]

The "Death" of El Azul

Interestingly, in 2014 media reported that El Azul had died.[49] El Azul appears to have either died or faked his own death to avoid wars and prosecution. Faking his own death would fit El Azul's low-profile trafficking-oriented character. In some respects this could increase violence. El Azul was a peacemaker and known as an alliance builder in Sinaloa and beyond.[50] Without his pacifying presence, there might be increased fragmentation within the network. However, given that law enforcement has been extremely skeptical of El Azul's "death,"[51] he is likely not getting what he really wanted—invisibility—and thus may continue to play a role in the Sinaloa cartel.

Risk and Business-Model Description

The Sinaloa cartel is widely considered to have a trafficking-oriented business model, as analysts such as Mazzitelli and Dudley, Mexican government officials, and others have argued.[52] Keefe refers in his writings to the Sinaloa cartel as keeping to its "core competency" of drug trafficking.[53] It "brands" itself through *narco-mantas* (notes left by drug traffickers) and public communications as being trafficking oriented and not territorial.[54] This minimizes the state and societal reaction to the network, thus minimizing risk.

As one security contractor related to me, the Sinaloa cartel engages in extortion of legitimate companies in the areas it controls, similar to other drug networks such as Los Zetas. It typically does this in ways indicative of what Bailey conceptualizes as "complex crime." Instead of simply demanding a percentage of the business, the Sinaloa cartel is likely to mask extortion through the control of local vendors, who are required to charge exorbitant markups. In this fashion, territorial extortion is masked.[55]

While the Sinaloa cartel does engage in kidnapping and extortion, it is generally to a lesser degree than other drug networks, and areas where it operates typically have lower kidnapping rates. For example, in the 2010 period when the Sinaloa cartel made inroads into the Tijuana plaza following the internecine conflict and weakening of the AFO, a dramatic decrease in kidnappings followed. This was likely due to an agreement between the AFO and the Sinaloa cartel to minimize kidnappings because it heated up the plaza for drug trafficking.[56]

As described by Grillo, innovation is built into the Sinaloa cartel's business model.[57] Employees on the Sinaloa cartel's payroll specialize in the development of new smuggling techniques. Chapo Guzmán is known to be one of the first major drug traffickers to build a tunnel into the United States, according to Beith.[58] Innovation provides options for smuggling techniques that, in turn, allows for a diverse portfolio, a common business mechanism for minimizing risk.

In cooperation with Amado Carrillo Fuentes, traffickers affiliated with the Juárez cartel in the 1990s were highly cooperative and generally pacific—the relationship with the Arellanos of Tijuana being an exception and not a large enough one to move national homicide rates.[59] The high profits of the transactional business model increase the ability to corrupt. As will be shown, throughout its history, the Sinaloa cartel was able to corrupt government officials, particularly at the state and federal levels. This can also be viewed a "transaction," as Reuter might argue, insofar as the network is buying the services of the state.[60] Data from bribery cases compiled by National Public Radio showed that the Sinaloa cartel prefers bribing at the state and federal levels, while the more territorial Zetas and LFM focused on local and state officials.[61] To deal with rival traffickers, the Sinaloa cartel is known for providing the state with information about rivals instead of engaging in violent confrontation, another strategy that minimizes risk.[62]

The Sinaloa cartel has been highly adaptive. In response to increased pressure on the land border, it has increased the use of pangas (open-hulled boats with outboard motors) in smuggling operations on the coast of California.[63] In these operations, it is known to utilize "blind mules"—individuals who think they are being hired for landscaping jobs, then are threatened to make sure they participate as off-loaders in a boat crew. While not all mules are "blind," their use minimizes risk to core network members.[64]

To deal with its high profits, the Sinaloa cartel engages in significant money laundering. As the Mexican government placed regulations on Mexican currency exchanges and the US government increased enforcement to prevent bulk cash smuggling into Mexico, the Sinaloa cartel resorted to increasingly clever mechanisms to reduce risk and maximize its ability to return profits to Mexico.[65] While all drug networks engage in money laundering, the Sinaloa cartel has been increasingly targeted by the Treasury Department's Office of Foreign Assets Control (OFAC) narcotics sanctions, further evidence of its high-profit and trafficking-oriented business model.[66]

Compartmentalization was built into the Sinaloa cartel business model, lending credence to the understanding of the Sinaloa cartel as a network.[67] One case illustrated this point. Following the arrest of El Teo, who led a confrontation against the AFO from 2008 to 2010 in Tijuana, the Sinaloa cartel began annexing El Teo's cells, including one led by a lieutenant, Jesús Israel "El Tomate" de la Cruz López. But the Sinaloa cartel did not simply make him a member of their network. He was treated as a rookie who would have to transport a certain number of drug loads. The Sinaloa cartel maintained this level of compartmentalization following the split with the BLO, which they believed had gained too much independent power. The leaders had learned from their mistake of giving one group of cells too much control. They also annexed other cells in the area and kept them in competition with each other so that no lieutenant could build an independent power base and break away from them in any region, according to El Tomate's interrogation.[68]

Case Study 2: The Gulf Cartel and Los Zetas

The Gulf cartel can trace its roots back to the smugglers in Matamoros who moved whiskey and alcohol into the United States during Prohibition.[69] When Prohibition ended, alcohol was replaced by marijuana (prohibited in the United States since 1937) and heroin, which had been outlawed by the Harrison Act earlier in the century. The volume and profits of heroin trafficking were dwarfed by alcohol trafficking until Prohibition's repeal. The Gulf cartel was the only major drug network that was not composed of traffickers from Sinaloa.[70] It was highly trafficking-oriented throughout much of its history. In the 1980s and 1990s, it became famous for high-level corruption in the administration of Carlos Salinas de Gortari. It was later discovered that the president's brother Raúl had accepted bribes from the Gulf cartel.[71] Some academics, such as Luis Astorga, have argued that this marked a significant challenge to the relationship between the state and the Sinaloa-based traffickers.[72] Others, such as Anabel Hernandez, have argued that despite these bribes, the government maintained a relationship with Sinaloa-based traffickers and that this only represented corrupt officials' double-dipping.[73]

As the work of Carlos Flores Pérez demonstrates, the Gulf drug cartel was successful in corrupting the political elite in the state of Tamaulipas.[74] The recent indictment of Tamaulipas governor Tomás Yarrington in the United States further demonstrates how high the levels of corruption went in the region.[75] The Gulf cartel also collected a toll from other cartels for trafficking through its territory, much like the AFO did in its territories in the 1990s. While this was an example of a territorial activity, it was subservient to the drug-trafficking business for the Gulf cartel in this period.[76]

Regardless of the view of which drug networks the state favored in this period, the weight of all drug-trafficking networks in this period were firmly trafficking oriented. In reality, the state was not moving effectively against any of the major trafficking networks, making only cursory arrests that did not significantly challenge the resilience of any of the networks. The arrest of Juan García Ábrego in 1996 was significant in that he was the head of the Gulf cartel, but it had little effect on the cartel's profits and operations, at least initially. Insofar as there was a power succession, it could be argued that there was a reorganization of the operation (a lower level of resilience), but the arrest had a limited effect. While the arrest left a leadership vacuum, it was filled by the younger, more violent Osiel Cárdenas Guillén. Cárdenas took the reins of the Gulf cartel in conjunction with his friend Salvador Gómez Herrera, whom he would kill, earning himself the nickname "Mata-Amigo," or the Friend Killer.[77]

Recruitment of Los Zetas

Osiel Cárdenas Guillén wanted a personal bodyguard force and began recruitment of Los Zetas in the late 1990s. There are many versions of how the recruitment began, but it centers on Cárdenas contacting Arturo "Z-1" Guzmán Decena of the Grupo Aeromóvil Fuerzas Especiales (GAFES), who agreed to leave the special operations unit and work as a bodyguard for him.[78] Guzmán Decena recruited other operatives from the GAFES and another unit with a similar level of training. Estimates range as to the number of original operatives recruited, but most center around thirty. Los Zetas quickly became a potent intelligence force, useful for the control of territory and expansion of the Gulf cartel into all of the strategic areas of northeastern Mexico in the late 1990s. The relationship between Los Zetas and the Gulf cartel in this period could be described as one in which the territorial Zetas were subservient to the traffickers of the Gulf cartel. Los Zetas were "transactionally" paid for services.[79] Cárdenas Guillén redistributed profits within the organization from the traffickers to the territorial enforcers.[80] This arrangement is highly susceptible to kingpin-strike disruption. Structurally, this changed rather quickly. Los Zetas as an intelligence force employed a network of *halcones*, or paid lookouts, and managed prostitutes known as *leopardos*, who were also valuable for gaining intelligence and controlling territory.[81] Like traditional mafias, they engaged in lending and debt collection. When debtors who were employees of local utilities could not meet their obligations, territorial networks were able to take control of the local utilities through the compromised employees. This allowed Los Zetas to enter the vast markets of electricity and telecommunications.[82]

Los Zetas also began extorting individuals and companies for protection taxes, in part through the threat of kidnapping for ransom. Their brutality became famous and gave them a strong reputation for violence.[83] Los Zetas also expanded into oil theft in Tamaulipas and Vera Cruz. This has led to direct confrontation with the Mexican military. Unlike other drug networks, Los Zetas did not retreat from escalated conflict with the Mexican state but instead used blockade tactics to mitigate the consequences of state action against them, as described by Sullivan:

For example, on August 14, 2010, members of the Zetas blocked off at least 13 major roads in Monterrey, preventing access to the city's international airport and major highways entering and exiting the north-ern industrial city. The narcobloqueos were deployed in the aftermath of a shootout between the military and Los Zetas that killed reputed Monter-rey Zeta leader "El Sonrics." Drivers were carjacked and their cars were used to close the roads. These blockades are a "show of force," a demon-stration of the Zetas' power.[84]

Many, such as Grillo, Brands, Sullivan, and Elkus, have referred to Los Zetas as examples of "narco insurgents" or "criminal insurgents."[85] Insurgencies aspire to statehood, which is a fundamentally territorial existence. Thus, the concept of Los Zetas as both territorial and insurgent should not surprise us, as they are not mutually exclusive.[86]

This expansion/diversification of criminal activities coincided similarly with the same territorial business-model rise in the El Teo network in the early 2000s. Los Zetas also began annexing local youth street gangs in this period, offering to pay them a salary and train them in Zeta tactics. This assisted their entry into retail drug sales, copyright piracy, gathering of local intelligence, and increased control over local communities.[87] Due to their direct confrontation with the state through assassinations and infantry tactics, Los Zetas also engaged in risk-mitigation strategies to minimize the state's response. These included imposing media blackouts by threatening journalists and throwing grenades into the offices of the newspaper *Reforma* but also putting journalists on their payroll for favorable coverage.[88] All of this demonstrated the emergence of a highly ter-ritorial business model.[89] But this business model was still controlled by a larger and highly profitable trafficking network.

Disruptive Event: Arrest of Osiel Cárdenas Guillén

Osiel Cárdenas Guillén, having a violent personality, made a mistake in the late 1990s that would trigger a strong state reaction against him from the US gov-ernment. Two FBI agents were driving in Matamoros with a confidential infor-mant (CI), who was pointing out the homes of drug traffickers and providing information about them. The vehicle was noticed by Gulf Cartel lookouts, who summoned Cárdenas Guillén and called other cars with gunmen to surround the vehicle. Cárdenas Guillén attempted to remove the CI from the vehicle, ostensibly to kill him. The agents refused to turn over the CI and were eventually escorted by the drug traffickers, including Cárdenas Guillén, to the border. Despite a peaceful resolution, the showdown was tense and enraged US law enforcement.[90]

Bureaucratically, US law-enforcement agencies emphasized the targeting of Cárdenas for arrest as a kingpin. In 2003, he was arrested and placed in a

Mexican prison. While there, Los Zetas asked Cárdenas for permission to engage in drug trafficking in Central America.[91] Cárdenas had little option but to allow them to expand.[92] As Dudley describes, Los Zetas were highly territorial in their expansion into Central America, particularly in Guatemala.[93] This period was one of significant territorial expansion for Los Zetas throughout southern Mexico and Central America. A reorganization was taking place within the drug network, and though there was no violence or conflict, this was a lower level of resilience for the Gulf–Zetas network.

The removal of Cárdenas from the network could thus be viewed as process that occurred over four years. Frustrated by his ability to run operations from behind bars, the Mexican and US governments agreed to extradite Cárdenas to a US prison cell in Houston in 2007.[94] Following this, Los Zetas, who had already gained increased financial independence through diversified territorial operations and an entry into drug trafficking, declared formal independence.[95] This demonstrates a lower level of resilience (fragmentation) in the model. While Los Zetas and their former masters cooperated in this period, they had fragmented into two disparate networks with their own identities. This situation limped along until its explosion in 2010.

The Gulf–Zeta war followed a personnel dispute in which an entire Gulf cartel cell was killed when it "failed to authenticate" a password to enter the city of Reynosa. "The Zetas admitted fault," according to former DEA Houston intelligence chief Gary Hale, but refused to turn over the responsible Zeta commander, and the spark ignited the powder keg.[96] Hale argues this was one of three potential "fog of war" events that led to the split, while Sullivan and Logan point to another Gulf–Zeta killing and demand for retribution.[97] The fact that multiple incidents can be pointed to as the precipitant of the split suggests that the split was in reality structurally preconditioned, based on the two networks' divergent business models.[98] The fragmentation had deepened into an internecine conflict that would spike levels of violence in northeastern Mexico. It was the traffickers (the Cárdenas brothers) against the territorial, paramilitary Los Zetas.[99] This period significantly weakened both groups, as the Mexican government dispatched federal troops to quell violence.[100]

Disruptive Events for the Gulf Cartel

The Gulf cartel suffered a series of high-level arrests, including that of Jorge Eduardo "El Coss" Costilla Sánchez (leader of the network) in 2012 and Arturo Ezequiel "Tony Tormenta" Cárdenas Guillén (another network leader and brother of Osiel Cárdenas Guillén) in 2010.[101] Interestingly, the state was punishing the Gulf cartel for high levels of violence in the area and the territorial business model of Los Zetas. These kingpin strikes laid bare further divisions within the Gulf cartel between Los Metros and Los Rojos, two trafficking groups that had long been within the Gulf cartel.[102] This is another example of fragmentation and internecine conflict of the network and reduced resilience as these groups battled with each other and Los Zetas.

The Gulf cartel appeared resurgent in 2012, supporting the argument that trafficking-oriented networks are more resilient. A report from Southern Pulse (a private investigation firm comprising network regional experts) as reported on by Insight Crime argued that the Gulf cartel had retaken 75 percent of the strategic city of Monterrey in northeastern Mexico.[103] Interviews with local law enforcement were also consistent with this conceptualization of the Gulf cartel as more trafficking oriented and Los Zetas as more mafia-like or territorially oriented.[104] More recently, however, the Gulf cartel appears to be suffering from increased fragmentation and internecine conflict. Since 2013, further splinter networks have split from the Gulf cartel, such as those calling themselves Dragones and Ciclones.[105]

Disruptive Events for Los Zetas

Following the death of Arturo "Z-1" Guzmán Decena in 2002 and the arrest of Rogelio "El Kelín / Z-2" González Pizaña in 2004, Los Zetas reorganized and deepened their territorial business model under the new leader, Heriberto "Z-3" Lazcano Lazcano, who took control of the network in 2004. Grayson and Logan argue in their book that Los Zetas make only 50 percent of their revenues from cocaine, while the rest comes from locally based crime such as kidnapping and extortion. Dudley and Pachico argue that the percentage of revenue derived from local crime by Los Zetas is higher.[106] Lazcano deepened the diversification of criminal activities with his second-in-command, Miguel "Z-40" Treviño Morales, who controlled the important Nuevo Laredo plaza.[107]

San Fernando Massacre

Part of the territorial business model of Los Zetas became the direct involvement and/or taxation of human smuggling/trafficking in the northeast. The killing of seventy-two migrants in 2010 in San Fernando, Tamaulipas, led to shock and outrage from the populace and the Mexican federal government. The massacre was discovered by the military when one of the migrants survived, despite serious injuries, by hiding among the dead and later reached a military checkpoint. Later, more mass graves were found in the same city, raising the death toll to more than 126. Speculation as to motives for the massacre included the possibilities that the migrants had been killed for refusing to join Los Zetas and that they were mistaken for Gulf cartel members.[108]

In 2011, Los Zetas members attacked a casino in Monterrey, killing fifty-three people. The gunmen set the casino on fire, apparently for its owners' failure to make extortion payments.[109] These attacks thus stem from the desire to tax their territory. These high-profile massacres resulted in significant state attention for Los Zetas and cemented their reputation as a brutal and ruthless drug network.[110] There is some evidence that Los Zetas have learned that this is a high-risk strategy, leading to increased government enforcement and negative consequences. For example, there have been suggestions that Zeta leadership has encouraged members to minimize violence when possible and hide bodies to minimize the perception of violence and public outcry. Further, they have engaged in media blackouts to prevent reporting of violence in the areas they control. These are examples of territorial drug networks attempting to minimize their risk of state reaction. This suggests that Los Zetas are a "learning" or "sense-making" organization that actively attempts to reduce risk to maximize resilience, as Kenney and Chabot might argue.[111]

Multiple factors in the model might explain why Los Zetas may be moving away from confrontational strategies. The Mexican state has significantly improved its ability to capture or kill high-value targets, suggesting that the consequences of confrontation are now higher. Thus, with new and higher consequences, the Zeta risk calculation may be shifting toward a low-profile model. The difficulty for Los Zetas is that the diversified business model, which should be risk minimizing, continues to necessitate territorial control and extortion capacity.

Despite a highly territorial business model and significant state attention, Los Zetas have suffered relatively little fragmentation in terms of internecine conflict compared to the Gulf cartel. This may in part be due to how I define internecine conflict here, where a group must split off from the main network and fight under a new banner. Rivals of Los Zetas can simply join the Gulf cartel and fight them, which may make splinter groups appear artificially limited.

While analysts expected a conflict between Z-3 and Z-40, causing fragmentation and internecine conflict within Los Zetas, this appears not to have been the case. Z-3's death in October of 2012 at the hands of Mexican marines in northeastern Mexico appears to have led to a fairly smooth transition to Z-40.[112] Z-40 was known for his violent temperament, and many expected that the Z-3's death might lead violence to surge under Z-40.[113]

The El Talibán Split and Los Zetas Fragmentation

Los Zetas experienced fragmentation and internecine conflict in 2012 when forces led by Iván "El Talibán/Z-50" Velázquez Caballero (an important but lower-ranking Zeta commander) believed that Z-40, second in command of Los Zetas at the time, had betrayed El Talibán's men to Mexican authorities. El Talibán formed a group known as El Sangre Zeta to fight Z-40.[114] This conflict was, however, short-lived, as El Talibán was apprehended in September 2012 and extradited to the United States in 2013.[115] This could be viewed as a drop in resilience, but, due to the short duration of the internecine conflict (a few months), it does not appear to have been a significant fragmentation for Los Zetas in historical hindsight.

The only other minor fragmentation that can be demonstrated following the death of Z-3 was the split of Los Legionarios, a group of former Los Zetas members that announced its existence in 2012 via narco-mantas that identified leadership figures already in jail. This splinter group claimed to blame Z-40 for their incarceration. This group appeared ineffectual until a year later when they released narco-mantas offering rewards for Los Zetas members. In the notes they also called for the support of relatives of El Talibán, suggesting this group had some sympathies with the former leader, and this minor fragmentation can be considered related to the earlier short-lived fragmentation within El Talibán.[116] While this is an example of fragmentation, it appears to have been fairly minor, ineffectual, and related to the El Talibán/El Sangre Zeta conflict.

Arrest of Z-40

Z-40 was arrested in 2013 in an operation involving a helicopter assault by Mexican marines, with no shots fired.[117] He attempted to bribe the marines, to no avail. This was considered a key disruptive event for the network, as leadership passed to Omar "Z-42" Treviño Morales, who was widely considered to be far weaker than his brother Z-40. Again there did not appear to be a major fragmentation of Los Zetas. No large spin-off groups appeared, reducing the resilience of the group through costly internecine conflict. Instead, the driving force of conflict in the region continued to be the conflict between Los Zetas and the Gulf cartel, which has become far more fragmented in the following two years despite what appeared to be a resurgence in late 2012 in the city of Monterrey.[118]

Arrest of Z-42

Los Zetas suffered what could be considered another major blow in March 2015 when Z-40's brother Z-42 was arrested in San Pedro, a wealthy suburb of Monterrey. His arrest also coincided with the arrest of one of his financial advisers. In the same month, US and Mexican law enforcement also arrested numerous other

potential Los Zetas successors. Whether or not the Mexican state has gained sufficient capability to fragment Los Zetas remains to be seen as this book goes to
press. The speed and rapid nature of these arrests suggests that Los Zetas will
fragment due to state pressure resulting from its territorial business model.

I am not the first analyst to make such predictions. Some, including Alejandro
Hope, have argued that Z-40's arrest marked the "beginning of the end" of Los
Zetas as a coherent national organization and that the future would see small,
independent local networks claiming to be Los Zetas and stealing their brand/
reputation for violence.[119] Thus far, that does not appear to be the case, and Los
Zetas continue to function. This may be due, as Guadalupe Correa-Cabrera
argues, to "cellular" leadership structures.[120] This raises the question of how
Los Zetas can be decentralized without suffering massive fragmentation. The
most likely explanation seems to be related to ideology, branding, and superior training.[121] While many have said that Los Zetas have been weakened,
there has been limited organizational restructuring of the group, such as frag-
mentations or breakaway networks. A recent *Reforma* report, based on PGR
freedom-of-information requests in Mexico, indicate that there are numerous
Los Zetas subcells, but many of those mentioned in the report have kept "Zeta"
in their name, unlike the breakaway cells from the Gulf cartel.[122] This suggests
that the regional Zeta cells are maintaining a pan-Zeta identity, allowing for
a decentralized "regional hierarchy" structure without significant conflict.[123]
Experts may agree that Los Zetas are weakened, but without open-source data
and limited internecine conflict, it is impossible to quantify. What is clear is that
the state has put a significant emphasis on targeting Los Zetas, as evidenced by
the establishment of a new government initiative called Plan Tamaulipas, which
includes the provision of four thousand federal support troops.[124]

Strengths and Weaknesses of the State-Reaction Argument

A weakness of my argument is that both Los Zetas and the Gulf cartel received
significant state attention and targeting but the more trafficking-oriented Gulf
cartel has had more fragmentation and internecine conflict and is thus less resilient according to the model. I attribute this to multiple factors. The state reaction
to the Gulf cartel was inspired initially when both networks were operating in
tandem. Thus, the Gulf cartel continued to be punished for the high levels of
violence and territorial business model of Los Zetas. In its confrontation with
Los Zetas, the Gulf cartel became more territorial in operations in its attempt to
wrest control of territory from them.

Further, the Gulf cartel had early developed some territorial/violent ten-
dencies due to the idiosyncrasies of its leader, Osiel Cárdenas Guillén. His

recruitment of Los Zetas and establishment of other paramilitary groups could be viewed as a personal, paranoid quirk.[125] But this should be tempered by the knowledge that the AFO also developed territorial paramilitaries in the same time period. This may have to do with the toll-collecting activities and the changing nature of drug trafficker–state relations. This may have been structurally determined and inevitable, based on Miguel Ángel Félix Gallardo's restructuring and division of territories among Mexican traffickers in the early 1990s. All of this is to say that the Gulf cartel was trafficking oriented but not perfectly so even without Los Zetas, and this may have helped to trigger the state reaction against both.

In the case of Los Zetas, which the resilience typology would suggest is resilient, the state is presently garnering a high number of arrests against the network. Given the long period following state attention required to fragment the AFO, this process is beginning rapidly in historical context for Los Zetas. The rapid leadership-arrest process will likely lead to fragmentation and, as state institutions strengthen, dissolution of the network.

Case Study 3: Los Caballeros Templarios

While the CT declared its birth in 2011, it is an outgrowth of its predecessor, the LFM, and must be understood in this context. According to Grayson, in the early 2000s, lieutenants of the Milenio cartel in Michoacán broke away to form an independent drug network. The new group contacted the Gulf cartel, which sent its armed wing, Los Zetas, to train the new network. Los Zetas trained it in their territorial extortion-based business model and abused the local population.[126] Eventually the lieutenants turned on their allies, and the LFM declared its existence in 2006 by throwing the severed heads of five Zetas onto a dance floor in a Michoacán nightclub along with a note that said, "La Familia doesn't kill for money, it doesn't kill women, it doesn't kill innocent people—only those who deserve to die. Everyone should know: this is divine justice."[127]

Led by Nazario "El Mas Loco / El Chayo" Moreno González, the LFM initially had success against Los Zetas and, according to Finnegan, removed them from most Michoacán plazas by 2008.[128] The LFM was initially popular for numerous reasons. First, it offered dispute-resolution mechanisms where the state failed. Second, it "branded" itself as opposed to methamphetamine (*cristal*) for Mexican citizens and as protectors of the regional population.[129] Los Zetas had cultivated an "internal market" for *cristal*, which was very unpopular. Third, in some areas the LFM minimized extortion and kidnapping. Fourth, its religious discourse was appealing.[130]

Business-Model and Risk-Mitigation Strategies

The LFM drug network and its successor/competitor, the CT, are known for high levels of religious ideology. As Grayson describes, they blend evangelical Christianity with regionalism and nationalism to gain legitimacy among the local population.[131] Sullivan argues that the CT is an example of Hobsbawn's "social bandit" concept, where, through "information operations," the CT attempts to gain tacit community support and create a situation of "dual sovereignty."[132] This is highly territorial but also moves the CT toward the insurgent portion of the state-reaction model.[133] This reduces risk by increasing intelligence from the local population and dulling the strength of the state reaction. On the other hand, it greatly increases the risk and threat of state reaction. The CT's resilience thus hinges on the calculated risk assessment that the state is weak and corruptible.

CT and LFM members carry Bibles or collections of sayings from their former leader El Chayo.[134] Some are recruited as recovered drug users. The LFM was a major producer and trafficker of methamphetamine.[135] These networks claimed both that they sold drugs only in the United States and that they fought drug use in Michoacán. As Canales argues, they attempted to brand themselves as the saviors of the people of Michoacán.[136] The high degree of LFM methamphetamine sales to the United States, as evidenced by US indictments, showed that the trafficking-oriented activity was a large part of their business model but played a limited role in comparison with other revenue streams such as extortion of mining and other industries.[137]

Branding can change perception, but when it diverges from reality, it can only help so much. The LFM began engaging in widespread abuses of the local population and industries: kidnappings (families in the United States were called for ransoms[138]), extortion of legal businesses such as mines and lime groves, wholesale theft of property and large land-holdings, rapes, and disappearances.[139] This led to a powerful societal backlash and increased the risk of state attack. The federal government had already long been targeting the LFM for these activities and attacks on federal authorities. Up to this point, the LFM had thoroughly corrupted local and state officials and co-opted any response from them.[140]

Following the 2010 "death" of El Chayo, the leader of LFM, in a shootout with government forces, a group of LFM leaders broke from that organization and founded the CT. In reality, they took the majority of the LFM network with them, and most of the remnants of the LFM were killed or fell to government arrest, though some survive in a highly fragmented form. Servando "La Tuta" Gómez Martínez, who led the CT, was a former schoolteacher who extorted the teachers' unions and mines and drew a teacher's salary while leading the drug network.[141] The CT continued the territorial LFM business model, including

control of the important port of Lázaro Cárdenas, which allowed for the importation of methamphetamine chemical precursors from India and China, sometimes in exchange for iron ore extorted from Michoacán mines.[142] Further supporting the notion that the CT is a territorial drug network, reports indicate
it has an annual income of $73 million before US drug profits are taken into
account. This income comes largely from extortion, kidnapping, car theft, and
retail drug sales in the territories it governs.[143] The CT also continued to utilize
extreme violence to portray itself as protectors of the people. This has included
crucifying an accused rapist in the name of protecting the population.[144]

The federal government response had little impact on the CT. State and local
governments were too thoroughly penetrated to respond to the CT abuses of the
population. Instead of a state reaction, the local population formed self-defense
forces to fight the CT in 2012.[145] These self-defense forces rose rapidly and began
armed confrontations with the CT, retaking territory and capturing CT leaders
and rank-and-file members. By 2013, a rapid succession of CT leaders had been
captured or killed by the self-defense forces, which sometimes coordinated with
federal government forces. The CT began to fragment as some CT cells switched
sides and joined the self-defense forces.[146] One notable 2014 event included
the death of El Chayo in a battle with government forces. The government was
forced to admit that he had not died in 2010 as it had previously claimed but that
he had been in hiding until his death, which was confirmed by DNA analysis.[147]

The federal government initially vacillated on the self-defense forces.[148] The
new Peña Nieto administration entered office in December of 2012 determined
to focus on economic and regulatory issues and not digress into the security
agenda that had swallowed the previous administration. The self-defense forces
would make ignoring the situation in Michoacán impossible.[149] The administration sent more federal troops and eventually decided to legitimize the
self-defense forces under a little-known proviso in the constitution that allows
the government to form *rurales*, or rural defense forces. The self-defense forces
have decimated the CT and may soon dissolve it. They have at a minimum
caused them to fragment, as evidenced by the breakaway CT cells now fight-
ing alongside the self-defense forces.[150] Audio recordings of La Tuta released
before his arrest indicate he was considering breaking away from the CT to focus
exclusively on extorting the local mining industry.[151] He believed that by simply
extorting the mining industry, he would reduce his personal and network risk.
Unfortunately for him, the damage was done, and the creation of self-defense
forces fixated on his death or capture would make diverting the state reaction
wishful thinking.

The Mexican government wants to co-opt and disband the self-defense forces
because of the challenge they pose to Mexican sovereignty. They are an amalgam
of various groups with various motivations.[152] It appears some are supported by

diaspora funding from the United States, though the CT claims they are sponsored by rival cartels.[153]

Arrest of La Tuta

The self-defense forces demanded that the Mexican government arrest key CT leaders, such as La Tuta, before they would disband. While he avoided arrest and detection for years while taunting the government with media interviews and audio recordings, his luck ran out in February 2015, when he was arrested in Morelia, Michoacán.[154] With his arrest, the dissolution of the CT appears a foregone conclusion, but only time will tell. It should be remembered that many predicted the death of the BLO years prior to the arrest of El H, suggesting that the trafficking portions of these groups have significant staying power.

While the reduced resilience of the LFM/CT due to its territorial business model is obvious, the interesting idiosyncrasy of this case for the argument here is that the CT was not fragmented by state action but by the spontaneous societal establishment of self-defense forces to provide the security the state had failed to provide. The state-reaction argument can be salvaged even here because the federal government co-opted the self-defense force movement by legitimizing it, but this suggests that the state-reaction argument is still tied to the institutional capacities of the state. If and where the state is too weak vis-à-vis a territorial drug network, the state has difficulty reducing the network's resilience. This suggests that the state must focus on capacity building in both kinetic and nonkinetic operations.[155]

Analysis

As with the study of all illicit networks, optimal data are inherently difficult to find.[156] To assess the resilience of a drug network optimally, the frequency of drug trafficking would need to be measured over time to understand the impact of disruptive events.[157] But those data do not exist in the public domain, so we must settle for the proxy provided here—the assessment of organizational shifts in response to disruptive events. The argument that territorial business models engender increased risk from state attack and thereby reduced resilience holds, though with some caveats derived from the idiosyncrasies of the various cases.

The trafficking-oriented Sinaloa cartel has proven resilient despite reduced resilience following its fragmentation and internecine conflict with the BLO. Despite significant arrests, it has not suffered significant further fragmentation and continues to be recognized as Mexico's most powerful drug network.[158] Of the major traffickers on the Calderón administration's kingpin list, El Azul, El Mayo, and now Chapo Guzmán, all of the Sinaloa cartel, are still believed to be running operations.[159]

The Gulf cartel is the quintessential case for the state-reaction argument. The rise of its highly territorial enforcers, Los Zetas, and the violent personal leadership of Osiel Cárdenas Guillén led to increased risk of state targeting and fragmented the network along its functional lines of specialization.[160] Unleashed from their masters, Los Zetas became even more territorial, though this territoriality was in some respects mitigated by the network's increased drug trafficking after 2003. While the model presented here has no difficulty explaining this period, the next is more challenging. The model would predict that the Gulf cartel, as a more trafficking-oriented network, would be more resilient than Los Zetas due to lower risk of state targeting. That appeared to be the case for a short period in 2012 when the Gulf cartel was resurgent, particularly in Monterrey. While the Gulf cartel did prove resilient in its ability to regain territory from Los Zetas there, state targeting continued, and the network fragmented between Los Metros and Los Rojos. It has further fragmented into so many small cells with various names that most analysts now have difficulty keeping track of them. A recent *Reforma* report based on freedom-of-information requests to the PGR resulted in a list of fragmented Gulf cartel cells, many of which have been in conflict with other former Gulf cartel cells.[161]

Los Zetas were also heavily targeted, as evidenced by the arrest of top leaders, but have not fragmented or been dissolved. I attribute this unexpected result, as Guadalupe Correa-Cabrera does, to their cell structure,[162] their training and esprit de corps,[163] and the fact that the Mexican government may not have been interested in distinguishing between the Gulf cartel and Los Zetas, given they were a unified force when Los Zetas committed many violent acts. Thus, the Gulf cartel continues to be punished for the territoriality of Los Zetas. Further, the Gulf cartel, in competition with Los Zetas, expanded into some territorial criminal activities such as the extortion of mines.[164]

The CT case provides a different challenge. The highly extortionist and territorial business model of the CT and its predecessor, the LFM, was at high risk of state attack from the federal government, though the territorial network was able to co-opt local and state government. The federal government's capacity to degrade the LFM/CT was limited until citizens founded their own self-defense forces, which, in conjunction with federal troops, have decimated the CT to the point where, based on audio recordings of its leader prior to his arrest, it may fragment yet again or equally likely dissolve.

Notes

1. George and Bennett, *Case Studies and Theory Development*, chaps. 3–4.
2. Canales, "Deadly Genius."
3. Thelen, "Historical Institutionalism"; Peters, *Institutional Theory in Political Science*, chapter on historical institutionalism.
4. Blancornelas, *El cártel*; Grayson, *Cartels*.
5. Caldwell, "Cartel Secrets"; Steve Duncan (law-enforcement investigator [CA Dept. of Justice] focused on the AFO), interview by the author, San Diego, 2010.
6. Both Hernandez and Beith separately describe in their books Guzmán's ability to operate as a trafficker from a maximum-security prison. Hernandez, *Narcoland*; Beith, *Last Narco*.
7. Reuter, "Systemic Violence"; Kilmer et al., *Reducing Drug Trafficking Revenues*.
8. Beith, *Last Narco*; Hernandez, *Narcoland*.
9. Parkinson, "Former Mexico Intelligence Chief."
10. Beith, *Last Narco*.
11. Hernandez, *Narcoland*, 92–93.
12. Miller, "In Mexico, Skepticism"; Schiller, "'La Barbie' Wants"; Siegal and Block, "Mexico Captures."
13. Burnett, "Nuevo Laredo Returns."
14. Bowden, *Murder City*.
15. Sullivan and Logan, "La Línea"; Sullivan, "Barrio Azteca."
16. Moore, "Myth of a 'Good Guy.'"
17. Sullivan and Logan, "La Línea."
18. Ibid.
19. Sullivan, "Barrio Azteca," 61.
20. Chindea, "Fear and Loathing."
21. Ibid.
22. Hernandez, *Narcoland*; Grillo, *El Narco*; Grayson, *Cartels*; Jones, "Appendix A"; Brands, "Los Zetas"; Brands, *Mexico's Narco-Insurgency*.
23. Grillo, *El Narco*.
24. Wilkinson, "Mexico Acknowledges."
25. Here Reuter cites Schelling's work on Mafia corruption. Reuter, "Systemic Violence."
26. Hernandez, *Narcoland*.
27. Grayson, *Cartels*.
28. Stevenson and Rivera, "Mexico Chief Pitches."
29. "Cable 09MEXICO3573."
30. Reuter, "Systemic Violence"; Wilkinson, "Drug Cartel Leader."
31. Marosi, "Tijuana Blood Bath."
32. Jones, "State Reaction."
33. McCleskey, "New Generation"; Gagne, "Bloody Attack on Police"; "Jalisco Cartel."

34. Keefe, "Hunt for El Chapo."

35. For impressive social-network maps of the Sinaloa cartel and networked part-ners, see Sánchez Valdéz, *Criminal Networks and Security Policies*. For integration of network-actor approaches and the concept of feral cities, see Bunker and Sullivan, "Inte-grating Feral Cities," and Sullivan, *From Drug Wars.*

36. Figueroa, "Analyst"; Corcoran, "'El Mayo' Rises."

37. "Detentions of 'El Chapo.'"

38. Keefe, "Hunt for El Chapo."

39. Ibid.

40. Ibid.

41. Shannon, *Desperados.*

42. Sullivan, "Will El Chapo Rule?"

43. Baker and Archibold, "U.S. Seeks Arrest."

44. Schoichet and Payne, "Mexican Drug Lord Joaquin 'El Chapo' Guzman Escapes."

45. Beith, *Last Narco.*

46. Reuters, "Mexico Arrests 13 in Connection with Chapo Escape."

47. Grillo, "Mexico's Fruitless Hunt for Justice."

48. Ahmed, "U.S. Sought 'El Chapo' Extradition."

49. Becerra, "Mexican Cartel Kingpin."

50. Grayson, *Cartels*; "Los secretos de Juan José Esparragoza."

51. Becerra, "Mexican Cartel Kingpin."

52. Dudley and Mazzitelli use the term "transportista vs. territorial" in lieu of "trans-actional/trafficking-oriented vs. territorial." The 2012 report of the United Nations Office on Drugs and Crime (UNODC) also describes the Zetas as territorial and the Sinaloa car-tel as trafficking-oriented. "Zetas in Guatemala"; Mazzitelli, "Mexican Cartel Influence"; "Outsmarted by Sinaloa"; Burnett, Penalosa, and Bennincasa, "Mexico Seems to Favor "; Burnett and Penalosa, "Mexico's Drug War"; Dudley, "Drug Trafficking Organizations."

53. Keefe, "How a Mexican Drug Cartel."

54. Canales, "Deadly Genius."

55. Bailey, *Politics of Crime in Mexico*; private security contractor with experience in Mexico, interview by the author by phone, 2015.

56. Jones, "Kidnapping in Tijuana"; Jones, "Unintended Consequences."

57. Grillo, *El Narco.*

58. Beith, *Last Narco.*

59. Duncan, interview.

60. Reuter, "Systemic Violence."

61. Burnett, Penalosa, and Bennincasa, "Mexico Seems to Favor"; Burnett and Pen-alosa, "Mexico's Drug War."

62. Duncan, interview.

63. Harris, *Gangs beyond Borders.*

64. Smith, "'Blind Mules' Unknowingly Ferry"; Siegal, "Architect and Opera Singer"; "Panga Boat Smuggling."

65. Mozingo, "L.A. Fashion District."

66. "Treasury Designates Additional."

67. Keefe, "Hunt for El Chapo."

68. "El Tomate Reveals"; "Tijuana's Cartel Landscape." The former article draws from *Zeta* magazine reporting.

69. Grayson, *Cartels*.

70. Astorga and Shirk, *Drug Trafficking Organizations*.

71. Flores Pérez, "Political Protection"; Flores Pérez, "El estado en crisis."

72. Astorga and Shirk, *Drug Trafficking Organizations*; Astorga, *Seguridad, traficantes y militares*; Astorga, *El siglo de las drogas*; Astorga, "Organized Crime," 76–77.

73. Hernandez, *Narcoland*, 97.

74. Flores Pérez, "Political Protection."

75. *United States vs Tomas Yarrington Ruvalcaba and Fernando Alejandro Cano Martinez*.

76. See Guerrero Gutiérrez, *Security, Drugs, and Violence* on the concept of toll collecting.

77. Grayson, *Cartels*.

78. Ibid.

79. Reuter, "Systemic Violence"; Felbab-Brown, *Calderón's Caldron*; Felbab-Brown, *Focused Deterrence*.

80. Prof. Raúl Benítez Manaut, conversation with the author, Tijuana, 2009.

81. Ibid.

82. Resa Nestares, "Los Zetas"; Brands, *Mexico's Narco-Insurgency*; Sullivan and Logan, "Los Zetas"; Grayson and Logan, *Executioner's Men*; Sullivan, "Extreme Narco Violence."

83. Konrad and Skaperdas, "Market for Protection"; Grayson and Logan, *Executioner's Men*.

84. Sullivan and Logan, "Los Zetas."

85. Felbab-Brown has also pointed to the similarities—in terms of impact upon the state and society—between organized crime groups such as Los Zetas and La Familia Michoacána (the precursor to the Caballeros Templarios) and insurgencies. See Sullivan and Bunker, "Drug Cartels, Street Gangs"; Brands, *Mexico's Narco-Insurgency*; Grillo, *El Narco*; Felbab-Brown, *Calderón's Caldron*.

86. Sullivan and Elkus have articulated the "criminal insurgent" framework that could be used to describe some of the territorial aspects of Los Zetas and move them on my continuum toward the insurgent type. Bunker and Sullivan, "Cartel Evolution Revisited"; Sullivan and Elkus, "State of Siege."

87. "'Zetas' usan a pandillas"; Guerrero Gutiérrez, "Pandillas y cárteles"; Balcázar Villarreal, *Pandillas en el siglo XXI*.

88. Sullivan and Logan, "Los Zetas."

89. Mazzitelli, "Mexican Cartel Influence"; Dudley, *Zetas and Battle for Monterrey*.

90. I also had the fortune of hearing FBI agent Daniel Fuentes, who was one of the agents in the standoff, describe the event at a speaking engagement at Sam Houston

State University, March 19, 2015. Grayson, *Cartels*; Grayson and Logan, *Executioner's Men*.

91. Mills, "Transnational Criminal Groups."

92. Ibid.

93. "Zetas in Guatemala."

94. Correa-Cabrera, "Violence on the 'Forgotten' Border"; Grayson and Logan, *Executioner's Men*; Grayson, *Cartels*.

95. Mills, "Transnational Criminal Groups"; Mazzitelli, "Mexican Cartel Influence."

96. Hale, *Mexico's Government Begins*, 5.

97. Ibid.; Logan and Sullivan, "Gulf-Zeta Split."

98. Eckstein, "On the Etiology."

99. Brands, *Mexico's Narco-Insurgency*; Grayson, *Cartels*.

100. Hale, *Mexico's Government Begins*.

101. Archibold, "Mexico Captures El Coss"; Cattan, "Killing of Top Mexico Drug Lord."

102. Hale, *Mexico's Government Begins*.

103. Dudley, "Two Mexico Cartel Rivals."

104. Municipal police officer with experience in Monterrey who now patrols a municipality near Monterrey, interview by the author, Monterrey, February 2014.

105. Jiménez, "Atomizan narco en Tamaulipas."

106. Dudley and Pachico, "Why a Zetas Split Is Inevitable."

107. Grayson and Logan, *Executioner's Men*; Grayson, *Cartels*.

108. "Two Mass Graves"; "Holy Week Vacations"; Dudley, *Transnational Crime in Mexico*.

109. Archibold, "After Fatal Casino Attack"; Ellingwood, "Mexico Gunmen Set Casino on Fire"; Ellingwood, "Fallout from Deadly."

110. Grayson, "Los Zetas."

111. Chabot, "Historical Case Study"; Kenney, *From Pablo to Osama*.

112. Llana, "Heriberto Lazcano."

113. Ibid.; Dudley, "Zetas Leader's First Task."

114. Pachico, "Breakaway Zetas."

115. Schiller and Althaus, "'El Taliban' Falls."

116. Stone, "Zetas Splinter Group."

117. "Repaso a carrera delictiva."

118. Dudley, *Zetas and Battle for Monterrey*; Dudley, "Two Mexico Cartel Rivals."

119. De Córdoba, "Mexico Captures Head."

120. Ibid.

121. Canales, "Deadly Genius"; Grayson and Logan, *Executioner's Men*.

122. Jiménez, "Atomizan narco en Tamaulipas."

123. See Salcedo-Albarán and Garay on decentralized structures of Los Zetas. *Results of a Pilot Survey*, 35; Salcedo-Albarán and Garay Salamanca, *Structure of a Transnational Criminal Network*.

124. Corcoran, "New Report Examines."

125. On the paramilitarization of northeastern Mexico and Los Zetas, see the excellent work of Correa-Cabrera, "Violence on the 'Forgotten' Border.'"

126. Finnegan, "Silver or Lead."

127. Ibid.

128. Ibid.; "Mexican Drug Cartels: Two Wars."

129. Canales, "Deadly Genius."

130. Finnegan, "Silver or Lead."

131. Grayson, *Cartels*.

132. Sullivan, "Los Caballeros Templarios."

133. Felbab-Brown describes La Familia as engaging in a "political project," lending credence to the insurgent conceptualization. Felbab-Brown, *Calderón's Caldron*; Felbab-Brown, *Focused Deterrence*.

134. Sullivan, "Los Caballeros Templarios."

135. "La Familia."

136. Canales, "Deadly Genius."

137. Fox, "Mexico Mining Ops."

138. Knight, "Families Fear Phone Call."

139. Fox, "Mexico Mining Ops."

140. "La Familia."

141. Grayson, *Cartels*.

142. Fausset, "Mexico's Lazaro Cardenas Port."

143. Parkinson, "Mexico's Knights Templar."

144. Sullivan, "Extreme Narco Violence"; Bunker, "Mexican Cartel Tactical Note #13."

145. McCrummen, "In Mexico, Self-Defense Groups."

146. Becerra, "To Fight the Cartel."

147. "El Chayo."

148. Archibold, "Quandary for Mexico"; Associated Press, "In Mexico, Vigilante Villagers."

149. Tony Payan (director, Mexico Center, Rice University), conversations with the author, Baker Institute, 2013–14. See also Hale, *Vigilantism in Mexico*.

150. Archibold, "Quandary for Mexico"; Krauze, "Mexico's Vigilantes on the March."

151. "'La Tuta' Says He's Sick and Tired."

152. Hale, *Vigilantism in Mexico*.

153. Corchado, "Immigrants in U.S."

154. Reuters, "Mexico Captures Most Wanted"; Michoacán, "'La Tuta' Audio."

155. Everton, *Disrupting Dark Networks*.

156. Van Schendel and Abraham, *Illicit Flows and Criminal Things*, introduction; Raab and Milward, "Dark Networks as Problems."

157. In Bakker, Raab, and Milward, "Preliminary Theory," the authors attempt to measure resilience in terrorist networks by assessing the tempo of bombings. Although

clandestine, terrorist-network bombings are far more public than drug-network smuggling runs.

158. Keefe, "Hunt for El Chapo."

159. Krauze, "Mexico's Disastrous Drug War 'Success.'"

160. Benítez, conversation; Resa Nestares, "Los Zetas."

161. Jiménez, "Atomizan narco en Tamaulipas."

162. De Córdoba, "Mexico Captures Head."

163. Grayson and Logan, *Executioner's Men*, chap. 5.

164. Fox, "Mexico Mining Ops."

Conclusion

THE STATE-REACTION ARGUMENT provides us with important insights into the resilience of drug networks, not just in Tijuana but also throughout Mexico. By assessing the proposed relationship between the variables of business strategy, risk, and the state reaction, we gain a conceptual framework for understanding the resilience of drug networks in Mexico. The state-reaction argument demonstrates which business strategies will increase the risk of state reaction and how strong that reaction will be, and it allows us to effectively measure the resultant drug network's resilience via the resilience typology. This answers important questions about Mexico's practical behavior in targeting some drug networks ahead of others, with significant policy and theoretical implications, including how changing the drug war could assist weak states in their battles with drug networks. The conclusion will discuss the lessons learned from the case-study comparisons, assess the weaknesses of the argument, and will conclude with theoretical and policy implications, including a discussion of alternative drug policies.

Lessons Learned from the Cases

Persistent kingpin strikes in the 2000s by the Mexican state with US support led to the splitting of Mexican drug networks along transactional and territorial lines.[1] Prior to US–Mexican decapitation of a drug network, both business strategies coexisted within the same network, though the transactional controlled the territorial in a clear hierarchy. Wealth was redistributed within the network by the transactional/strategic leadership.[2] After suffering the arrest or killings of its first generation of leadership, the AFO split along territorial and transactional lines in 2008. The kidnapping and extortion wave of the independent El Teo territorial network from 2008 to 2010 led to a strong backlash, as both the state and society converged to dissolve it.[3] The state, society, and a rival network led by El Ingeniero reacted viscerally and immediately against the territorial El Teo drug network. The El Teo network has since dissolved, while the El Ingeniero drug network reorganized and formed a truce with the Sinaloa cartel in 2010.

The willingness of local-government actors to spend more on capacity building in the police forces was a precondition for the success in Tijuana.[4] The successful state reaction focused on the critical elements of intelligence, the removal of corrupt police officers, and cooperation from local civil-society groups, businessmen, rival drug networks, and the populace. The surviving network led by El Ingeniero (arrested June 2014) was a smaller transactional drug network. It focused on money laundering, drug trafficking, and maintaining a truce with other drug networks, such as the Sinaloa cartel, which began to supplant the AFO in Baja California.[5]

The surviving AFO has, since 2011, faced significant pressure from authorities and rivals. While it is a trafficking-oriented network, it was less so than the recent challenger, the Sinaloa cartel. Competition with a more trafficking-oriented drug network explains why the AFO was targeted so heavily from 2012 to the present. The Tijuana plaza is now in flux, with traffickers recently released from prison permitting a resurgence of the AFO there. The AFO has been severely fragmented and is now in internecine conflict with former members who have joined the Sinaloa cartel. The remaining AFO members are attempting a reorganization of the network in the midst of conflict with the rival Sinaloa cartel, while some loyalists maintain a low profile in Guadalajara. The possibility of the remaining AFO loyalists changing their name and operating under a new banner is real.[6] If this were to happen, the AFO would be considered dissolved, the lowest level of resilience in the typology.

The Gulf Cartel and Los Zetas

The pattern of the state inadvertently splintering drug networks along business-strategy lines through kingpin strikes and then targeting the resultant territorial networks is apparent throughout Mexico. As others have argued, the best example is the Gulf cartel–Los Zetas split.[7] This split continues to play out throughout Mexico and continues to be a major driver of drug-related violence. After the arrest of Osiel Cárdenas Guillén, head of the Gulf cartel, that network splintered between its transactional traffickers and its former armed wing, Los Zetas.[8] While Cárdenas was arrested in 2003 and extradited to the United States in 2007, the formal split occurred in 2010, which is why the resilience typology treats fragmentation and internecine conflict as two separate levels of resilience. The Gulf cartel continued its trafficking orientation but moved toward a more territorial business model in the violent conflicts with Los Zetas.[9] During the conflict, the Gulf cartel appeared to become more territorial by adopting the same traits and business lines of its rival. These new business lines may have been present all along but were subservient to the trafficking-oriented upper echelons, or they may have been learned from Los Zetas as Los Zetas expanded their activities and extortion in the early 2000s. Los Zetas, with fewer drug-trafficking contacts, focused on extortion of licit and illicit businesses, copyright piracy, murder for hire, oil theft, human trafficking, and kidnapping.[10] Nonetheless, the Gulf cartel was still heavily targeted by the state and fragmented into severe internecine conflict.

Despite the increased drug-market penetration, Los Zetas continues their territorial strategy. They have become famous for spectacular acts of violence, especially when entering new territories. This is designed to demonstrate to the local population and rival networks that they have arrived and are in control.[11] They have established drug-trafficking contacts with suppliers in Colombia, penetration into Central America, and relationships with transnational street gangs such as Mara Salvatrucha (MS-13).[12] The conflict turned Monterrey, known as a peaceful haven and Mexico's northern industrial hub, into a drug-network war zone in 2010.[13]

Los Zetas' territorial business model follows directly from the sophisticated training they brought with them from the Mexican special forces when they defected. Los Zetas' original training comes from the Mexican-state military, which specializes in the control of territory. Even when the battle is for the local population, as is the case in counterinsurgency, the state's control of the population is only a means toward asserting territorial control.[14] Los Zetas' training may make them more resilient in their fight with Mexican authorities than the El Teo network of the AFO.[15]

Comparing the Los Zetas case and the case of the Gulf cartel can be useful in understanding the fragmentation of drug networks. While Los Zetas suffered severe targeting by the Mexican government due to their territorial activities, the more trafficking-oriented Gulf cartel has been targeted as well. In fact, the Gulf cartel has felt those effects more severely, having fragmented into many cells engaged in internecine conflict. Despite appearing resurgent in 2012, especially in the city of Monterrey, the Gulf cartel has since fragmented more heavily than any network in Mexico.[16] This finding runs counter to the state-reaction prediction that territorial networks will dissolve first. The strength of the Los Zetas brand and the group's training, decentralized structures, and esprit de corps may explain its ability to mitigate the risk and consequences of state targeting.[17] It may also be on the verge of extreme fragmentation, internecine conflict, and possible dissolution, given the state's recent systematic arrests.

The Sinaloa Cartel

The Sinaloa cartel's split with its partners, the BLO, followed a pattern similar to the AFO split. One interesting difference, however, is that both the Sinaloa cartel and the BLO were largely transactional in their activities at the time of their split. The Sinaloa cartel had long included the Beltrán Leyva brothers, who were in charge of corrupting government officials, as well as handling important intelligence and drug-trafficking operations. Despite that largely transactional activity, following the split, the BLO converted to a territorial focus and engaged in violent conflict with the Sinaloa cartel throughout Mexico. As Hernandez points out, this occurred because the Sinaloa cartel was better able to maintain its government officials and contacts, forcing the newly fragmented BLO to ally with Los Zetas, a highly territorial network.[18] This territoriality may have influenced the BLO, which has maintained its alliance with Los Zetas. As Grillo points out, because the BLO and the Sinaloa cartel had been such longtime partners and knew each other's business operations, their split was violent and bloody.[19] The conflict between the territorial Los Zetas alliance and the transactional Sinaloa cartel alliance is now the driving force behind drug-related violence in Mexico.[20]

It should be noted that the CT is generally territorial but is still allied with the Sinaloa cartel against Los Zetas. Conflict between territorial networks is to be expected because territorial drug networks tax their territory exclusively and thus cannot share territory with other territorial networks. The CT and its precursor organization, La Familia Michoacána (LFM), have had ongoing conflicts with Los Zetas. The business strategy of the CT has focused on branding itself as the saviors and protectors of the people of Michoacán, which moves its territorial business strategy toward insurgent.[21] Not everyone in Michoacán was impressed by the LFM and CT attempts to win hearts and minds through propaganda, branding, and public acts of violence. Self-defense forces rose up in small villages to resist the extortion and violence of the CT.[22]

In response to the increasing influence of the CT, the Peña Nieto administration, which was previously intent on minimizing discussion of drug-related violence, was forced to send federal troops and police to Michoacán in the hope of regaining control of the important agricultural state. The navy also took control of the port of Lazaro Cárdenas because it became obvious the CT used it to import chemical precursors for methamphetamine in exchange for iron ore stolen from local mines.[23] This state reaction was predictable and is the essence of why, all other things being equal, territorial networks are less resilient than their transactional counterparts.

All of the top leaders of the CT have been arrested or killed, including La Tuta. Already suffering from fragmentation and internecine conflict, the CT appears on the verge of dissolution. The future of the region will depend upon the new relationship between emergent drug networks (such as Los Viagras), the self-defense forces, and the federal government. Over the long term, the federal government will need to rebuild and strengthen local law-enforcement capability in the region.

Defeating the CT and fragmenting Los Zetas has taken far longer than the destruction of the El Teo network. I attribute this to multiple factors. Los Zetas and the CT are better-run networks, with training acquired from the state itself. How long the state will need in order to dissolve them or turn them into a more manageable problem will depend upon the ability of the Mexican state to improve its capacity to defeat these networks vis-à-vis the quality and resources of the networks.[24]

One of the counterintuitive lessons of the cases analyzed is that actions that strengthen the state that are positive in the long term can have negative unintended consequences in the short term. Improvements to the judicial system to increase its long-term effectiveness can result in short-term security losses, such as released traffickers changing drug-network dynamics in potentially violent locales. We have seen this in the release of traffickers arrested by the military in Tijuana and the release of Z-2. This is not an argument against a stronger judiciary, which should be viewed as a necessary prerequisite for improved security. An improved judiciary, with oral trials and strict rules of evidence, will minimize the number of innocents incarcerated and allow the penal system to focus on the guilty. Further, faith in the judicial system will improve the public's perception of law enforcement and the state-security apparatus at all levels. Improving the judicial system and the capability of investigators and prosecutors to pursue organized-crime cases is of fundamental importance to Mexico's success against transactional, territorial, and even insurgent-like networks. As Buscaglia, Gonzalez-Ruiz, and Ratliff point out, the creation of specialized antimafia units has proven successful. What they call "the team model" has been proven in the Tijuana case study by the US–Mexican task force established under Operation United Eagles.[25]

Drug-Network Risk Mitigation

By assessing drug-network resilience according to the DHS risk-management framework and breaking it into its components (risk as a function of threat, vulnerability, and consequence), we can systematically assess risk-mitigation strategies employed by drug networks. For a multitude of reasons, territorial and insurgent business strategies increase the risk of state reaction.

In all of the drug networks assessed, intriguing risk-mitigation strategies were used by the drug networks to minimize the consequences of the state-imposed

disruptions (decapitations). These included corruption payments to state officials before and after disruptive events to mitigate their impact, recording and
photographing meetings with narcos and politicians to ensure cooperation
and gain leverage over state officials, attempts to brand themselves through
narco-mantas as serving society, media manipulation (blackouts), investment
in local communities, adoption of low-profile strategies that moved toward the
transactional point of the continuum, succession mechanisms, the use of sophisticated communication technology, decentralizing structure and compartmen-
talizing operations, and other conscious attempts to minimize the network vulnerability and the consequences of state reaction. Some of these strategies are
effective in attenuating risk, but over the long term, state targeting of territorial
groups will increase the risk of state disruption of drug networks with high consequence to a near certainty. Those drug networks that failed to learn the lesson
of shifting toward exclusively trafficking-based operations to minimize the state
reaction found themselves weakened or eliminated completely (for example,
La Tuta).

The Future of Mexico's Drug Networks

The Peña Nieto administration has scored impressive successes against the big-
gest capos in Mexico. It has arrested the true heads of every major drug network
in fairly rapid succession since taking office in December of 2012. These arrests
include Il Ingeniero (AFO), El Chapo (Sinaloa cartel), El H (BLO), Vicente
Carrillo Fuentes (CFO), La Tuta (CT), and Z-40 and then his brother Z-42
(Los Zetas). The only major capos who have not been killed or arrested are El
Mayo and El Azul of the Sinaloa cartel, while Chapo Guzmán has escaped and
Caro Quintero was released from prison.[26] This is another key piece of evidence
fitting the state-reaction argument.

While the state-reaction argument emphasizes the resilience of trafficking networks, it also makes the argument that trafficking networks are not
impervious to state attack but that states will attack territorial networks *first*.[27]
The sheer number of small turf-oriented network nodes that emerge from the
wreckage of larger networks limits the capacity of the state to target the myriad
small turf-oriented groups rapidly.[28] This may lead to a false impression that
turf-oriented territorial network nodes are resurgent, when in reality they are in
the process of being broken down and dissolved as state institutions strengthen.

Some newly released traffickers such as Caro Quintero (Sinaloa cartel) and
Z-2 (Los Zetas) are believed to have learned these lessons and may be trying
to move their networks toward highly trafficking-oriented, old-school business
strategies that focus on drug trafficking.[29] The release of Caro Quintero preceded

the arrest of Chapo Guzmán, leading some observers to question whether this was a managed transition. Some speculated that Caro Quintero was a "boss of bosses" in the Mexican underworld.[30] Since Guzmán's escape, the more plausible explanation is that Guzmán and Caro Quintero continue to cooperate, amassing power with their Sinaloa compatriots.

The recent release from prison of Rogelio "Z-2 / El Kelín" González Pizaña could also represent a shift in the drug-network equilibrium in northeastern Mexico. He has issued narco-mantas claiming to have united elements of the Gulf cartel and Los Zetas. In them, he references returning to old-school trafficking and refraining from victimizing the local population.[31] This illustrates that he is aware that territorial business models trigger stronger state and societal reactions and that he has attempted to mitigate this risk by branding himself as not engaging in extortion activities. This suggests a learning curve with regard to risk and the state reaction that time in prison and age may facilitate.[32]

The capacity of the Mexican government to disrupt drug networks through engaging high-value targets has rapidly increased. This improved capacity is most noticeable in the marines and navy, which have proven to be a force of national presence and power projection while remaining small enough to prevent leaks. Over the long term, this is a capacity best suited for law-enforcement institutions such as those used in Operation United Eagles.[33]

One way to improve that capacity is to deepen ties with the United States and European partners in the context of training and capacity building for the gendarmerie. While the Peña Nieto administration initially appeared fixated on sovereignty concerns and wary of US cooperation on anything but its own terms, it has warmed to US cooperation. One example of this that goes beyond even the intense US–Mexican cooperation under the Calderón administration is the Peña Nieto administration's proposal to allow US law enforcement to carry weapons in Mexico. While this has been hotly debated, the fact that it was proposed suggests that the hypernationalist PRI party is willing to acknowledge the value of US cooperation.[34]

Weaknesses of the Argument

As with any typological theory, real-world cases do not always perfectly fit the ideal type descriptions. Some transactional drug networks, such as the El Ingeniero–led AFO, did engage in some extortion and kidnapping activities, as evidenced by court documents and recent arrests.[35] Overall, however, these extortion activities were much more limited, and kidnappings tended to be of wealthy individuals or a small number of low-profile, middle-class targets, as opposed to the large number of middle-class people and small business owners targeted by the territorial El Teo network.[36] Also, some transactional drug networks engage in highly territorial behaviors, such as in the case of the Sinaloa cartel's behavior in its battle for Ciudad Juárez against the CFO (Juárez cartel).

This raises an important question. If the Sinaloa cartel is considered transactional but initiates conflicts and works with territorial networks such as the Artistas Asesinas to take plazas,[37] does the state-reaction argument hold? I would answer, yes. Generally, the Sinaloa cartel focuses on its "core competence"—the trafficking of highly profitable drugs.[38] It engages in combat for strategic corridors, and when it needs to use violence it usually contracts that out to local territorial nodes, specialized squads of hit men such as Los Ántrax, or corrupted elements of the state security apparatus.[39] Thus, the majority of its business strategy is transactional, though that might be of little comfort to a resident of a contested plaza.[40]

My resilience typology uses organizational structural changes as a proxy for operational capacity after a disruptive event. Resilience is typically defined as the ability to bounce back from disruptive events or shocks and is conceptualized as operational capacity. For a drug network, the best measure of operational capacity would be the tempo of successful drug trafficking, but due to the nature of clandestine networks, that data does not exist. Thus, organizational changes as measured by surviving intact, restructuring, fragmenting, engaging in internecine conflict, and dissolving serve as a proxy for resilience levels.

One of the weaknesses found in the case studies was that when networks had already experienced internecine conflict, assessing their resilience through increased fragmentation was not easy, given that the new splinter network would not announce itself with a new name but could simply join the enemy camp. This could have the effect of creating false negatives. For example, Los Zetas may be more fragmented or in internecine conflict than my analysis suggests because the group's splinter cells have joined the Gulf cartel.

The unique nature of the border between Mexico and the United States limits the generalizability of any argument based on Mexican case studies. The criticism is mitigated, however, because other illicit networks demonstrate that these patterns also exist in other illicit networks.

International Applicability of the Argument

The argument that the business model increases the risk of a strong state reaction and thereby reduces the resilience of an illicit network can be applied far beyond Mexico. Insurgent networks with the aim of overthrowing the state will generally trigger a visceral state reaction and be targeted as a higher priority than either transactional or territorial criminal networks. All insurgent networks are likely to have some component of all three business models.[41]

Colombian cartels such as those of the Medellín and Cali in the 1980s and 1990s are interesting tests of the state-reaction argument. The Medellín cartel led by Pablo Escobar was largely transactional in its business strategy and was tolerated by the Colombian government throughout much of the 1980s. That changed when Escobar moved the cartel toward insurgency on the illicit-network typology established in chapter 1, by engaging in the kidnappings of politicians and the random assassination of police officers in an effort to change government policy on extradition.[42] After Escobar's death in 1993, the Cali cartel was also dissolved as a coherent network despite the Colombian state's reticence because it had not directly threatened the state through political violence.[43] This was prompted by the United States, which as a consolidated democracy in a prohibitionist drug regime has a low tolerance for even transactional drug networks. The resultant decentralized cartelito trafficking model in Colombia could be described as more transactional and more focused on the specific aspects of drug trafficking.[44]

Theoretical Implications

The state-reaction argument provides us with significant theoretical implications. First, the state-reaction argument suggests that state attacks will split drug networks along territorial or transactional lines largely in response to the actions of territorial portions of large networks. These splits inadvertently unleash territorial networks from the bonds of their transactional masters, which leads to increased violence. Second, states will then target the resultant territorial networks, reducing their resilience over time and removing them from the system. This will have the salubrious effect of reducing violence and the victimization of society that occurs through kidnapping and extortion. Third, transactional networks will be more apt to survive these conflictive periods through either tacit or explicit alliances with the state and civil society. Thus, the long-term problem that states will face after the defeat of territorial networks is not violence but corruption. While states cannot maintain legitimacy with high levels of violence because it challenges their claims to sovereignty, they can survive high levels of corruption. States choose transactional networks by targeting their territorial enemies first because transactional networks are "the lesser evil."[45] Fourth, at the systemic level, the state-reaction argument suggests that states will cooperate to maintain themselves as the dominant unit of the international system when challenged by "alternative governance structures."[46] This, combined with the fact that they have a preponderance of power and resources, suggests that states have long-term staying power vis-à-vis illicit networks despite reduced technological advantages due to the empowerment of private sectors.[47]

Policy Implications

Policymakers can draw important lessons from the state-reaction argument. First, kingpin strategies may play important roles for states attempting to assert dominance over illicit networks, but they may have unintended consequences such as increases in homicides, kidnappings, and extortion cases.[48] Second, states must prepare for the resultant splits between drug networks along their lines of functional specialization. Third, states will need to build stronger law-enforcement and penal institutions while paying careful attention to development funding to address territorial networks. Failing to invest in the society results in weak institutions and a ready recruitment base for drug networks. The question of security versus development is not a choice. Both security and development funding and programs must be developed in tandem. Mexico has shown proof of successful social development in places such as Ciudad Juárez, through Todos Somos Juárez, a government program to engage civil society in what was once one of Mexico's most violent cities. These programs can be scaled up to engage civil society on a national level.[49]

Fourth, in regard to transactional drug networks, Mexico will have to focus on money-laundering legislation and investigative capabilities to eliminate the ability of drug networks to use their ill-gotten gains in the political system. Mexico cannot continue to rely on the US Treasury Department's Office of Foreign Assets Control (OFAC) to build financial crime cases against its most prolific traffickers. While the increased number of OFAC sanctions against all Mexican drug networks has been impressive, it is not a panacea.[50] Mexico needs its own financial-crimes enforcement capacity with the ability to build cases against not just the most prolific traffickers and their families but also against even midlevel narcos using the financial system to launder their profits. This will require a vast investment in the appropriate state agencies and will be built over decades. Finally, the international community must fundamentally rethink the underlying political economic forces of the drug war.

Political Economic Structures

The key to improving state capacity and development programs will be finding the resources and the will to pay for them.[51] In the relationships between states and illicit networks, states usually maintain the preponderance of power. The tax base of the licit markets of states provides the ability to marshal incredible resources but often goes untapped. Mexico, for example, has been dependent upon oil and the state oil company PEMEX for between 30 and 40 percent of government revenues over the last decade, though that percentage may be shrinking due to declining production. Mexico raises less than 8.5 percent of GDP in taxes when fuel subsidies are taken into account, while the top income earners pay only 30 percent of income in taxes.[52] Prompted by declining oil revenues, the Peña Nieto administration has expressed a desire to change these structures through economic and energy reforms.[53] Increased revenues are necessary to improve the judiciary and the military and to reform/professionalize the thousands of independent police agencies throughout the country.[54]

Free-market norms such as privatization, low taxation, and "smaller government" are not always consistent with the goals of states. The ability to tax is the lifeblood of the state and provides the resources to manage organized crime at tolerable levels. The goals of states include not only eliminating illicit flows but also strengthening themselves and state capacity by eliminating "alternate governance structures" as potential threats.[55] The ultimate goal is not the elimination of the illicit flow but security. The Colombia case of the last decade best embodies the security priority in the face of illicit networks. Mexico appears to be following the same path, emphasizing security over the elimination of illicit narcotics flows.[56]

Successful transactional drug networks often penetrate the state through corruption. Through the consolidation of democracy—including reforms such as the government funding of political campaigns—this relationship can be weakened. Also imperative is an improved judicial system that can solve a substantial portion of crimes and increase the public's willingness to report crime to authorities.[57] Large transactional drug networks can then be dismantled, and drug networks will assume decentralized network forms. This decentralization of drug networks was achieved in Colombia with the destruction of the Medellín and Cali cartels and deepened with the weakening and disbandment of the AUC and the FARC when state-security institutions were improved under the Álvaro Uribe administration.[58] A similar transition is occurring in Mexico where the state is attempting to improve security institutions and weaken drug-network capacity to challenge governability.

The battle against territorial drug networks can in many ways strengthen the state and borders because it can serve to justify what Andreas calls "escalation," the increased emphasis on law enforcement and the hardening of borders.[59] Transactional drug networks pose a long-term threat because of their resilience and their ability to corrupt and deflect the reaction of the state. They can, even in democratic and quasi-democratic states, make the state dependent and beholden to them through the funding of elections and the ability to embed themselves within the society in a parasitic and symbiotic fashion—for example, Russian organized crime's role in reinforcing the state.[60]

Considering Alternatives to Prohibition

The resilience of all drug networks is made possible by the profits stemming from the consumption of drugs. While most of these profits come from the developed world, developing states such as Mexico are also increasingly becoming consumer nations.[61] While territorial drug networks are most threatening to the raison d'être of the state, transactional illicit networks are the long-term threat. They are able to weaken state responses to them through corruption, and in democratic societies drug networks are able to fund elections, leaving the state beholden to them. Stronger institutions to regulate elections, professionalized bureaucracies, and market regulators could manage and mitigate the power of these illicit networks, but that requires significant political will and state expenditures.[62] The ability of the state to raise revenues through taxation to fund stronger, more effective state institutions will prove critical to Mexico's success as a transitioning democracy combating illicit networks.[63]

Challenging the drug-prohibition regime is no longer an academic debate, nor is it an unrealistic and politically unviable fringe position. The legalization of medical marijuana in twenty-three states and the District of Columbia has shown it to be a topic of mainstream policy discussion.[64] Ballot initiatives in 2012 legalizing recreational marijuana that were implemented in Colorado and Washington the subsequent year (personal cultivation, then retail stores in Colorado) have taken this a step further, fundamentally challenging the "drug war" mentality that has been politically dominant in the United States since the Richard Nixon administration. Changing public opinion has no doubt supported these policy shifts. For the first time, both Pew and Gallup national polls now show a majority of Americans supporting marijuana legalization.[65]

The legalization of marijuana has the potential to deny significant profits to drug networks. A study by Alejandro Hope and Eduardo Clark of the Mexican Competitiveness Institute (IMCO) demonstrated how legalization in three US states (Washington, Colorado, and Oregon had ballot initiatives in 2012) could cut Mexican cartel profits from those states by approximately 30 percent and would impact the Sinaloa cartel particularly hard.[66] As if to prove the accuracy of the study's findings, reporting from National Public Radio's John Burnett found that wholesale marijuana prices in Culiacán had already dropped by 30 percent despite implementation in only two of the three states (Washington and Colorado) considered in the study. With the additional marijuana-legalization efforts passing in Oregon, Alaska, and the District of Columbia, the wholesale marijuana price seems likely to drop even further, cutting Mexican drug networks out of the market.[67] While drug networks will likely shift to other drugs and activities, this process will deny them significant profits, and those other activities will engender greater state reaction. The shift to other drugs does not create a new market but can only serve the market that presently exists, meaning profits will be divided among a greater number of networks.

Calls for drug-policy change have also become powerful in Latin America. The sitting presidents of Colombia, Guatemala, and Uruguay have all urged the international community to revisit the global drug-prohibition regime, and Uruguay in 2014 even legalized marijuana in quantities associated with personal use, although not mass production.[68] These presidents have joined the calls of former Latin American presidents of Brazil, Mexico, and Colombia for alternative drug policies.[69] Even conservative center-right Mexican president Felipe Calderón (2006–12) used the phrase "market alternatives" to signal a willingness to challenge the prohibition regime following the organized-crime killing of more than fifty people in a Monterrey casino.[70]

Opponents of the initiatives regularly point out that legalization would not eliminate Mexican drug networks. While ending drug prohibition in favor of a public-health approach to addiction does not need to eliminate Mexican drug networks to improve upon the status quo, it is important to consider how Mexican drug networks could survive such laws. Two relevant characteristics of drug networks are their adaptability and resilience.[71] While the drug networks may have started as a result of drug prohibition, their networks historically find new activities and commodities to sustain themselves when these markets are legalized.

The US alcohol analogy is illustrative. The end of Prohibition did not eliminate organized crime in the United States. It did, however, deny it significant profits, which in conjunction with improved state law-enforcement capacity helped to turn organized crime into a manageable problem over the subsequent decades. As economists would predict, alcohol consumption increased following the end of Prohibition.[72] Alcohol demand is elastic; as price drops, more individuals buy. Researchers have used liver cirrhosis as a proxy for alcohol use and found that there were more cases after Prohibition ended.[73] But even with higher consumption and all of its negative externalities, the market was in the hands of licit actors instead of illicit actors and was thus subject to legal dispute-resolution mechanisms and government regulation.[74] The transition away from Prohibition denied significant profits to illicit networks.

Illicit network resilience does not mean that a shift in the global drug-prohibition regime is futile. Indeed, eliminating significant profits for organized crime helps to weaken these networks and allows the state to more effectively combat them. With so much profit, illicit networks are able to corrupt state officials. This makes the institutional reforms critical to improving state capacity all but impossible. Organized crime is a problem that can be controlled, not eliminated, and that control requires strong state capacity and depriving illicit networks of significant profits.[75] Though Mexico has generally had weak state capacity, this is changing slowly through efforts to improve the judicial sector and the state's security apparatus, as well as increased social spending.[76]

The Future of States and Illicit Networks

The question of the future of the territorial sovereign state in the international system hangs heavy in the political science discipline and the debates on states versus markets and illicit networks. My analysis of the AFO suggests that the challenge drug networks pose to the state is not in their direct violent confrontation with the state, which is a short-term problem, but in the long-term capability of transactional drug networks to graft themselves to the state, eroding democracy and the rule of law, as well as stunting economic development. Wherever the state can utilize market solutions effectively to address the powerful supply-and-demand forces that fuel drug networks, they can strengthen themselves by reducing the cost of combating illicit networks. If the state is unwilling to lift prohibition regimes, or is unable to do so due to negative political consequences, the state will continue to face both territorial and transactional drug networks.

The future of the state as the dominant unit of the international system is bright if it prudently applies the resources it has at its disposal. A list of reforms that strengthen states vis-à-vis drug networks is less important than the ability of the state to fund capacity building through taxation. Without resources, no reforms or increases in state capacity are possible. In so far as norms of "privatization," "smaller government," and low taxation prevail, the state is weakened in its capacity to marshal these resources. These norms, when taken to extremes, are incompatible with the concept of the state itself.[77] States can also draw upon the advantage of cooperation with other states in their battles against illicit networks. Mexico, for example, drew upon US-provided signals-intelligence capability for its battles against illicit networks during the Calderón administration, drawing not just on equipment, but also capability and training that could not be bought on the open market.[78]

Democratic transition and its concomitant features, including transparency, rule of law, and effective judicial institutions, appear to reduce corruption. Thus, we can surmise that the elimination of corruption through democratization is a likely mechanism that many developing states will use in their struggles with the transactional drug networks that arise following the defeat of territorial drug networks.[79] These transitions will be hindered by the transactional network penetration of the state during conflicts with territorial networks. Only deepened democratization will motivate states to eliminate the lesser evil of transactional networks.

The victory of states over territorial drug networks is not inevitable. If state institutions are weak, corrupted, and suffer from a lack of legitimacy while territorial drug networks are strong, well organized, violent, and profitable, the networks can potentially supplant the state.[80] Most developing states are not in this position. Strong states will be able to manage both transactional and territorial drug-network business strategies. Weak states can piggyback on the "economies of scale" and technological advantages of strong states to combat drug networks. The motivation of states to engage in these battles is the strengthening of the concept of the state itself and the achievement of security from political threat, not the elimination of "illicit flows."[81] Territorially sovereign states will target territorial drug networks first because they most resemble the state and also because they trigger a visceral societal backlash, necessitating even stronger responses from democratic states. States and profit-seeking illicit networks are enemies because they are so much alike.[82] Transactional networks, the lesser evil,[83] will be a lower priority but can be reduced over time through the development of capacities for democracy and rule of law.

Notes

1. Mazzitelli, "Mexican Cartel Influence"; "Mexico, Central America and the Caribbean"; Reuter, "Systemic Violence in Drug Markets."

2. Prof. Raúl Benítez Manaut, conversation with the author, Tijuana, 2009.

3. Marosi, "Mystery Man Blamed."

4. For the concepts of precipitants and preconditions, see Eckstein, "On the Etiology."

5. It is impossible to confirm the exact illicit arrangements that existed between the AFO and the Sinaloa cartel, but it did appear that the latter deferred to the former as the AFO's power increased in Tijuana in 2010. The Sinaloa cartel may have been avoiding conflict in Tijuana due to the ongoing conflict in Ciudad Juárez with the Carrillo Fuentes Organization. Given recent events, this no longer appears to be the case as the Sinaloa and the fragmented AFO fight small battles over key areas of the city. These conflicts do not appear to rise to the level of the battles of 2008–10. Mexican official, interview by the author, Mexico City, 2010; family member of Tijuana doctor, interview by the author, Tijuana, 2011; Tijuana businessman, interview by the author, Tijuana, 2011; Tijuana municipal police officer, interview by the author, Tijuana, February 2011.

6. Steve Duncan (law-enforcement investigator [CA Dept. of Justice] focused on the AFO), correspondence with the author, 2015; Gagne, "Tijuana Cartel Resurgent"; "Balaceras, 'se reorganiza el CAF'"; "Guerritas del CAF y Sinaloa."

7. Mazzitelli, "Mexican Cartel Influence"; Reuter, "Systemic Violence in Drug Markets."

8. Benítez, conversation.

9. Brands, "Los Zetas"; Grayson, "Los Zetas"; Rodriguez, "Mexican Drug Cartels"; "'Zetas' usan a pandillas"; Logan and Sullivan, "Gulf–Zeta Split."

10. "Mexico Drug Cartel Unleashes"; Payan and Correa Cabrera, *Energy Reform and Security*; Grayson and Logan, *Executioner's Men*.

11. Canales, "Deadly Genius"; Sullivan, "Extreme Narco Violence"; Dudley and Rios Contreras, "Why Mexico's Zetas."

12. Dudley, "5 Things the El Salvador Gang"; Felbab-Brown and Olson, "Better Strategy"; Dudley and Corcoran, "InSight Map"; *Los Zetas Factsheet*.

13. Hale, *"Failed State" in Mexico*.

14. On needing the support of the population in counterinsurgency, see Petraeus and Amos, *FM 3-24*, 51; Galula, *Counterinsurgency Warfare*; Thompson, *Defeating Communist Insurgency*.

15. Grayson and Logan, *Executioner's Men*.

16. Dudley, "Two Mexico Cartel Rivals."

17. The possibility of a highly resilient Los Zetas was presciently speculated on by Eduardo Guerrero Gutiérrez in *Nexos* magazine in 2011: "Nonetheless, one mustn't discard the possibility that the Zetas have developed an operational model that is unique among the Mexican cartels that enables them to expand geographically very quickly without taking a toll on their internal cohesion." For more on the esprit de corps of Los Zetas, see Grayson and Logan, *Executioner's Men*, chap. 5. Guerrero Gutiérrez, "At the Root of the Violence," 15–16; Grayson, "Los Zetas," 83; Sullivan and Logan, "Los Zetas"; Salcedo-Albarán and Garay Salamanca, *Structure of a Transnational Criminal Network*.

18. Hernandez, *Narcoland*.

19. Grillo, *El Narco*.

20. Jones, "Monopoly of Force"; Chindea, "Fear and Loathing."

21. Canales, "Deadly Genius."

22. Carillo, "Mexico Self-Defense Groups"; Parkinson, "Arrest of Mexico Self-Defense Leader."

23. Fausset, "Mexico's Lazaro Cardenas Port."

24. Buscaglia, Gonzalez-Ruiz, and Ratliff, "Undermining the Foundations."

25. Ibid.; *DEA History 2003–2008*.

26. Krauze, "Mexico's Disastrous Drug War 'Success.'"

27. Felbab-Brown, *Focused Deterrence*.

28. Bailey, *Politics of Crime in Mexico*.

29. Esquivel, "'El Kelin' revelo"; Gagne, "Announced Zetas, Gulf Alliance Could Change Mexico's Criminal Landscape."

30. Beith, "Narco of Narcos."

31. Gagne, "Announced Zetas, Gulf Alliance"; Esquivel, "'El Kelin' revelo."

32. Felbab-Brown points to more violent youth leadership to explain increased violence in drug markets with high leadership turnover, while Beith points to Chapo

Guzmán's time in prison as a possible factor for his improved managerial skills, which allow him to minimize conflict. Felbab-Brown, "Stemming the Violence in Mexico"; Beith, *Last Narco*.

33. See Grayson, *Cartels*, on the preferred use of law enforcement. On high-value targeting, see "Cable 09MEXICO3573"; Ellingwood, "Mexico Drug War"; Booth and Miroff, "DEA Intelligence Aids."

34. Longmire, "US Agents Could Soon Carry."

35. Wiretap recordings in the Luz Verde indictment describe the AFO engaging in kidnapping operations, and the recent arrest of a kidnapping cell demonstrates the low-profile kidnapping strategy that eschewed well-known targets. "Desmantelan banda"; "Indictment: United States vs. Armando Villareal Heredia et al."

36. Jones, "Unintended Consequences."

37. "Mexican Attorney General Identifies."

38. Keefe, "How a Mexican Drug Cartel."

39. For a discussion of networked actors cooperating, see Sullivan. See Canales on branding. Bunker and Sullivan, "Integrating Feral Cities "; Sullivan, *From Drug Wars*; Canales, "Deadly Genius."

40. Keefe, "How a Mexican Drug Cartel."

41. UC Irvine professor Caesar Sereseres (a specialist in insurgency and Latin America), phone conversation with the author, 2015; Dra. Patricia Escamilla Hamm (Latin America specialist), phone conversation with the author about illicit networks, 2015.

42. Felbab-Brown, "Violent Drug Market"; Felbab-Brown, *Shooting Up*.

43. For an excellent empirical account of the fall of the Medellín and Cali cartels, see Felbab-Brown, "Violent Drug Market"; Felbab-Brown, *Shooting Up*; Bowden, *Killing Pablo*.

44. Pardo, "Colombia's Two-Front War"; Garzón, *Mafia & Co.*

45. Moore, "Myth of a 'Good Guy.'"

46. Clunan and Trinkunas, *Ungoverned Spaces*, 5.

47. Kenney discusses the force advantage of state bureaucracies. Kenney, *From Pablo to Osama*; Nye, "Changing Nature of World Power," 184.

48. Guerrero Gutiérrez, "Cómo reducir la violencia"; Jones, "Unintended Consequences."

49. Jones, "Understanding and Addressing Youth."

50. "Treasury Designates."

51. That the tax-revenue rates in Mexico are low is an important point made by Dr. Samuel Gonzalez-Ruiz, "Public Safety in Mexico."

52. Hughes, "Analysis"; Bailey, *Politics of Crime*, 33–39; Gonzalez-Ruiz, "Public Safety."

53. Hughes, "Analysis."

54. See Camp, *Mexico's Military*, for low funding of the Mexican military.

55. Andreas, *Border Games*; Van Schendel, *Bengal Borderland*; Clunan and Trinkunas, *Ungoverned Spaces*, 5.

56. Ford, *Plan Colombia*.

57. "Study: 98.5% of Crimes."

58. Bowden, *Killing Pablo*; "Study: 98.5% of Crimes"; "Latin America Most Dangerous"; Oppenheimer, "Mexico's Big Hope"; Guerrero Gutiérrez, "Cómo reducir la violencia"; Garzón, *Mafia & Co*; Pardo, "Colombia's Two-Front War."

59. Andreas, *Border Games*; Sadiq, *Paper Citizens* ; Van Schendel and Abraham, *Illicit Flows*.

60. Naím, "Mafia States"; Lupsha, "Transnational Organized Crime"; Arias, *Drugs and Democracy*.

61. Gray, *Why Our Drug Laws*; "Mexico's Drug War: Stories"; Payan, Staudt, and Kruszewski, *War That Can't Be Won*.

62. Buscaglia and Ratliff, *War and Lack of Governance*; Buscaglia, Gonzalez-Ruiz, and Ratliff, "Undermining the Foundations"; Buscaglia, *Judicial Corruption*; Gonzalez-Ruiz, "Public Safety in Mexico."

63. Gonzalez-Ruiz, "Public Safety in Mexico."

64. Hefler, "Medical Marijuana Law."

65. Carpenter, *Bad Neighbor Policy*.

66. Hope and Clark, *Si los vecinos legalizan*; Ramsey, "Study: US Marijuana Legalization."

67. Burnett, "Legal Pot in the U.S."

68. Bosworth, "Why Military Hawks"; Parsons and Bennett, "At Latin America Summit"; "AP Interview."

69. Cardoso, Gaviria, and Zedillo, "War on Drugs a Failure."

70. Archibold, "After Fatal Casino Attack"; Ellingwood, "Fallout from Deadly"; Johnson, "Mexican Leader Hints."

71. Kenney, *From Pablo to Osama*; Jones, "State Reaction"; Chabot, "Historical Case Study."

72. MacCoun and Reuter, *Drug War Heresies*.

73. Kleiman, "Targeting Drug-Trafficking Violence."

74. Ibid.

75. Buscaglia, Gonzalez-Ruiz, and Ratliff, "Undermining the Foundations."

76. Shirk, "Judicial Reform in Mexico."

77. Rawls, *Theory of Justice*; Polanyi, *Great Transformation*.

78. "Cable 09MEXICO2882."

79. Arias, *Drugs and Democracy*; Sandholtz and Koetzle, "Accounting for Corruption"; Buscaglia, Gonzalez-Ruiz, and Ratliff, "Undermining the Foundations."

80. Felbab-Brown, "Conceptualizing Crime as Competition"; Clunan and Trinkunas, *Ungoverned Spaces*; Williams, "Here Be Dragons."

81. Andreas, *Border Games*; Bowden, *Killing Pablo*; Felbab-Brown, *Shooting Up*; Andreas, "Redrawing the Line."

82. Jones, "State Reaction."

83. Moore, "Myth of a 'Good Guy.'"

Appendix: Comparison of Territorial versus Transactional Drug-Trafficking Networks

Business Strategies	Territorial Drug Networks	Transactional Drug Networks
1. Treatment of territory	Focus on control and taxation of territory.	Emphasis on trafficking over territorial control.
2. Degree of hierarchy	More hierarchical due to need for enforcers.	Flatter structures but can be hierarchical. A smaller number of highly sophisticated individuals.
3. Profile	Flashy lifestyle (e.g., gold-plated guns).	Low-profile lifestyle (no conspicuous consumption), or lifestyle is explained by front businesses. May contain territorial cells that eschew the low-profile strategy.
4. Extortion as a source of profit	Extortion of illegitimate and legitimate businesses used en masse. Extortion of petite bourgeoisie.	Extort illicit businesses but profit mostly from trafficking drugs. Establish norms of paying extortion tax regularly for illicit businesses. Provide protection/ business services.
5. Kidnapping	Kidnappings of citizens uninvolved in underworld. Less intelligence on targets. Targets held for short periods of time.	Kidnappings limited to enforcing drug debts and those involved in crime. Sometimes used when network is profit-starved but always high-profile targets. Punish freelance kidnappers.
6. Violence against police	Killing of police officers in large numbers.	More emphasis on corrupting police or evading altogether. Pay off high-level commanders.
7. Use of extreme violence	Heavy use of extreme violence (e.g., decapitations). YouTube postings, public hangings of bodies from bridges.	Focus on bribery of officials over extreme violence or threats but use extreme violence in confrontations with territorial traffickers.

(Continued)

Comparison of Territorial versus Transactional Drug-Trafficking Networks (Continued)

Business Strategies	Territorial Drug Networks	Transactional Drug Networks
8. Political campaigns	Some funding of local political campaigns. Heavy use of intimidation.	Greater funding of political campaigns, especially on the federal and state levels but also local.
9. Management	Typically younger leadership. Often more violent (ephemeral). Leaders tend to be those who specialize in violence. Heavy use of franchise model.	Experienced managers. Typically have, or hire those with, degrees in business, law, accounting, etc.
10. Use of enforcers	More enforcers.	Fewer enforcers, more smugglers and intelligence. Enforcers focus on bodyguard and security operations. Preference for corruption.
11. Size	Larger organizations in terms of numbers of individuals involved.	Large organizations but higher profit margins due to relative numbers involved.
12. Violence toward society	More violence toward society and rival traffickers. More likely to have street gun battles for turf and come into conflict with police.	Less violence toward society. Some violence directed at rival traffickers. More apt to use intelligence to tip off state-security apparatus to rivals.
13. Source of profits	Profit primarily from kidnapping/extortion, human trafficking, prostitution, drugs, and taxing small smugglers for use of territory. Diversified activities.	Profit from trafficking drugs, money laundering, financing drug production, high-profile kidnapping victims, legitimate businesses, front businesses, government contracts, etc.
14. Retail drug sales	More retail drug sales in their territory.	Fewer retail drug sales in their home territories.
15. Domestic use of street gangs	More use of local street gangs domestically.	Lower use of local street gangs domestically.
16. Crime rates	Higher crime in areas controlled by these groups.	Lower crime rates in areas controlled by these groups.
17. Corruption/ bribes	Tend to bribe lower levels of government (e.g., municipal police).	Tend to bribe higher levels of government (federal/state government and law enforcement).
18. Adaptability	Less adaptable in smuggling methods but able to diversify activities to compensate.	Highly adaptable in smuggling methods.
19. Alliance stability	Fewer alliances, less stable. More likely to annex local street gangs and change their identity. Heavy use of franchise model.	More alliances with other groups. Alliances more stable and based on business interests. More likely to create "federations" with other trafficking-oriented drug networks.

Business Strategies	Territorial Drug Networks	Transactional Drug Networks
20. Trafficking-method sophistication	Sophistication of trafficking dependent upon smuggling group being taxed.	More sophisticated trafficking methods (e.g., sea-submersibles, ventilated tunnels, air transport), all of which may require large initial investment.
21. Capital reserves	Lower capital reserves, resulting in a diversification of criminal activity to cover overhead of enforcers when drug profits drop due to market forces or border enforcement.	Higher capital reserves. Less need to diversify criminal activity.
22. Violence toward state, society, and political elites	Highly violent threat to state, society, and political elites.	Less violent threat to state, society, and political elites. Dangerous corrupting influence.
23. Investment in local population	Invest heavily in local population for political capital but also tax local population. Net loss for local population.	Invest heavily in local population and central government corruption. Often a net gain for local population in underdeveloped regions. Corruption can also hinder economic development.
24. Use of firepower	Heavy emphasis on firepower.	Lower emphasis on firepower.
25. Assassination	Random assassination strategies (e.g., bounties for killing any police officers).	Strategic assassinations targeting specific high-ranking individuals for specific reasons.
26. Terrorist bombing	More likely to engage in terrorist bombings.	More likely to ally with state than use terrorism.

Sources: The main categories were inspired by Reuter, "Systematic Violence," and an anonymous Mexican government official's 2010 statement quoted in the *Economist,* January 7, 2010. Dudley, "Drug Trafficking Organizations"; Beith, *Last Narco*; Keefe, "How a Mexican Drug Cartel"; Jones, "Unintended Consequences"; Steve Duncan (law-enforcement investigator [CA Dept. of Justice] focused on the AFO), interview by the author, San Diego, 2010; Sullivan, "Barrio Azteca, Los Aztecas Network"; Burnett, Penalosa, and Bennincasa, "Mexico Seems to Favor"; Burnett and Penalosa, "Mexico's Drug War"; Grayson, *Cartels*; Grayson and Logan, *Executioner's Men*; Buscaglia, Gonzalez-Ruiz, and Ratliff, "Undermining the Foundations"; Sullivan and Logan, "Los Zetas"; Mazzitelli, *Mexican Cartel Influence*; "Outsmarted by Sinaloa"; Kenney, *From Pablo to Osama*; Resa Nestares, "Los Zetas"; Ramsey, "Study: US Marijuana Legalization"; Hope and Clark, *Si los vecinos legalizan*; Marosi, "Mexico General Battles"; Guerrero Gutierrez, "Pandillas y cárteles"; "'Zetas' usan a pandillas"; Keefe, "Hunt for El Chapo"; Bunker and Sullivan, "Cartel Evolution Revisited"; Felbab-Brown, "Stemming the Violence"; Hampson, "Extreme Violence"; Sullivan, "Extreme Narco Violence"; Sabet, "Confrontation, Collusion and Tolerance"; anonymous Tijuana businessman, interview by the author, Tijuana, 2011; Marosi, "Mystery Man Blamed"; UNODC, *Transnational Organized Crime in Central America and the Caribbean.*

Bibliography

"Activos secuestradores del CAF." *Semanario Zeta*, March 3, 2015. http://zetatijuana.com/noticias/reportajez/19069/activos-secuestradores-del-caf.

Ahmed, Azam. "U.S. Sought 'El Chapo' Extradition before Escape." *New York Times*, July 17, 2015. http://www.nytimes.com/2015/07/18/world/americas/joaquin-guzman-loera-extradition-request.html.

"Al Día: Merida Initiative and Pillar IV; Addressing the Causes of Mexican Criminal Violence—What Role for the USAID?" Mexico Institute, Woodrow Wilson International Center for Scholars, December 15, 2010. http://mexicoinstitute.wordpress.com/2010/12/15/al-dia-merida-initiative-pillar-iv-%e2%80%93-addressing-the-causes-of-mexican-criminal-violence-what-role-for-the-usaid/.

Allison, Graham T. *Essence of Decision: Explaining the Cuban Missile Crisis*. Boston: Little, Brown, 1971.

Alvarado, Ignacio. "Leyzaola: Héroe, villano ¿o ambos?" *El Universal*, November 8, 2010, sec. Sociedad. http://archivo.eluniversal.com.mx/notas/721865.html.

Andreas, Peter. *Border Games: Policing the US–Mexico Divide*. Ithaca, NY: Cornell University Press, 2009.

———. "Illicit Globalization: Myths, Misconceptions, and Historical Lessons." *Political Science Quarterly* 126, no. 3 (2011): 403–25. http://dx.doi.org/10.1002/j.1538-165X.2011.tb00706.x.

———. "Redrawing the Line." *International Security* 28, no. 2 (2003): 78–111. http://dx.doi.org/10.1162/016228803322761973.

———. *Smuggler Nation: How Illicit Trade Made America*. New York: Oxford University Press, 2013.

"AP Interview: Guatemala Prez Urges Drug Legalization While Escalating War on Cartel Gangs." *Washington Post*, September 25, 2012, sec. World. http://www

.washingtonpost.com/world/the_americas/ap-interview-guatemala-prez
-urges-drug-legalization-while-escalating-war-on-cartel-gangs/2012/09/25
/89cf3f4e-0742–11e2–9eea-333857f6a7bd_story.html.

Archibold, Randal C. "After Fatal Casino Attack, Mexican Officials Focus on Organized Crime's Link." *New York Times*, August 26, 2011, sec. World/ Americas. http://www.nytimes.com/2011/08/27/world/americas/27mexico .html.

———. "Mexican Navy Believes It Killed Ruthless Gang Kingpin." *New York Times*, October 9, 2012, sec. World/Americas. http://www.nytimes .com/2012/10/10/world/americas/mexico-zetas.html.

———. "Mexico Captures El Coss, Head of Gulf Cartel." *New York Times*, September 13, 2012, / Americas. http://www.nytimes.com/2012/09/14/ world/americas/el-coss-head-of-gulf-cartel-captured-mexico-says.html.

———. "A Quandary for Mexico as Vigilantes Rise." *New York Times*, January 15, 2014. http://www.nytimes.com/2014/01/16/world/americas/a -quandary-for-mexico-as-vigilantes-rise.html.

Arias, Enrique Desmond. *Drugs and Democracy in Rio de Janeiro: Trafficking, Social Networks, and Public Security*. Chapel Hill: University of North Carolina Press, 2006.

Arquilla, John, and David F. Ronfeldt. *The Advent of Netwar*. Santa Monica, CA: RAND, 1996.

———. *In Athena's Camp: Preparing for Conflict in the Information Age*. Santa Monica, CA: RAND, 1997. http://www.rand.org/pubs/monograph_ reports/MR880.html.

Arquilla, John, and David F. Ronfeldt, eds. *Networks and Netwars: The Future of Terror, Crime, and Militancy*. Santa Monica, CA: RAND, 2001. http://www .rand.org/pubs/monograph_reports/MR1382.html.

Arrow, K. J. *The Limits of Organization*. New York: Norton, 1974.

Asal, Victor, H. Brinton Milward, and Eric W. Schoon. "When Terrorists Go Bad: Analyzing Terrorist Organizations' Involvement in Drug Smuggling." *International Studies Quarterly* 59 (2015): 112–23.

Associated Press. "In Mexico, Vigilante Villagers Plan to Try 53 Prisoners." *New York Times*, January 31, 2013, sec. World/Americas. http://www .nytimes.com/2013/02/01/world/americas/in-mexico-vigilante-villagers -plan-to-try-53-prisoners.html.

———. "Mexico Says Cartels Turning Attacks on Authorities." *New York Times*, April 25, 2010. http://www.nytimes.com/aponline/2010/04/25/world/ AP-LT-Drug-War-Mexico.html?ref=americas.

———. "¡Porqué se fue Leyzaola!: EU." *El Mexicano*, November 28, 2010. http:// www.el-mexicano.com.mx/informacion/noticias/1/3/estatal/2010/11/ 28/440646/porque-se-fue-leyzaola-eu.aspx.

Astorga, Luis. *El siglo de las drogas.* Mexico City: Plaza & Janés, 2005.

———. "Organized Crime and the Organization of Crime." In *Organized Crime and Democratic Governability: Mexico and the U.S.–Mexican Borderlands,* edited by John Bailey and Roy Godson. Pittsburgh: University of Pittsburgh Press, 2000.

———. *Seguridad, traficantes y militares: El poder y la sombra.* Mexico City: Tusquets, 2007.

Astorga, Luis, and David Shirk. *Drug Trafficking Organizations and Counter-Drug Strategies in the U.S.–Mexican Context.* Woodrow Wilson International Center for Scholars. http://www.wilsoncenter.org/sites/default/files/Chapter%20 1-Drug%20Trafficking%20Organizations%20and%20Counter-Drug%20 Strategies%20in%20the%20U.S.-Mexico%20Context.pdf.

Bagley, Bruce. *Drug Trafficking and Organized Crime in the Americas: Major Trends in the Twenty-First Century.* Washington, DC: Woodrow Wilson International Center for Scholars, August 2012. http://www.wilsoncenter.org/ sites/default/files/BB%20Final.pdf.

Bailey, John. *The Politics of Crime in Mexico: Democratic Governance in a Security Trap.* Boulder, CO: First Forum Press, 2014.

Bailey, John, and Jorge Chabat. *Transnational Crime and Public Security: Challenges to Mexico and the United States.* U.S.–Mexico Contemporary Perspectives Series. La Jolla, CA: Center for U.S.–Mexican Studies, University of California, San Diego, 2002. http://www. loc.gov/catdir/toc/fy022/2001059874.html.

Bailey, John J., and Roy Godson. *Organized Crime and Democratic Governability: Mexico and the U.S.–Mexican Borderlands.* Pittsburgh: University of Pittsburgh Press, 2000.

Baker, Peter, and Randal C. Archibold. "U.S. Seeks Arrest of Mexican Kingpin Who Was Freed in American's Murder." *New York Times,* August 14, 2013, sec. World/Americas. http://www.nytimes.com/2013/08/15/world/americas/us-asks-for-arrest-of-mexican-kingpin-who-was-freed-in-americans-murder.html.

Bakker, René M., Jörg Raab, and H. Brinton Milward. "A Preliminary Theory of Dark Network Resilience." *Journal of Policy Analysis and Management* 31, no. 1 (2012): 33–62. http://dx.doi.org/10.1002/pam.20619.

"Balaceras, 'se reorganiza el CAF': Lares." *Semanario Zeta,* February 3, 2015. http://zetatijuana.com/noticias/reportajez/17622/balaceras-se-reorganiza-el -caf-lares.

Balcázar Villarreal, Manuel, ed. *Pandillas en el siglo XXI: El reto de su inclusión en el desarollo nacional.* Mexico City: Secretaría de Seguridad Pública Federal, 2012.

Bargent, James. "Tijuana Cartel Leader Arrest Could Mean End of Drug Empire." InSight Crime. June 24, 2014. http://www.insightcrime.org/news-briefs/ tijuana-cartel-leader-arrest-could-spell-end-of-arellano-felix-drug-empire.

Becerra, Hector. "Mexican Cartel Kingpin Reported Dead—of a Heart Attack." *Los Angeles Times*, June 9, 2014. http://www.latimes.com/world/mexico-americas/la-fg-mexican-cartel-kingpin-dead-20140609-story.html.

———. "To Fight the Cartel, Mexican Emigrants Return to Their Hometowns." *Los Angeles Times*, January 25, 2014. http://www.latimes.com/local/la-me-michoacan-la-20140126-story.html.

Beith, Malcom. *The Last Narco: Inside the Hunt for El Chapo, the World's Most Wanted Drug Lord*. New York: Grove, 2010.

———. "The Narco of Narcos: Fugitive Mexican Drug Lord Rafael Caro Quintero." InSight Crime, April 14, 2014. http://www.insightcrime.org/news-analysis/the-narco-of-narcos-fugitive-mexican-drug-lord-rafael-caro-quintero.

Benson, Bruce L. "Review of *The Sicilian Mafia: The Business of Private Protection* by Diego Gambetta." *Public Choice* 80, no. 1/2 (1994): 217–19. http://www.jstor.org/stable/30026921.

Bergman, Lowell. "Drug Wars." Documentary. PBS's *Frontline*, 2000. http://www.pbs.org/wgbh/pages/frontline/shows/drugs/business/afo/narcojunior.html.

———. "Drug Wars: Interviews: 'Steve.'" Documentary. PBS's *Frontline*, 2000. http://www.pbs.org/wgbh/pages/frontline/shows/drugs/interviews/steve.html.

———. "Murder, Money, and Mexico: Family Tree; The Hanks." Documentary. PBS's *Frontline*, 2000. http://www.pbs.org/wgbh/pages/frontline/shows/mexico/family/bergman.html.

Betanzos, Said. "Leyzaola 'pactó' con los Arellano." *El Mexicano*, March 17, 2011. http://www.el-mexicano.com.mx/informacion/noticias/1/3/estatal/2011/03/17/461166/leyzaola-pacto-con-los-arellano.aspx.

Blancornelas, Jesús. *El cártel: Los Arellano Félix, la mafia más Poderosa en la historia de América Latina*. Mexico City: Plaza y Janés, 2002.

Bloomekatz, Ari. "Federal Marijuana Memo Could Affect Other Countries, Expert Says." *Los Angeles Times*, August 30, 2013. http://www.latimes.com/local/lanow/la-me-ln-pot-memo-20130829,0,6615623.story.

Booth, William, and Nick Miroff. "DEA Intelligence Aids Mexican Marines in Drug War." *Washington Post*, December 4, 2010. http://www.washingtonpost.com/wp-dyn/content/article/2010/12/03/AR2010120306820.html?hpid=topnewswashingtonpost.com.

Booth, William, and Steve Fainaru. "Widespread Oil Theft by Drug Traffickers Deals Major Blow to Mexico's Government." *Washington Post*. December 13, 2009. http://www.washingtonpost.com/wp-dyn/content/article/2009/12/12/AR2009121202888_pf.html.

Bosworth, James. "Why Military Hawks Are Leading Drug Legalization Debate in Latin America." *Christian Science Monitor*, February 15, 2012.

http://www.csmonitor.com/World/Americas/2012/0215/Why-military
-hawks-are-leading-drug-legalization-debate-in-Latin-America.

Bowden, Charles. *Murder City: Ciudad Juárez and the Global Economy's New Killing Fields.* New York: Nation Books, 2010.

Bowden, Mark. *Killing Pablo: The Hunt for the World's Greatest Outlaw.* New
York: Penguin, 2001.

Brands, Hal. "Los Zetas: Inside Mexico's Most Dangerous Drug Gang." December 29, 2009. http://www.airpower.maxwell.af.mil/apjinternational/
apj-s/2009/3tri09/brandseng.htm.

———. *Mexico's Narco-Insurgency and U.S. Counterdrug Policy.* Strategic Studies
Institute, 2009. www.strategicstudiesinstitute.army.mil/pdffiles/pub918.pdf.

"Brian Terry Family Sues ATF Officials in Fast and Furious–CBS News." Broad-
cast news. CBS News, December 17, 2012. http://www.cbsnews.com/8301
-250_162-57559582/brian-terry-family-sues-atf-officials-in-fast-and-furious/.

Bunker, R. J., and J. P. Sullivan. "Cartel Evolution Revisited: Third Phase
Cartel Potentials and Alternative Futures in Mexico." *Small Wars &
Insurgencies* 21, no. 1 (March 12, 2010): 30–54. http://dx.doi.org/10.1080/
09592310903561379.

Bunker, Robert J. "Mexican Cartel Tactical Note #13: Man Crucified in Michoacán, Mexico." *Small Wars Journal,* September 10, 2012. http://smallwarsjournal
.com/blog/mexican-cartel-tactical-note-13-man-crucified-in-michoac%C3%
A1n-mexico.

Bunker, Robert J., and John P. Sullivan. "Integrating Feral Cities and Third Phase
Cartels/Third Generation Gangs Research: The Rise of Criminal (Narco)
City Networks and BlackFor." *Small Wars & Insurgencies* 22, no. 5 (2011):
764–86. http://dx.doi.org/10.1080/09592318.2011.620804.

Burnett, John. "Legal Pot in the U.S. May Be Undercutting Mexican Marijuana." NPR, December 1, 2014. http://www.npr.org/blogs/parallels/
2014/12/01/367802425/legal-pot-in-the-u-s-may-be-undercutting-mexican-
marijuana.

———. "Nuevo Laredo Returns to Normal as Violence Slows" NPR, January 23,
2009. http://www.npr.org/templates/story/story.php?storyId=99742620.

Burnett, John, and Marisa Penalosa. "Mexico's Drug War: A Rigged Fight?" May 19,
2010. http://www.npr.org/templates/story/story.php?storyId=126890838.

Burnett, John, Marisa Penalosa, and Robert Bennincasa. "Mexico Seems
to Favor Sinaloa Cartel in Drug War." NPR, May 19, 2010. http://www
.npr.org/2010/05/19/126906809/mexico-seems-to-favor-sinaloa-cartel
-in-drug-war.

Burnett, John, and Renée Montagne. "On the Trail of Mexico's Vicious Sinaloa
Cartel." NPR. May 18, 2010. http://www.npr.org/templates/story/story.php?
storyId=126894829.

Burt, Ronald S. "Structural Holes versus Network Closure as Social Capital." *Social Capital: Theory and Research*, 2001, 31–56.

Burt, R. S. *Structural Holes: The Social Structure of Competition*. Cambridge, MA: Harvard University Press, 1995.

Burton, Fred. "Mexico: The Price of Peace in the Cartel Wars." Stratfor, May 2, 2007. https://www.stratfor.com/mexico_price_peace_cartel_wars.

Buscaglia, Edgardo. *Judicial Corruption in Developing Countries: Its Causes and Economic Consequences*. Vienna: United Nations Office of Drug Control and Crime Prevention, March 2001.

Buscaglia, Edgardo, Samuel Gonzalez-Ruiz, and William Ratliff. "Undermining the Foundations of Organized Crime and Public Sector Corruption: An Essay on Best International Practices." Hoover Institution, August 1, 2005. http://www.hoover.org/sites/default/files/uploads/documents/epp_114 .pdf.

Buscaglia, E., and J. Van Dijk. "Controlling Organized Crime and Corruption in the Public Sector," *Forum on Crime and Society* 3 (2003): 3–34.

Buscaglia, E., and W. E. Ratliff. *War and Lack of Governance in Colombia: Narcos, Guerrillas, and US Policy*. Stanford, CA: Hoover Institution Press, 2001.

"Cable 09MEXICO2882: Elements of GOM Policy Team Interested in Focusing Together on Improving Security in a Few Key Cities." WikiLeaks, October 5, 2009. https://wikileaks.org/plusd/cables/09MEXICO2882_a.html.

"Cable 09MEXICO3573: Mexican Navy Operation Nets Drug Kingpin Arturo." WikiLeaks, 2009. https://wikileaks.org/plusd/cables/09MEXICO3573_a .html.

" SCENESETTER FOR THE OPENING OF THE DEFENSE BILATERAL WORKING GROUP, WASHINGTON, D.C., FEBRUARY 1." WikiLeaks, January 29, 2010. https://wikileaks.org/plusd/cables/10MEXICO83_a .html

"Cae 'El Tigrillo' Arellano Félix." *AP*. August 17, 2006. http://www.tabascohoy .com.mx/nota.php?id_nota=114426.

Caldwell, Robert. "Captured." *San Diego Union-Tribune*, August 29, 2004. http:// www.utsandiego.com/uniontrib/20040829/news_mz1e29caldwe.html.

———. "Cartel Secrets." *San Diego Union-Tribune*, July 1, 2007. http://www .uniontrib.com/uniontrib/20070701/news_lz1e1cartel.html.

———. "Cold-Blooded Killers." *San Diego Union-Tribune*, July 1, 2007. http:// www.utsandiego.com/uniontrib/20070701/news_lz1e1killers.html.

Camp, Roderic Ai. *Mexico's Military on the Democratic Stage*. Westport, CT: Praeger Security International, in cooperation with the Center for Strategic and International Studies, 2005.

Canales, Rodrigo. "The Deadly Genius of Drug Cartels." TED Talk, November 4, 2013. https://www.youtube.com/watch?v=VYU25aJpg5o.

Cardoso, F. H., C. Gaviria, and Ernesto Zedillo. "The War on Drugs Is a Failure." *Wall Street Journal*, February 23, 2009. http://www.wsj.com/articles/SB123535114271444981.

Carillo, Mario. "Mexico Self-Defense Groups Coach Businesses on Counter-Extortion." InSight Crime, June 19, 2013. http://www.insightcrime.org/news-briefs/mexico-self-defense-groups-coach-businesses-on-counter-extortion.

Carpenter, T. G. *Bad Neighbor Policy: Washington's Futile War on Drugs in Latin America*. Palgrave Macmillan, 2003.

Carroll, Rory. "US Has Lost Faith in Mexico's Ability to Win Drugs War, WikiLeaks Cables Show." *Guardian*, December 2, 2010. http://www.theguardian.com/world/2010/dec/02/us-mexico-drugs-war-wikileaks.

Cattan, Nacha. "Killing of Top Mexico Drug Lord 'Tony Tormenta' May Boost Rival Zetas Cartel." *Christian Science Monitor*, November 7, 2010. http://www.csmonitor.com/World/Americas/2010/1107/Killing-of-top-Mexico-drug-lord-Tony-Tormenta-may-boost-rival-Zetas-cartel.

Cearley, Anna. "Many Ignore Official's Alleged Link to Arellanos." *San Diego Union-Tribune*. October 31, 2005. http://legacy.signonsandiego.com/uniontrib/20051031/news_1m31carrillo.html.

Central Intelligence Agency. "Mexico." In *The World Factbook*. Washington, DC: CIA, June 14, 2008. https://www.cia.gov/library/publications/the-world-factbook/geos/mx.html#Military.

Chabot, Paul. "An Historical Case Study of Organizational Resiliency within the Arellano-Felix Drug Trafficking Organization." PhD diss., George Washington University, 2008. http://www.paulchabot.com/PDF/PaulChabotDissertationMar272008.pdf.

Chindea, Irina. "Fear and Loathing in Mexico: Narco-Alliances and Proxy Wars." *Fletcher Security Review* 1, no. 2 (Spring 2014). http://media.wix.com/ugd/c28a64_4f406b0a66314668aae6a81a4066465a.pdf.

———. "Man, the State and War against Drug Cartels: A Typology of Drug-Related Violence in Mexico." *Small Wars Journal*, March 19, 2014. http://smallwarsjournal.com/jrnl/art/man-the-state-and-war-against-drug-cartels-a-typology-of-drug-related-violence-in-mexico.

Chivis. "Mexican Army Captures 'El Melvin', Second in Command of Tijuana Cartel." *Borderland Beat*, March 15, 2013. http://www.borderlandbeat.com/2013/03/mexican-army-captures-el-melvin-second.html.

———. "Trial Begins of AFO Cell in San Diego, Prosecutor: Victims Kidnapped and Dissolved in Acid." *Borderland Beat*, February 23, 2012. http://www.borderlandbeat.com/2012/02/trial-begins-of-afo-cell-in-san-diego.html.

Clark Alfaro, Víctor. "El 'modelo' Tijuana." *Proceso*, August 22, 2012. http://www.proceso.com.mx/?p=317763.

Clunan, A. L., and H. A. Trinkunas. *Ungoverned Spaces: Alternatives to State Authority in an Era of Softened Sovereignty*. Stanford, CA: Stanford Security Studies, 2010.

Conery, Ben. "Mexican Drug Cartels 'Hide in Plain Sight' in U.S." *Washington Times*, June 7, 2009. http://www.washingtontimes.com/news/2009/jun/07/mexican-drug-cartels-hide-in-plain-sight-in-us/print/.

Conroy, Bill. "US, Mexican Officials Brokering Deals with Drug 'Cartels,' WikiLeaks Documents Show." *Narco News Bulletin*, August 20, 2012. http://www.narconews.com/Issue67/article4621.html.

Cook, Colleen W. *CRS Report for Congress: Mexico's Drug Cartels*. Congressional Research Service, December 10, 2007. www.fas.org/sgp/crs/row/RL34215.pdf.

Cook, Colleen, Rebecca G. Rush, and Clare Ribando Seelke. *Merida Initiative: Proposed U.S. Anticrime and Counterdrug Assistance for Mexico and Central America*. Woodrow Wilson International Center for Scholars. March 18, 2008. http://fpc.state.gov/documents/organization/103694.pdf.

Corchado, Alfredo. "Immigrants in U.S. Sending Money to Fight Mexican Cartels." *Dallas Morning News*, February 28, 2014. http://www.dallasnews.com/news/nationworld/mexico/20140228-immigrants-in-u.s.-sending-money-to-fight-mexican-cartels.ece.

———. "Mexican Drug Cartels Gaining Strength in Peru: Worry Spreads as Their Presence Increases Coca Production, Violence." *Dallas Morning News*, January 8, 2007. www.dallasnews.com.

Corcoran, Patrick. "'El Mayo' Rises to Lead a Sinaloa Cartel Whose Future Is Uncertain." InSight Crime, July 24, 2014. http://www.insightcrime.org/news-analysis/el-mayo-rises-to-lead-a-sinaloa-cartel-whose-future-is-uncertain.

———. "New Report Examines Tamaulipas Security Strategy." InSight Crime, January 27, 2015. http://www.insightcrime.org/news-analysis/new-report-examines-tamaulipas-security-strategy.

Correa-Cabrera, Guadalupe. "Violence on the 'Forgotten' Border: Mexico's Drug War, the State, and the Paramilitarization of Organized Crime in Tamaulipas in a 'New Democratic Era.'" *Journal of Borderlands Studies* 29, no. 4 (2014): 419–33.

Coscia, Michele, and Viridiana Rios. *Knowing Where and How Criminal Organizations Operate Using Web Content*. CIKM, 2012. http://dx.doi.org/10.1145/2396761.2398446.

Creechan, James. "Cartels, Gangs, Near-Groups and Mobs: The Different Organizational Structures of Mexican Crime Organizations." Conference presentation. Latin American Studies Association, Chicago, May 24, 2014.

Curtis, Glenn E., and Tara Karacan. *The Nexus among Terrorists, Narcotics Traffickers, Weapons Proliferators, and Organized Crime Networks in Western Europe*.

Study commissioned by Congress. Washington, DC: Federal Research Division, Library of Congress, December 2002. http://www.loc.gov/rr/frd/.

Danelo, David. "A New Approach Is Needed in Anti-Crime Fight in Mexico." Banderas News, December 23, 2010. http://www.banderasnews.com/1012/edop-fpri23.htm.

DEA History 2003–2008. Drug Enforcement Administration, 2008. http://www.dea.gov/about/history/2003-2008.pdf.

"DEA Programs, Organized Crime Drug Enforcement Task Force (OCDETF)." Drug Enforcement Administration, 2010. http://www.justice.gov/criminal/organized-crime-drug-enforcement-task-forces.

De Córdoba, José. "Mexico Captures Head of Zetas Cartel." Wall Street Journal, July 16, 2013, sec. World. http://www.wsj.com/articles/SB10001424127887323848804578608470625724206.

De Mauleon, Hector. "Tijuana: En la colina de El Pozolero." Nexos, January 8, 2009. http://www.nexos.com.mx/?p=13252.

DePalma, Anthony. "Mexico Reports Troops Capture Powerful Narcotics Trafficker." New York Times, June 25, 1995, sec. World. http://www.nytimes.com/1995/06/25/world/mexico-reports-troops-capture-powerful-narcotics-trafficker.html.

"Desmantelan banda de secuestradores ligada al CAF." Semanario Zeta, February 21, 2015. http://zetatijuana.com/noticias/generalez/18629/desmantelan-banda-de-secuestradores-ligada-al-caf.

"The Detentions of 'El Chapo' and 'Mayito Gordo' Have Had No Effect on CDS." Borderland Beat, January 24, 2015. http://www.borderlandbeat.com/2015/01/the-detentions-of-el-chapo-and-mayito.html.

DHS Risk Lexicon 2010 Edition. Department of Homeland Security, 2010. https://www.dhs.gov/xlibrary/assets/dhs-risk-lexicon-2010.pdf.

Diaz, Tom. "Before the Subcommittee on National Security and Foreign Affairs, Committee on Oversight and Government Reform, Hearing on 'Money, Guns, and Drugs: Are U.S. Inputs Fueling Violence on the U.S./Mexico Border?'" March 12, 2009. House of Representatives: Violence Policy Center, 2009. http://democrats.oversight.house.gov/index.php?option=com_content&view=article&id=4429:subcommittee-holds-hearing-on-money-guns-and-drugs-are-us-inputs-fueling-violence-on-the-us-mexico-border&catid=140:hearings-nshdfo.

Dibble, Sandra. "Soldiers Arrest Drug Trafficking Suspect in Tijuana." San Diego Union-Tribune, March 15, 2013. http://www.sandiegouniontribune.com/news/2013/mar/15/soldiers-arrest-drug-trafficking-suspect-in-tijuan/.

———. "Split within Arellano Félix Cartel Leads to More Violence." San Diego Union-Tribune, January 4, 2009. http://www.utsandiego.com/news/2009/jan/04/n52766113653-arellano-f233lix-drug-cartel-split-sm/.

————. "Tijuana Police to Use Body Cameras." *San Diego Union-Tribune,* March 1, 2015. http://www.utsandiego.com/news/2015/mar/01/tijuana -police-use-body-cameras/.

————. "Tijuana's Bloodiest Year." *San Diego Union-Tribune,* January 4, 2009. http://www.signonsandiego.com/news/2009/jan/04/lz1n4tijuana23134 -tijuanas-bloodiest-year/?zIndex=31756.

————. "Tijuana Violence Slows, Drops from Spotlight." *San Diego Union-Tribune.* April 26, 2010. http://www.signonsandiego.com/news/2010/ apr/26/tijuana-violence-slows-drops-out-of-spotlight/.

Díez, J., and I. Nicholls. *The Mexican Armed Forces in Transition.* Carlisle, PA: Strategic Studies Institute, US Army War College, 2006.

Dillon, Sam. "Mexican Traffickers Recruiting Killers in the U.S." *New York Times,* December 4, 1997. http://www.nytimes.com/1997/12/04/world/ mexican-traffickers-recruiting-killers-in-the-us.html?pagewanted=2&page wanted=print.

Do, Quynhanh. "The Evolution of ISIS." *New York Times,* February 18, 2015. http://www.nytimes.com/video/world/middleeast/100000003240417/ the-evolution-of-isis.html.

Dolnick, Sam. "The Sinaloa Cartel's 90-Year-Old Drug Mule." *New York Times,* June 11, 2014. http://www.nytimes.com/2014/06/15/magazine/ the-sinaloa-cartels-90-year-old-drug-mule.html.

Dorn, Nicholas, Lutz Oette, and Simone White. "Drugs Importation and the Bifurcation of Risk: Capitalization, Cut Outs and Organized Crime." *British Journal of Criminology* 38, no. 4 (1998): 537–60. http://dx.doi.org/10.1093/ bjc/38.4.537.

Downie, Richard Duncan. *Learning from Conflict: The U.S. Military in Vietnam, El Salvador, and the Drug War.* Westport, CT: Praeger, 1998.

Dudley, Steven. "Bin Laden, the Drug War and the Kingpin Strategy." InSight Crime, May 2, 2011. http://www.insightcrime.org/news-analysis/insight -bin-laden-the-drug-war-and-the-kingpin-strategy.

————. "Drug Trafficking Organizations in Central America: Transportis- tas, Mexican Cartels and Maras." In *Shared Responsibility: U.S.-Mexico Policy Options for Confronting Organized Crime,* edited by David Shirk, Andrew Selee, and Eric Olson. San Diego: Trans-Border Institute, 2010. https://justiceinmexico.org/wp-content/uploads/2014/09/2010_Shared Responsibility.pdf.

————. "5 Things the El Salvador Gang Truce Has Taught Us." InSight Crime, March 12, 2013. http://www.insightcrime.org/news-analysis/5-things-el -salvador-gang-truce-taught-us.

————. "InSight: Who Controls Tijuana?" *Insight Crime,* May 3, 2011. http:// www.insightcrime.org/investigations/who-controls-tijuana.

———. "Tijuana Cartel." InSight Crime, 2010. http://www.insightcrime.org/mexico-organized-crime-news/tijuana-cartel-profile.

———. *Transnational Crime in Mexico and Central America: Its Evolution and Role in International Migration*. Regional Migration Study Group. Washington, DC: Migration Policy Institute and the Woodrow Wilson International Center for Scholars, November 2012. http://www.migrationpolicy.org/pubs/RMSG-TransnationalCrime.pdf.

———. "Two Mexico Cartel Rivals, Once Reeling, Now Resurging." InSight Crime, February 3, 2013. http://www.insightcrime.org/news-analysis/2-mexico-cartels-once-reeling-now-resurging.

———. *The Zetas and the Battle for Monterrey*, December 18, 2012. http://www.insightcrime.org/reports/zetas_monterrey.pdf.

———. *The Zetas in Guatemala*. InSight Crime, September 8, 2011. http://www.insightcrime.org/media/k2/attachments/insight_crime_the_zetas_in_guatemala.pdf.

———. "Zetas Leader's First Task: Hold Nuevo Laredo." InSight Crime, July 22, 2013. http://www.insightcrime.org/investigations/zetas-leaders-first-task-holding-nuevo-laredo.

Dudley, Steven, and Elyssa Pachico. "Why a Zetas Split Is Inevitable." InSight Crime, August 24, 2012. http://www.insightcrime.org/news-analysis/why-a-zetas-split-is-inevitable.

Dudley, Steven, and Patrick Corcoran. "InSight Map: The Most Dangerous Migrant Routes in Mexico." InSight Crime, April 2011. http://www.insightcrime.org/news-analysis/insight-map-the-most-dangerous-migrant-routes-in-mexico-refreshed.

Dudley, Steven, and Viridiana Rios Contreras. "Why Mexico's Zetas Expanded Faster than Their Rivals." InSight Crime, April 21, 2013. http://www.insightcrime.org/news-analysis/why-mexicos-zetas-expanded-faster-rivals.

Duran-Martinez, Angelica, and Richard Snyder. "Does Illegality Breed Violence? Drug Trafficking and State-Sponsored Protection Rackets." *Crime, Law, and Social Change* 52, no. 3 (September 2009): 253–73.

Easton, David. *A Framework for Political Analysis*. Englewood Cliffs, NJ: Prentice Hall, 1965.

Eban, Katherine. "The Truth about the Fast and Furious Scandal." *Fortune*, June 27, 2012. http://fortune.com/2012/06/27/the-truth-about-the-fast-and-furious-scandal/.

Eckstein, H. "On the Etiology of Internal Wars." *History and Theory* 4, no. 2 (1965): 133–63. http://dx.doi.org/10.2307/2504149.

Edmonds-Poli, Emily, and David A. Shirk. *Contemporary Mexican Politics*. Lanham, MD: Rowman & Littlefield, 2009.

"'El Chapo' y 'El Mayo' reclutan jefes de célula para traficar droga en Tijuana: Delata estructura de Sinaloa." *Semanario Zeta*, January 2011. http://amigos-detamaulipas2.mforos.com/1817565/9771923-delata-estructura/.

"El Chayo." Accessed November 10, 2014. http://www.insightcrime.org/mexico-organized-crime-news/nazario-moreno-gonzalez-el-chayo-el-mas-loco.

Ellingwood, Ken. "Actually Violence Is Down—So Say the Numbers." *Los Angeles Times*, August 22, 2009. http://www.latimes.com/la-fg-mexico-murder22-2009aug22-story.html.

———. "Fallout from Deadly Mexico Casino Fire Sparks Political Brawl." *Los Angeles Times*, September 22, 2011. http://articles.latimes.com/2011/sep/22/world/la-fg-mexico-casino-fallout-20110922.

———. "Mexico Drug War: Mexican Marines Arrest Beltran Leyva Group's Sergio Villarreal Barragan." *Los Angeles Times*. September 14, 2010. http://articles.latimes.com/2010/sep/14/world/la-fg-mexico-beltran-20100914.

———. "Mexico Gunmen Set Casino on Fire, Killing at Least 53." *Los Angeles Times*, August 26, 2011. http://articles.latimes.com/2011/aug/26/world/la-fgw-mexico-casino-20110827.

"El Tomate Reveals the Sinaloa Cartel's Methods of Operation." *Borderland Beat*, January 12, 2010. http://www.borderlandbeat.com/2011/01/el-tomate-reveals-sinaloa-cartels.html.

Enrique Osorno, Diego. *El Cartel de Sinaloa*. Mexico City: Grijalbo, 2009.

Escalante Gonzalbo, Fernando. "Homicidios 2008–2009: La Muerte Tiene Permiso." *Nexos*, March 1, 2011. http://www.nexos.com.mx/?P=leerarticulo&Article=1943189.

Esquivel, J. Jesus. "'El Kelín' revelo de unos Zetas venidos a menos." *Proceso*, March 7, 2015. http://www.proceso.com.mx/?p=397804.

Everton, Sean F. *Disrupting Dark Networks*. New York: Cambridge University Press, 2012. http://dx.doi.org/10.1017/CBO9781139136877.

"FBI Informant Details Mexican Mafia's Control over Prisons." News story. KGTV San Diego, February 9, 2010. http://www.10news.com/news/22516591/detail.html.

Fausset, Richard. "Mexico's Lazaro Cardenas Port Thrives—with Commerce and Crime." *Los Angeles Times*, November 7, 2013. http://www.latimes.com/world/la-fg-mexico-port-20131107,0,5911836.story#axzz2jyasNu8t.

Felbab-Brown, Vanda. *Calderón's Caldron: Lessons from Mexico's Battle against Organized Crime and Drug Trafficking in Tijuana, Ciudad Juárez, and Michoacán*. Brookings Institution, 2011. http://www.brookings.edu/~/media/research/files/papers/2011/9/calderon-felbab-brown/09_calderon_felbab_brown.pdf.

———. "Conceptualizing Crime as Competition in State-Making and Designing an Effective Response." Brookings Institution, May 21, 2010. http://

www.brookings.edu/research/speeches/2010/05/21-illegal-economies
-felbabbrown.

―――. *Focused Deterrence, Selective Targeting, Drug Trafficking and Organised Crime: Concepts and Practicalities.* Modernizing Drug Law Enforcement. United Kingdom: International Drug Policy Consortium, February 23, 2013. http://www.brookings.edu/research/reports/2013/02/deterrence-drugs-crime-felbabbrown.

―――. "Mexican Drug War." Brookings Institution, April 8, 2010. http://www.brookings.edu/research/interviews/2010/04/08-mexico-narcotics-felbab brown.

―――. *Shooting Up: Counterinsurgency and the War on Drugs.* Washington, DC: Brookings Institution Press, 2009.

―――. "Stemming the Violence in Mexico, but Breaking the Cartels." Brookings Institution, September 2010. http://www.brookings.edu/research/articles/2010/09/mexico-violence-felbabbrown.

―――. "The Violent Drug Market in Mexico and Lessons from Colombia." Foreign Policy at Brookings: Policy Paper, September 30, 2009. http://www.brookings.edu/research/papers/2009/03/mexico-drug-market-felbabbrown.

Felbab-Brown, Vanda, and Eric Olson. "A Better Strategy to Combat Organized Crime in Mexico and Central America." Brookings Institution, April 13, 2012. http://www.brookings.edu/blogs/up-front/posts/2012/04/13-crime-central-america-felbabbrown.

Figueroa, Lorena. "Analyst: Sinaloa Cartel Losing Power in Juárez." *El Paso Times,* April 17, 2014. http://www.elpasotimes.com/news/ci_25583946/analyst-sinaloa-cartel-losing-power-ju-rez.

Finnegan, William. "In the Name of the Law: A Colonel Cracks Down on Corruption." *New Yorker,* October 18, 2010. http://www.newyorker.com/magazine/2010/10/18/in-the-name-of-the-law#ixzz12ONN9dAn.

―――. "Silver or Lead." *New Yorker,* May 31, 2010. http://www.newyorker.com/reporting/2010/05/31/100531fa_fact_finnegan.

Flores Pérez, Carlos Antonio. *El estado en crisis: Crimen organizado y política; Desafíos para la consolidación democrática.* Mexico City: Centro de Investigaciones y Estudios Superiores en Antropología Social (CIESAS): 2009.

―――. "Organized Crime and Official Corruption in Mexico." In *Police and Public Security in Mexico,* edited by David Shirk and Robert Donnelly. Trans-Border Institute, 2009.

―――. "Political Protection and the Origins of the Gulf Cartel." *Crime, Law, and Social Change* 61, no. 5 (2014): 517–39. http://dx.doi.org/10.1007/s10611-013-9499-x.

Ford, Jess. *Plan Colombia: Drug Reduction Goals Were Not Fully Met, but Security Has Improved; U.S. Agencies Need More Detailed Plans for Reducing Assistance.*

Government Accountability Office, 2008. http://www.gao.gov/products/ GAO-09-71.

"40 años de cárcel a Chuy Labra." *San Diego Union-Tribune*, April 5, 2010. http://www.sandiegouniontribune.com/news/2010/apr/05/40-anos-de -carcel-chuy-labra/.

Fox, Edward. "Mexico Mining Ops Pay Hefty Extortion Fees to Cartels," InSight Crime, May 8, 2012. http://www.insightcrime.org/news-briefs/ mexico-mining-ops-pay-hefty-extortion-fees-to-cartels.

Friman, H. R., and Peter Andreas. *The Illicit Global Economy and State Power.* Lanham, MD: Rowman & Littlefield, 1999.

Gagne, David. "Announced Zetas, Gulf Alliance Could Change Mexico's Criminal Landscape." InSight Crime, November 12, 2014. http://www .insightcrime.org/news-briefs/new-zetas-gulf-cartel-alliance-in-mexico ?highlight=WyJ6ZXRhcyIsInpldGFzJyIsIid6ZXRhcyIsIid6ZXRhcyci LCJndWxmIiwiZ3VsZidzIiwiJ2d1bGYiLCJ6ZXRhcyBndWxmIl0=.

———. "Bloody Attack on Police in Mexico Raises Jalisco Cartel's Profile." InSight Crime, April 8, 2015. http://www.insightcrime.org/news-analysis/ bloody-attack-police-mexico-raises-jalisco-cartel-profile?utm_source= Master+ List&utm_campaign=3aac997e0c-04_10_20154_9_2015&utm_ medium=email&utm_ term=0_e90c5425f9–3aac997e0c-206740657.

———. "Tijuana Cartel Resurgent in Mexico: Official." Insight Crime, February 13, 2015. http://www.insightcrime.org/news-briefs/tijuana-cartel -resurgent-in-mexico-official.

Galula, David. *Counterinsurgency Warfare: Theory and Practice.* New York: Praeger, 1964.

Gambetta, Diego. *The Sicilian Mafia: The Business of Private Protection.* Cambridge, MA: Harvard University Press, 1996.

Garzón, Juan Carlos. *Mafia & Co.* Bogota, Colombia: Editorial Planeta Colombiana, 2008.

George, Alexander L., and Andrew Bennett. *Case Studies and Theory Development in the Social Sciences.* BCSIA Studies in International Security. Cambridge, MA: MIT Press, 2005.

The Globalization of Crime: A Transnational Organized Crime Threat Assessment. Vienna: United Nations Office on Drugs and Crime, 2010. http://www.unodc .org/documents/data-and-analysis/tocta/TOCTA_Report_2010_low_res.pdf.

Gonzalez Ruiz, Samuel. "Public Safety in Mexico and Strengthening the Rule of Law." Paper presented at conference, "México: How to Tap Progress," Federal Reserve Bank of Dallas, Houston Branch, November 2, 2012. http://www .dallasfed.org/research/events/2012/12mexico.cfm.

Granovetter, Mark. "The Strength of Weak Ties: A Network Theory Revisited." *Sociological Theory* 1 (1983): 201–33. http://dx.doi.org/10.2307/202051.

Gray, J. P. *Why Our Drug Laws Have Failed and What We Can Do about It: A Judicial Indictment of the War on Drugs*. Philadelphia: Temple University Press, 2001.

Grayson, George W. *The Cartels: The Story of Mexico's Most Dangerous Criminal Organizations and Their Impact on U.S. Security*. Westport, CT: Praeger, 2014.

———. "Los Zetas: The Ruthless Army Spawned by a Mexican Drug Cartel." Foreign Policy Research Institute, June 13, 2008. http://www.fpri.org/articles/2008/05/los-zetas-ruthless-army-spawned-mexican-drug-cartel.

———. "Mexico and the Drug Cartels." Foreign Policy Research Institute, December 19, 2008. http://www.fpri.org/enotes/ 200708.grayson.mexico-drugcartels.html.

———. *Mexico: Narco-Violence and a Failed State?* New Brunswick, NJ: Transaction, 2009.

Grayson, George W., and Samuel Logan. *The Executioner's Men: Los Zetas, Rogue Soldiers, Criminal Entrepreneurs, and the Shadow State They Created*. New Brunswick, NJ: Transaction, 2012.

Grillo, Ioan. *El Narco: Inside Mexico's Criminal Insurgency*. New York: Bloomsbury, 2011.

———. "Mexico's Fruitless Hunt for Justice." *New York Times*, September 18, 2015. http://www.nytimes.com/2015/09/18/opinion/mexicos-fruitless-hunt-for-justice.html.

"Growing Drug Abuse in Mexico Adds to Crime and Violence—Frontera Norte Sur." *Mexidata.info*, February 1, 2010. http://mexidata.info/id2541.html.

Guerrero Gutiérrez, Eduardo. *At the Root of the Violence*. Translated by Charlie Roberts. Washington Office for Latin American Affairs, June 2011. http://www.wola.org/sites/default/files/downloadable/Drug%20Policy/2011/September/E_Guerrero_-_Root_of_Violence_-_WOLA_9-9-11.pdf.

———. "Cómo reducir la violencia en México." *Nexos*, November 3, 2010. http://www.nexos.com.mx/?P=leerarticulo&Article=1197808.

———. "Pandillas y cárteles: La gran alianza." *Nexos*, January 6, 2010. http://www.nexos.com.mx/?P=leerarticulo&Article=73224.

———. *Security, Drugs, and Violence in Mexico: A Survey*. 2011. http://iis-db.stanford.edu/evnts/6716/NAF_2011_EG_%28Final%29.pdf.

"Guerritas del CAF y Sinaloa." *Semanario Zeta*, March 16, 2015. http://zetatijuana.com/noticias/reportajez/19451/guerritas-del-caf-y-sinaloa.

Gurney, Kyle. "Colombia Takes Down Another Oficina de Envigado Leader." InSight Crime, January 12, 2015. http://www.insightcrime.org/news-briefs/colombia-takes-down-oficina-de-envigado-leader.

Hale, Gary. *A "Failed State" in Mexico: Tamaulipas Declares Itself Ungovernable*. Policy report. James A. Baker III Institute for Public Policy, July 26, 2011. http://bakerinstitute.org/research/a-failed-state-in-mexico-tamaulipas-declares-itself-ungovernable/.

————. *Mexico's Government Begins to Retake Northeastern Mexico.* Policy report. James A. Baker III Institute for Public Policy, December 9, 2011. http://bakerinstitute.org/files/465/.

————. "Targeting Criminals, Not Crimes: The Kingpin Strategy Works." *Baker Institute Blog,* October 24, 2012. http://blog.chron.com/bakerblog/2012/10/targeting-criminals-not-crimes-the-kingpin-strategy-works/.

————. *Vigilantism in Mexico: A New Phase in Mexico's Security Crisis.* Policy paper. James A. Baker III Institute for Public Policy, April 18, 2014. http://bakerinstitute.org/media/files/Research/3e645892/BI-Brief-041814-Vigilantism.pdf.

Hammes, Thomas X. *The Sling and the Stone: On War in the 21st Century.* St. Paul, MN: Zenith Press, 2004. http://catdir.loc.gov/catdir/enhancements/fy0704/2004559123-b.html.

Hampson, Michael. "The Extreme Violence of Uganda's Militant LRA." *Baker Institute Blog,* October 10, 2012. http://blog.chron.com/bakerblog/2012/10/the-extreme-violence-of-uganda%E2%80%99s-militant-lra/.

————. "Rationalizing the Profane: Explaining the Violence of the LRA." Diss. draft, University of California, Irvine, 2013.

Harris, Kamala D. *Gangs beyond Borders: California and the Fight against Transnational Organized Crime.* March 2014. https://oag.ca.gov/sites/all/files/agweb/pdfs/toc/report_2014.pdf.

Harrod, Scharf and Ziegler. Drug Enforcement Administration Lecture Series. Drug Enforcement Administration, 2008. http://www.deamuseum.org/education/transcripts/Harrod_Scharf.pdf.

Hefler, Jeff. "Medical Marijuana Law Sponsors Surprised Christie Wants to Impose Sales Tax on It." *Inquirer,* December 3, 2012. http://articles.philly.com/2012-12-04/news/35572496_1_ken-wolski-medical-marijuana-sales-tax.

Hernandez, Anabel. *Narcoland: The Mexican Drug Lords and Their Godfathers.* Translated by Iain Bruce. New York: Verso, 2013.

"Holy Week Vacations Marred by Violence; San Fernando Body Count Reaches 196." Sensitive cable. US Consulate, Matamoros, April 29, 2011. http://www2.gwu.edu/~nsarchiv/NSAEBB/NSAEBB445/docs/20110429.pdf.

Hope, Alejandro, and Eduardo Clark. *Si los vecinos legalizan: Reporte técnico.* IMCO, October 2012. http://imco.org.mx/images/pdf/reporte-tecnico-legalizacion-marihuana.pdf.

Hughes, Krista. "Analysis: Mexico Aims to Overhaul Tax System, Raise Revenue." Reuters. May 6, 2013. http://www.reuters.com/article/2013/05/06/us-mexico-tax-idUSBRE9450A520130506.

"Imparables comandos de 'El Teo.'" *Semanario Zeta,* 2010. http://www.zetatijuana.com/html/EdcionesAnteriores/Edicion1748/Principal.html.

"Indictment: United States vs. Armando Villareal Heredia et al." United States District Court, Southern District of California, July 23, 2010.

Ines Zamudio, Maria. "Fear and Loathing at the Border." *Chicago Reporter*, September 1, 2013. http://chicagoreporter.com/fear-and-loathing-border/#.UoU4b43gJT4.

"Jalisco Cartel: New Generation (CJNG)." InSight Crime. Accessed April 10, 2015. http://www.insightcrime.org/mexico-organized-crime-news/jalisco-cartel-new-generation.

Jiménez, Benito. "Atomizan narco en Tamaulipas." *Reforma*, March 20, 2015. http://www.reforma.com/aplicaciones/articulo/default.aspx?id=494178.

Johnson, David T. "The Merida Initiative: Examining U.S. Efforts to Combat Transnational Criminal Organizations." June 5, 2008. http://2001-2009.state.gov/p/inl/rls/rm/105695.htm.

Johnson, Tim. "Mexican Leader Hints Again at U.S. Drug Legalization." McClatchy, September 20, 2011. http://www.bendbulletin.com/csp/mediapool/sites/BendBulletin/News/story.csp?cid=1606741&sid=497&fid=151.

Jones, Calvert, and Mette Eilstrup-Sangiovanni. "Assessing the Dangers of Illicit Networks: Why Al-Qaida May Be Less Threatening Than Many Think." *International Security* 33, no. 2 (2008): 7–44.

Jones, Nathan. "Appendix A: Goat Horns, Blackbirds and Cop Killers; U.S. Guns in Mexico's Drug Violence." In Sidney Weintraub and Duncan Wood, *Cooperative Mexican–U.S. Antinarcotics Efforts*. Washington, DC: Center for Strategic and International Studies, November 22, 2010, 52–73. http://csis.org/files/publication/101108_Weintraub_MexicanUSAntinarc_web.pdf.

———. "Applying Lessons from Colombia to Mexico." Mexico Institute, Woodrow Wilson International Center for Scholars, December 3, 2010. http://mexicoinstitute.wordpress.com/2010/12/03/applying-lessons-from-colombia-to-mexico/.

———. "Arrest of Tijuana Ex-Mayor: Putting Crime in the 'Freezer'?" InSight Crime, June 5, 2011. http://www.insightcrime.org/news-analysis/arrest-of-tijuana-ex-mayor-putting-crime-in-the-freezer

———. "Captured Tijuana Cartel Boss Confirms Sinaloa Truce." InSight Crime, December 12, 2011. http://www.insightcrime.org/news-analysis/captured-tijuana-cartel-boss-confirms-sinaloa-truce.

———. "Cartel Lieutenant's Capture Could Bring Tijuana a Step Closer to War." InSight Crime, July 18, 2011. http://www.insightcrime.org/news-analysis/cartel-lieutenant-s-capture-could-bring-tijuana-a-step-closer-to-war.

———. Explaining the Slight Uptick in Violence in Tijuana. Policy paper. James A. Baker III Institute for Public Policy, September 17, 2013. http://bakerinstitute.org/files/3825/.

————. "Kidnapping in Tijuana: The New Normal." InSight Crime, May 31, 2011. http://www.insightcrime.org/investigations/kidnapping-in-tijuana-the-new-normal.

————. "Monopoly of Force Does Not Always Explain Peace: Illicit Network Evolution Does." In *Mexican Cartel Essays and Notes: Strategic, Operational, and Tactical*, edited by Robert Bunker. A Small Wars Journal–El Centro Anthology, vol. 2. Bloomington: iUniverse, 2013.

————. "Report Tracks How Intra-Cartel Wars Exploded in Mexico." InSight Crime, February 9, 2011. http://www.insightcrime.org/news-analysis/insight-report-tracks-how-intra-cartel-wars-exploded-in-mexico.

————. "The Resilience and Destruction of Mexican Drug Networks: Sinaloa, Los Zetas, and Los Caballeros Templarios." Paper presented at the ISAC-ISSS Conference, Austin, TX, November 10, 2014.

————. "The State Reaction: A Theory of Illicit Network Resilience." Diss., University of California, Irvine, 2011.

————. "Understanding and Addressing Youth in 'Gangs' in Mexico." In *Building Resilient Communities in Mexico: Civic Responses to Crime and Violence*, edited by David A. Shirk, Duncan Wood, and Eric L. Olson. Washington, DC: Mexico Institute, Woodrow Wilson International Center for Scholars, 2013. http://www.wilsoncenter.org/publication/understanding-youth-gangs-mexico.

————. "The Unintended Consequences of Kingpin Strategies: Kidnap Rates and the Arellano-Félix Organization." *Trends in Organized Crime* 16, no. 2 (2013): 156–76. http://dx.doi.org/10.1007/s12117-012-9185-x.

Jordan, Mary, and Kevin Sullivan. "Mexican Police Linked to Tijuana Cartel." *Washington Post*, April 12, 2002. http://www.latinamericanstudies.org/drugs/cartel.htm.

"Juez falla a favor de extradición del capo Benjamín Arellano Félix a EU." *Cronica.com*, April 23, 2010. http://www.cronica.com.mx/notas/2010/502299.html.

Kahler, Miles. *Networked Politics: Agency, Power and Governance*. Ithaca, NY: Cornell University Press, 2009.

Kaldor, Mary. *New and Old Wars: Organized Violence in a Global Era*. Stanford, CA: Stanford University Press, 1999.

Kean, Thomas H., et al. *9/11 Commission Report*, July 22, 2004. http://www.9-11commission.gov/report/911Report.pdf.

Keefe, Patrick Radden. "How a Mexican Drug Cartel Makes Its Billions." *New York Times*, June 15, 2012, sec. Magazine. http://www.nytimes.com/2012/06/17/magazine/how-a-mexican-drug-cartel-makes-its-billions.html.

————. "The Hunt for El Chapo." *New Yorker*, May 5, 2014. http://www.newyorker.com/magazine/2014/05/05/the-hunt-for-el-chapo.

Kenney, Michael. "The Architecture of Drug Trafficking: Network Forms of Organisation in the Colombian Cocaine Trade." *Global Crime* 8, no. 3 (2007): 233–59. http://dx.doi.org/10.1080/17440570701507794.

———. "From Pablo to Osama: Counter-Terrorism Lessons from the War on Drugs." *Survival* 45, no. 3 (2003): 187–206. http://dx.doi.org/10.1093/survival/45.3.187.

———. *From Pablo to Osama: Trafficking and Terrorist Networks, Government Bureaucracies, and Competitive Adaptation.* University Park: Pennsylvania State University Press, 2007.

Keohane, Robert O. *After Hegemony: Cooperation and Discord in the World Political Economy.* Princeton, NJ: Princeton University Press, 2005.

Kilmer, Beau. "Debunking the Mythical Numbers about Marijuana Production in Mexico and the United States." In *Rethinking the "War on Drugs" through the US–Mexico Prism*, 168–75. Yale Center for the Study of Globalization, 2012. http://www.ycsg.yale.edu/assets/downloads/rethinking-war-on-drugs.pdf.

Kilmer, Beau, Jonathan P. Caulkins, Brittany M. Bond, and Peter Reuter. *Reducing Drug Trafficking Revenues and Violence in Mexico: Would Legalizing Marijuana in California Help?* Santa Monica, CA: RAND, 2010. http://www.rand.org/pubs/occasional_papers/OP325.html.

Kilmer, Beau, S. Everingham, Jonathan P. Caulkins, G. Midgette, R. Pacula, Peter Reuter, R. Burns, B. Han, and Russell Lundberg. *What America's Users Spend on Illegal Drugs: 2000–2010.* Santa Monica, CA: Prepared by RAND for the Executive Office of the President of the United States, February 2014. https://www.whitehouse.gov/sites/default/files/ondcp/policy-and-research/wausid_results_report.pdf.

Kleiman, M. "Surgical Strikes in the Drug Wars: Smarter Policies for Both Sides of the Border." *Foreign Affairs* 90 (2011): 97–101.

———. "Targeting Drug-Trafficking Violence in Mexico: An Orthogonal Approach." In *Rethinking the "War on Drugs" through the US–Mexico Prism*, edited by Ernesto Zedillo and Haynie Wheeler. Yale Center for the Study of Globalization, 2012. http://www.ycsg.yale.edu/assets/downloads/rethinking-war-on-drugs.pdf.

Klotz, Audie, and Cecelia Lynch. *Strategies for Research in Constructivist International Relations: International Relations in a Constructed World.* Armonk, NY: M. E. Sharpe, 2007.

Knight, Meribah. "Families Fear Phone Call from Mexico's Cartels." Chicago News Cooperative/*New York Times*, July 31, 2010. http://www.nytimes.com/2010/08/01/us/01cnccartel.html?scp=1&sq=kidnappings&st=cse.

Konrad, K. A., and S. Skaperdas. "The Market for Protection and the Origin of the State." *Economic Theory* 50, no. 2 (2012): 417–43.

Krasner, Stephen D. *Sovereignty: Organized Hypocrisy.* Princeton, NJ: Princeton University Press, 1999.

Kraul, Chris. "Weakened Tijuana Drug Cartel Still Deadly." *Los Angeles Times,* July 17, 2004. http://articles.latimes.com/2004/jul/17/world/fg-tijuana17.

Krauze, Enrique. "Mexico's Vigilantes on the March." *New York Times,* February 3, 2014. http://www.nytimes.com/2014/02/04/opinion/krauze-mexicos-vigilantes-on-the-march.html.

Krauze, Leon. "Mexico's Disastrous Drug War 'Success.'" *Daily Beast,* March 31, 2015. http://www.thedailybeast.com/articles/2015/03/31/mexico-s-disastrous-drug-war-success.html.

Krebs, Valdis E. "Uncloaking Terrorist Networks." *First Monday* 7, no. 4 (April 2002). http://dx.doi.org/10.5210/fm.v7i4.941

Lacey, Marc. "At Least 6 People Abducted in Mexican Hotel Raids." *New York Times.* April 21, 2010. http://www.nytimes.com/2010/04/22/world/americas/22mexico.html?hp.

———. "Drug Wars: When a 'Cartel' Really Isn't." *Economix,* October 10, 2009. http://economix.blogs.nytimes.com/2009/09/21/drug-wars-when-a-cartel-really-isnt/?scp=1&sq=merida%20initiative&st=cseID%20-%20526.

———. "Report Says U.S. Fails to Assess Drug Aid to Mexico." *New York Times,* July 20, 2010. http://www.nytimes.com/2010/07/21/world/americas/21mexico.html?_r=1&hp.

"La Familia." InSight Crime. Accessed August 2, 2011. http://www.insightcrime.org/mexico-organized-crime-news/familia-michoacana-mexico-profile.

Larano, Chris, and Josephine Cuneta. "Philippines Says Drug Raid Shows Presence of Mexican Cartel." *Wall Street Journal,* December 27, 2013. http://www.wsj.com/articles/SB10001424052702304753504579283753590616152.

"Latin America Most Dangerous Region for Journalists in 2010." *Latin American Herald Tribune,* 2011. http://www.laht.com/article.asp?ArticleId=382446&CategoryId=12394.

"'La Tuta' Says He's Sick and Tired of the Caballeros Templarios." *Borderland Beat,* November 1, 2014. http://www.borderlandbeat.com/2014/11/la-tuta-says-hes-sick-and-tired-of.html.

"Leaders of Arellano-Felix Criminal Organization Plead Guilty." San Diego Division, Federal Bureau of Investigation, November 30, 2009. http://sandiego.fbi.gov/dojpressrel/pressrel09/sd102109a.htm.

Llana, Sara Miller. "Heriberto Lazcano, a Zetas Leader, Was Killed in Mexico—but Is the Cartel Done?" *CSM Blog: Latin America Blog,* October 9, 2012. http://www.csmonitor.com/World/Americas/Latin-America

-Monitor/2012/1009/Heriberto-Lazcano-a-Zetas-leader-was-killed-in -Mexico-but-is-the-cartel-done.

Logan, Samuel, and John P. Sullivan. "The Gulf–Zeta Split and the Praetorian Revolt." *ISN Security Watch,* April 7, 2010. http://www.isn.ethz.ch/isn/ Current-Affairs/Security-Watch/Detail/?lng=en&id=114551.

Longmire, S. *Cartel: The Coming Invasion of Mexico's Drug Wars.* New York: Palgrave Macmillan, 2011.

———. "Some US Agents Could Soon Carry Firearms in Mexico." *Breitbart,* March 16, 2015. http://www.breitbart.com/texas/2015/03/16/ some-us-agents-could-soon-carry-firearms-in-mexico/.

"Los asesinos de la mafia." *Semanario Zeta,* November 18, 2013. http:// zetatijuana.com/noticias/reportajez/7443/los-asesinos-de-la-mafia.

"Los secretos de Juan José Esparragoza 'El Azul.'" *Proceso,* April 2010. http://www .proceso.com.mx/?p=107493.

"'Los Teos' rentan sicarios." *Semanario Zeta,* October 2010. http://amigos detamaulipas2.mforos.com/1817565/9542754-los-teos-rentan-sicarios/.

Los Zetas Factsheet. Houston Field Division, Drug Enforcement Agency, February 2010. http://www2.gwu.edu/~nsarchiv/NSAEBB/NSAEBB445/ docs/20100200.PDF.

Lupsha, P. "Transnational Organized Crime versus the Nation State." *Transnational Organized Crime* 2, no. 1 (1996): 21–48.

MacCoun, Robert, Beau Kilmer, and Peter Reuter. *Research on Drugs–Crime Linkages: The Next Generation.* National Institute of Justice, 2003. https:// www.ncjrs.gov/pdffiles1/nij/194616c.pdf.

MacCoun, Robert J., and Peter Reuter. *Drug War Heresies: Learning from Other Vices, Times, and Places.* Cambridge: Cambridge University Press, 2001. http://ebooks.cambridge.org/ebook.jsf?bid=CBO9780511754272.

"Major Cartel Lieutenants Arrested in Mexico." Press release. Drug Enforcement Administration. June 7, 2004. http://www.dea.gov/pubs/states/sandiego_ news_releases2004.html.

Makarenko, T. "The Crime–Terror Continuum: Tracing the Interplay between Transnational Organised Crime and Terrorism." *Global Crime* 6, no. 1 (2004): 129–45. http://dx.doi.org/10.1080/1744057042000297025.

Manwaring, Max. *A Contemporary Challenge to State Sovereignty: Gangs and Other Illicit Trafficking Organizations in Central America, El Salvador, Mexico, Jamaica and Brazil.* Strategic Studies Institute, December 2007. http://www .strategicstudiesinstitute.army.mil/pdffiles/PUB837.pdf.

———. *A "New" Dynamic in the Western Hemispheric Security Environment: The Mexican Zetas and other Private Armies.* Strategic Studies Institute, September 2009. http://www.strategicstudiesinstitute.army.mil/pdffiles/pub940.pdf.

————. *Street Gangs: The New Urban Insurgency*. Strategic Studies Institute, 2005. http://www.strategicstudiesinstitute.army.mil/pdffiles/pub597.pdf.

Marks, T. A. "Counterinsurgency in the Age of Globalism." *Journal of Conflict Studies* 27, no. 1 (2008): 22–29.

Marosi, Richard. "Diagnosis: Irony." *Los Angeles Times*, May 3, 2008. http://articles.latimes.com/2008/may/03/local/me-tijuana3/2.

————. "Flying High for the Sinaloa Drug Cartel." *Los Angeles Times*. July 27, 2011. http://www.latimes.com/news/local/cartel/la-me-cartel-20110727, 0,4934932,print.story.

————. "Mexico General Battles Tijuana Drug Traffickers." *Los Angeles Times*, April 18, 2009. http://www.latimes.com/news/nationworld/world/la-fg -mexico-drugs-general18-2009apr18,0,917553.story

————. "Mystery Man Blamed for Gruesome Tijuana Deaths." *Los Angeles Times*, December 18, 2008. http://www.latimes.com/la-fg-tijuanadruglord 18-2008dec18,0,5864824.story.

————. "Reputed Drug Cartel Leader 'Muletas' and Another Suspected Gang-ster Are Arrested in Baja California." *Los Angeles Times*, April 14, 2010. http://latimesblogs.latimes.com/laplaza/2010/02/mexico-cartel-leaders -arrested-baja-california-la-paz-muletas-raydel-lopez-uriarte-manuel -simentel.html.

————. "A Tijuana Blood Bath." *Los Angeles Times*, October 16, 2008. http://articles.latimes.com/2008/oct/06/world/fg-arellano6.

————. "Tijuana Drug Cartels Feel Crackdown." *Los Angeles Times*, February 25, 2008. http://latimesblogs.latimes.com/laplaza/2008/02/tijuana-cartels. html.

————. "Tijuana Reels amid a Surge of Violence." *Los Angeles Times*, January 11, 2010. http://articles.latimes.com/2010/jan/11/world/la-fg-tijuana-violence 11-2010jan11.

————. "Tijuana's Security Chief Needs All of It He Can Get: Julian Leyza-ola Lives with Threats and Worse, plus the Accusations." *Los Angeles Times*, December 20, 2009. http://articles.latimes.com/2009/dec/20/world/la-fg -tijuana-police20-2009dec20.

Marosi, Richard, and Ken Ellingwood. "Mexico Drug War: Troops Kill Top Sinaloa Cartel Figure." *Los Angeles Times*, July 30, 2010. http://articles .latimes.com/2010/jul/30/world/la-fg-mexico-cops-20100730.

Mason, Caleb E. "Blind Mules: New Data and New Case Law on the Border Smuggling Industry." *Criminal Justice* 26 (2011): 17–24.

"Massive Gunbattles Break Out in Tijuana; 13 Dead, 9 Wounded." Fox News, December 29, 2009. http://www.foxnews.com/story/2008/04/27/massive -gunbattles-break-out-in-tijuana-13-dead-wounded.html.

Mazzitelli, Antonio L. "Mexican Cartel Influence in Central America." Florida International University: *Western Hemispheric Security Analysis Center*, Paper 45. September 2011. http://digitalcommons.fiu.edu/cgi/viewcontent.cgi?article=1044&context=whemsac.

———. "Transnational Organized Crime in West Africa: The Additional Challenge." *International Affairs* 83, no. 6 (2007): 1071–90. http://dx.doi.org/10.1111/j.1468-2346.2007.00674.x.

McCleskey, Claire O'Neill. "New Generation Jalisco Cartel Leader Captured in Mexico." InSight Crime, July 22, 2013. http://www.insightcrime.org/news-briefs/new-generation-jalisco-cartel-leader-captured-in-guadalajara.

McCrummen, Stephanie. "In Mexico, Self-Defense Groups Battle a Cartel." *Washington Post*, September 13, 2013, sec. World. https://www.washingtonpost.com/world/the_americas/in-the-hills-of-michoacan-self-defense-groups-battle-a-mexican-drug-cartel/2013/09/09/6947e47a-119f-11e3-a2b3-5e107edf9897_story.html.

McDermott, Jeremy. "4 Reasons Why Peru Became World's Top Cocaine Producer." Insight Crime, December 25, 2013. http://www.insightcrime.org/news-analysis/why-peru-top-cocaine-producer.

Mearsheimer, John J. *The Tragedy of Great Power Politics: Vol. 1*. New York: Norton, 2001.

Burton, Fred, and Stephen Meiners. "Mexico and the War against the Drug Cartels in 2008." Stratfor, December 9, 2008. https://www.stratfor.com/weekly/20081209_mexico_and_war_against_drug_cartels_2008.

"Members of Arellano-Felix Organization." PBS's *Frontline* ("Drug Wars"), January 30, 2010. http://www.pbs.org/wgbh/pages/frontline/shows/drugs/business/afo/afomembers.html.

Merlos, Andrea, and Maria de La Luz Gonzalez. "Pone gobierno federal en marcha Operativo Tijuana." *El Universal*, January 2, 2007. http://archivo.eluniversal.com.mx/notas/397765.html.

"Mexican Attorney General Identifies Most Wanted Criminals." Insight Crime, January 6, 2011. http://www.insightcrime.org/news-analysis/mexican-attorney-general-identifies-most-wanted-criminals.

"Mexican Drug Cartels: Government Progress and Increasing Violence." Stratfor, December 11, 2008. https://www.stratfor.com/analysis/mexican-drug-cartels-government-progress-and-growing-violence.

"Mexican Drug Cartels: Two Wars and a Look Southward." Stratfor, 2009. https://www.stratfor.com/analysis/mexican-drug-cartels-two-wars-and-look-southward.

"Mexican Drug Wars Update: Targeting the Most Violent Cartels." Stratfor, 2011. https://www.stratfor.com/analysis/mexican-drug-wars-update-targeting-most-violent-cartels.

"Mexico, Central America and the Caribbean." United Nations Office on Drugs and Crime. Accessed July 10, 2012. http://www.unodc.org/unodc/en/drug-trafficking/mexico-central-america-and-the-caribbean.html.

"Mexico Drug Cartel Unleashes New Levels of Violence." Reuters, 2012. http://www.reuters.com/video/2012/05/22/mexico-drug-cartel-unleashes-new-levels?videoId=235434205.

"Mexico's Drug War: Stories, Photos, Videos; Mexico under Siege." *Los Angeles Times*, 2011 2010, sec. Mexico under Siege. http://www.latimes.com/world/drug-war/#/its-a-war.

"Mexico's Drug War: Storm Clouds with Silver Linings." *Economist*, May 19, 2012. http://www.economist.com/node/21555593.

"Mexico Security Memo November 10, 2008." Stratfor. https://www.stratfor.com/analysis/mexico-security-memo-nov-10-2008.

Michoacán, Morelia. "'La Tuta' Audio: I Regret Commanding Los Viagra." *Borderland Beat*, February 3, 2015. http://www.borderlandbeat.com/2015/02/la-tuta-audio-i-regret-commanding-los.html.

Migdal, Joel S. *Strong Societies and Weak States: State-Society Relations and State Capabilities in the Third World*. Princeton, NJ: Princeton University Press, 1988.

Miller, Sarah Llana. "In Mexico, Skepticism That Arrest of Edgar Valdez Villarreal—'La Barbie'—Will Stem Drug Trade." *Christian Science Monitor*, August 31, 2010. http://www.csmonitor.com/World/Americas/2010/0831/In-Mexico-skepticism-that-arrest-of-Edgar-Valdez-Villarreal-La-Barbie-will-stem-drug-trade

Mills, Eduardo. "Transnational Criminal Groups in Central America." Director of Investigations for Southern Pulse. Cultural Knowledge Consortium, 2013. https://www.youtube.com/watch?v=QWwHgTWYyhQ&feature=youtube_gdata_player.

Moore, Gary. "The Myth of a 'Good Guy' Drug Cartel in Mexico." InSight Crime, 2011. http://www.insightcrime.org/investigations/the-myth-of-a-good-guy-drug-cartel-in-mexico.

Moore, Solomon. "War without Borders: How U.S. Became Stage for Mexican Drug Feud." *New York Times*, December 8, 2009. http://www.nytimes.com/2009/12/09/us/09border.html.

Mozingo, Joe. "L.A. Fashion District Firms Raided in Cartel Money Laundering Probe." *Los Angeles Times*, September 10, 2014. http://www.latimes.com/local/crime/la-me-fashion-district-raids-20140911-story.html#page=1.

Naím, Moisés. *Illicit: How Smugglers, Traffickers and Copycats Are Hijacking the Global Economy*. Washington, DC: Centro Cultural del BID, 2005.

———. "Mafia States: Organized Crime Takes Office." *Foreign Affairs* 91 (2012): 100–111.

National Research Council of the National Academies. *Review of the Department of Homeland Security's Approach to Risk Analysis*. Washington, DC: National

Academy of Science, 2010. http://www.nap.edu/catalog/12972/review-of
-the-department-of-homeland-securitys-approach-to-risk-analysis.

Neher, Julian. "Mexico Cleared for U.S. Anti-Drug Aid as Army Accused of
Crimes." Bloomberg, April 22, 2009. http://www.bloomberg.com/apps/
news?pid=20601086&sid=ag0Y1liddYzg.

Nye, Joseph S. "The Changing Nature of World Power." Political Science
Quarterly 105, no. 2 (1990): 177–92. http://dx.doi.org/10.2307/2151022.

Ojeda, Nestor. "Ruffo y Franco Ríos protegían a los Arellano Félix: 'El
Chapo.'" El Mexicano, July 8, 2002. http://www.el-mexicano.com.mx/
informacion/noticias/1/1/internacional/2002/07/08/1878/ruffo-y-franco
-rios-protegian-a-los-arellano-felix-el-chapo.aspx.

Olson, Eric, and Miguel Salazar. A Profile of Mexico's Major Organized Crime
Groups. Washington, DC: Woodrow Wilson International Center for Scholars, February 16, 2011. https://www.wilsoncenter.org/sites/default/files/
profile_organized_crime_groups.pdf.

Olson, Mancur. "Dictatorship, Democracy, and Development." American Political
Science Review 87, no. 3 (1993): 567–76. http://dx.doi.org/10.2307/2938736.

———. Power and Prosperity: Outgrowing Communist and Capitalist Dictator-
ships. New York: Basic Books, 2000.

Oppenheimer, Andres. "Mexico's Big Hope: Get 5 Million U.S. Retir-
ees." Miami Herald, April 17, 2010. https://mexicoinstitute.wordpress
.com/2010/04/17/op-ed-mexicos-big-hope-get-5-million-u-s-retirees/.

Orama, Juan L. "U.S. Military Evolution in Counternarcotics Operations in
Latin America." Strategy Research Project, US Army War College, 2001.
http://oai.dtic.mil/oai/oai?verb=getRecord&metadataPrefix=html&
identifier=ADA391652.

"Organized Crime." United Nations Office on Drugs and Crime, 2010. http://
www.unodc.org/unodc/en/organized-crime/index.html?ref=menuside.

"Organized Crime Drug Enforcement Task Forces (OCDETF)." US Department of Justice. Accessed October 17, 2013. http://www.justice.gov/
criminal/organized-crime-drug-enforcement-task-forces.

Ortiz Aguilera, Lauro. "Operativo Tijuana." Accessed March 16, 2011. http://
www.zetatijuana.com/html/EdcionesAnteriores/Edicion1714/Reportajez
OperativoTijuana.html.

"Outsmarted by Sinaloa: Why the Biggest Drug Gang Has Been Least Hit."
Economist, January 7, 2010. http://www.economist.com/node/15213785.

Pachico, Elyssa. "Breakaway Zetas Form New 'Zeta Blood' Cartel." InSight
Crime, February 18, 2013. http://www.insightcrime.org/news-briefs/
sangre-zeta-new-generation-mexico-cartel.

———. "Mexico Cartels Operate in 16 Countries." InSight Crime, September 19, 2012. http://www.insightcrime.org/news-analysis/mexico-cartels
-connections-abroad.

———. "Re-Emergence of Splinter Criminal Group Is Bad Sign for Mexico." InSight Crime, September 10, 2012. http://www.insightcrime.org/news-analysis/guerrero-gang-mexico-cartel-fragments.

"Panga Boat Smuggling Suspects' Operation Detailed in Affidavit." *Daily Breeze.* November 1, 2012. http://www.dailybreeze.com/20121101/panga-boat-smuggling-suspects-operation-detailed-in-affidavit.

Pardo, R. "Colombia's Two-Front War." *Foreign Affairs* 79, no. 4 (2000): 64–73. http://dx.doi.org/10.2307/20049809.

Parkinson, Charles. "Arrest of Mexico Self-Defense Leader Reveals Selfish Motives of Group." InSight Crime, August 15, 2013. http://www.insightcrime.org/news-briefs/self-defense-force-leader-arrested-for-claiming-mining-royalties.

———. "Former Mexico Intelligence Chief Brands El Chapo 'Business Genius.'" InSight Crime, December 13, 2013. http://www.insightcrime.org/news-briefs/former-mexico-intelligence-chief-brands-el-chapo-business-genius.

———. "Mexico's Knights Templar Earns $73 Mn before US Drug Profits." InSight Crime, November 8, 2013. http://www.insightcrime.org/news-briefs/mexicos-knights-templar-earns-73-mn-before-us-drug-profits.

Parsons, Christi, and Brian Bennett. "At Latin America Summit, Obama to Face Push for Drug Legalization." *Los Angeles Times,* April 13, 2012. http://articles.latimes.com/2012/apr/13/world/la-fg-latin-america-summit-20120414.

Payan, Tony, and Guadalupe Correa Cabrera. *Energy Reform and Security in Northeastern Mexico.* Issue brief. James A. Baker III Institute for Public Policy, May 16, 2014. http://bakerinstitute.org/media/files/files/21e1a8c8/BI-Brief-050614-Mexico_EnergySecurity.pdf.

Payan, Tony, Kathleen Staudt, and Z. Anthony Kruszewski. *A War That Can't Be Won: Binational Perspectives on the War on Drugs.* Tucson: University of Arizona Press, 2013.

Perkins, Kevin, and Anthony Placido. "Drug Trafficking Violence in Mexico: Implications for the United States." Federal Bureau of Investigation, May 5, 2010. https://www.fbi.gov/news/testimony/drug-trafficking-violence-in-mexico-implications-for-the-united-states.

Peters, B. Guy. *Institutional Theory in Political Science: The New Institutionalism.* New York: Pinter, 1999.

Petraeus, D. H., and J. F. Amos. *FM 3-24: Counterinsurgency.* Washington, DC: Department of the Army, 2006.

Podolny, J. M., and Karen L. Page. "Network Forms of Organization." *Annual Review of Sociology* 24, no. 1 (1998): 57–76. http://dx.doi.org/10.1146/annurev.soc.24.1.57.

Polanyi, Karl. *The Great Transformation: The Political and Economic Origins of Our Time,* 2nd ed. Boston: Beacon, 2001.

Powell, Walter W., and Paul DiMaggio. *The New Institutionalism in Organizational Analysis*. Chicago: University of Chicago Press, 1991.

Privette, W. H. "Organized Crime in the United States: Organizational Analogies for Counterinsurgency Strategy." Thesis, Naval Postgraduate School, 2006. http://calhoun.nps.edu/bitstream/handle/10945/2490/06Dec_Privette.pdf?sequence=1.

Raab Jorg, and H. Brinton Milward. "Dark Networks as Problems." *Journal of Public Administration: Research and Theory* 13, no. 4 (2003): 413–39. http://dx.doi.org/10.1093/jopart/mug029.

Ramsey, Geoffrey. "Study: US Marijuana Legalization Could Cut Cartel Profits by 30%." InSight Crime, November 5, 2012. http://www.insightcrime.org/news-analysis/study-legalization-cut-cartel-profits-by-30.

Ravelo, Ricardo. *Los capos: Las narco-rutas de México*. Mexico City: Plaza & Janes Mexico, 2005.

Rawls, John. *A Theory of Justice*. Cambridge, MA: Belknap Press of Harvard University Press, 1999.

"Reconocen al General Alfonso Duarte Mújica." *El Mexicano*, September 13, 2010. http://www.el-mexicano.com.mx/informacion/noticias/1/3/estatal/2010/09/13/425134/reconocen-al-general-alfonso-duarte-mujica.

"Repaso a carrera delictiva de Miguel Ángel Treviño Morales, 'El Z-40.'" *SIPSE*, July 16, 2013. http://sipse.com/mexico/el-z-40-comenzo-como-mensajero-de-pandilla-41922.html.

Replogle, Jill. "Street Dealers Fuel Spike in Violence in Tijuana." KPBS, June 12, 2013. http://www.kpbs.org/news/2013/jun/12/street-dealers-fuel-spike-violence-tijuana/.

Resa Nestares, Carlos. "Los Zetas: De narcos a mafiosos." El Comercio de Drogas Ilegales en Mexico, Investigation Notes. April 9, 2003. https://www.uam.es/personal_pdi/economicas/cresa/nota0403.pdf.

Results of a Pilot Survey of Forty Selected Organized Criminal Groups in Sixteen Countries. Office of Drugs and Crime, United Nations, September 2002. http://www.unodc.org/pdf/crime/publications/Pilot_survey.pdf.

Reuter, Peter. "Systemic Violence in Drug Markets." *Crime, Law, and Social Change* 52, no. 3 (2009): 275–84. http://dx.doi.org/10.1007/s10611-009-9197-x.

Reuter, Peter, and Mark A. R. Kleiman. "Risks and Prices: An Economic Analysis of Drug Enforcement." *Crime and Justice* 7 (1986): 289–340. http://dx.doi.org/10.1086/449116.

Reuters. "Mexico Arrests 13 in Connection with Chapo Escape." *New York Times*, September 18, 2015. http://www.nytimes.com/reuters/2015/09/18/world/americas/18reuters-mexico-chapo-arrests.html.

———. "Mexico Captures Most Wanted Drug Kingpin, Former Teacher 'La Tuta.'" February 27, 2015. http://www.reuters.com/article/2015/02/28/us-mexico-drugs-idUSKBN0LV1B620150228.

Reiss, Albert J., Jr., and Jeffrey A. Roth. *Understanding and Preventing Violence*, vol. 1. Washington, DC: National Academies Press, 1993.

Reza Gonzalez, Yamile. "'Cae' narco miembros del CAF." *El Mexicano*, February 7, 2011. http://www.el-mexicano.com.mx/informacion/noticias/1/22/policiaca/%202011/02/07/453559/cae-narco-miembros-del-caf.aspx.

Ribando Seelke, Clare, and Kristin Finklea. *U.S.–Mexican Security Cooperation: The Mérida Initiative and Beyond*. Congressional Research Services, May 7, 2015. https://www.fas.org/sgp/crs/row/R41349.pdf.

Rios Contreras, Viridiana. "How Government Structure Encourages Criminal Violence: The Causes of Mexico's Drug War." Harvard University, 2012. http://www.gov.harvard.edu/files/Rios_PhDDissertation.pdf.

———. *Mexico's* Petite Révolution: *Justice and Security Implications of Approving a Fully New Code of Judicial Procedures*. Mexico Institute, Woodrow Wilson International Center for Scholars. Accessed April 20, 2015. http://www.wilsoncenter.org/sites/default/files/rios_single_code.pdf.

Roberts, Nancy, and Sean F. Everton. "Strategies for Combating Dark Networks." *Journal of Social Structure* 12 (2011): 1–32. http://www.cmu.edu/joss/content/articles/volume12/RobertsEverton.pdf.

Rodriguez, Olga. "Mexican Drug Cartels Join Forces to Destroy Rival Gang." Associated Press. June 13, 2010. http://www.huffingtonpost.com/2010/04/13/mexican-drug-cartels-join_n_535406.html.

Romero, Simon. "Coca Production Makes a Comeback in Peru." *New York Times*, June 13, 2010. http://www.nytimes.com/2010/06/14/world/americas/14peru.html?ref=americas.

Ross, Ashley D. *Local Disaster Resilience: Administrative and Community Preparedness: Administrative and Political Perspectives*. New York: Routledge, 2013.

Rotella, Sebastian. "Mexico's Cartels Sow Seeds of Corruption, Destruction: Fight for Control of U.S.-Bound Drug Trade Is Deadly Competition; Gangs Enlist Police and Politicians." *Los Angeles Times,* June 16, 1995. http://articles.latimes.com/1995-06-16/news/mn-13754_1_federal-police/2.

Rothstein, Hy S. *Afghanistan and the Troubled Future of Unconventional Warfare*. Annapolis, MD: Naval Institute Press, 2006. http://www.loc.gov/catdir/toc/ecip063/2005031132.html.

Rubin, Alissa J., and Damien Cave. "In a Force for Iraqi Calm, Seeds of Conflict." *New York Times*, December 23, 2007, sec. International/Middle East. http://www.nytimes.com/2007/12/23/world/middleeast/23awakening.html.

Sabet, Daniel. "Confrontation, Collusion and Tolerance: The Relationship between Law Enforcement and Organized Crime in Tijuana." *Mexican Law Review* 2, no. 2: 3–29 (September 2009). http://biblio.juridicas.unam.mx/revista/pdf/MexicanLawReview/4/arc/arc1.pdf.

———. *Police Reform in Mexico: Informal Politics and the Challenge of Institutional Change*. Stanford, CA: Stanford University Press, 2012.

Sadiq, Kamal. *Paper Citizens: How Illegal Immigrants Acquire Citizenship in Developing Countries*. Oxford/New York: Oxford University Press, 2009.

Salazar, Miguel, and Eric Olson. *A Profile of Mexico's Major Organized Crime Groups*. Washington, DC: Woodrow Wilson International Center for Scholars, February 16, 2011. https://www.wilsoncenter.org/sites/default/files/profile_organized_crime_groups.pdf.

Sánchez Valdéz, Victor Manuel. *Criminal Networks and Security Policies*. Mexico Institute, Woodrow Wilson International Center for Scholars. Accessed April 13, 2015. http://www.wilsoncenter.org/sites/default/files/criminal_networks_sanchez.pdf.

Sandholtz, W., and W. Koetzle. "Accounting for Corruption: Economic Structure, Democracy, and Trade." *International Studies Quarterly* 44, no. 1 (2000): 31–50. http://dx.doi.org/10.1111/0020-8833.00147.

Salcedo-Albarán, Eduardo, and Luis Jorge Garay Salamanca. *Structure of a Transnational Criminal Network: "Los Zetas" and the Smuggling of Hydrocarbons*. Vortex, 2014. http://www.scivortex.org/12TCNsMexUsV2.pdf.

Scott, John. *Social Network Analysis: A Handbook*, 2nd ed. Thousand Oaks, CA: Sage Publications, 2000.

Schelling, Thomas C. *Arms and Influence*. New Haven, CT: Yale University Press, 1966.

———. "What Is the Business of Organized Crime?" *American Scholar* 40, no. 4 (1971): 643–52.

Schiller, Dane. "'La Barbie' Wants to Be Tried in U.S." *Houston Chronicle*, September 9, 2010. http://www.mysanantonio.com/news/local_news/article/La-Barbie-wants-to-be-tried-in-U-S-694556.php?showFullArticle=y.

Schiller, Dane, and Dudley Althaus. "'El Taliban' Falls in Mexico: House Smashed by Drug Rivals." September 28, 2012. http://blog.chron.com/narcoconfidential/2012/09/taliban-falls-in-mexico-and-narco-wars-take-another-twist/#7584101=2.

Schoichet, Catherine E., and Ed Payne. "Mexican Drug Lord Joaquin 'El Chapo' Guzman Escapes." *CNN*. July 12, 2015. http://www.cnn.com/2015/07/12/world/mexico-el-chapo-escape/index.html.

Serrano, Richard. "Family of U.S. Agent Slain in Mexico Demands to Know Source of Guns." *Los Angeles Times*, July 17, 2011. http://articles.latimes.com/2011/jul/17/nation/la-na-guns-cartel-20110718.

Shannon, Elaine. *Desperados: Latin Drug Lords, U.S. Lawmen, and the War America Can't Win*. New York: Viking, 1988.

Shirk, David. "Democratization and Party Organization: The Growing PAiNs of Mexico's Partido Acción Nacional." Latin American Studies Association International Congress, 1998.

————. "Drug Violence in Mexico: Data and Analysis from 2001–2009." January 17, 2010. https://justiceinmexico.files.wordpress.com/2010/04/drug_violence.pdf.

————. "Judicial Reform in Mexico: Change and Challenges in the Justice Sector." *Mexican Law Review* 3, no. 2 (January–June 2011).

————. "Law Enforcement Challenges and 'Smart Borders.'" In *Homeland Security: Protecting America's Targets*, vol. 1. Edited by James J. D. Forest. Westport, CT: Praeger, 2006.

————. *Mexico's New Politics: The PAN and Democratic Change.* Boulder, CO: Lynne Rienner, 2005.

Shirk, David, and Viridiana Rios. *Drug Violence in Mexico: Data and Analysis through 2010.* Trans-Border Institute, University of San Diego, February 2011. http://www.gov.harvard.edu/files/RiosShirk2011_DrugViolenceReport.pdf.

Siegal, Erin. "The Architect and the Opera Singer: A Tale of Two Drug Mules." *Fronteras Desk*, December 21, 2012. http://www.fronterasdesk.org/content/architect-and-opera-singer-tale-two-drug-mules.

Siegal, Robert, and Melissa Block. "Mexico Captures Reputed Drug Lord 'La Barbie.'" NPR, August 31, 2010. http://www.npr.org/templates/story/story.php?storyId=129558719..

"Sinaloa Drug Cartel Said to Infiltrate Executive Branch." *SourceMex Economic News & Analysis on Mexico*, February 23, 2005. http://www.thefreelibrary.com/SINALOA+DRUG+CARTEL+SAID+TO+INFILTRATE+EXECUTIVE+BRANCH.-a0129178856.

Skaperdas, S. "Cooperation, Conflict, and Power in the Absence of Property Rights." *American Economic Review* 82, no. 4 (1992): 720–39.

————. "The Political Economy of Organized Crime: Providing Protection When the State Does Not." *Economics of Governance* 2, no. 3 (2001): 173–202. http://dx.doi.org/10.1007/PL00011026.

Skaperdas, S., and C. Syropoulos. "Gangs as Primitive States." Working paper, Department of Economics, Pennsylvania State University, 1993.

Smith, Emily. "'Blind Mules' Unknowingly Ferry Drugs across the U.S.–Mexico Border." CNN, January 24, 2012. http://www.cnn.com/2012/01/23/world/americas/mexico-blind-drug-mules/index.html.

Solingen, E. "The Domestic Sources of Regional Regimes: The Evolution of Nuclear Ambiguity in the Middle East." *International Studies Quarterly* 38, no. 2 (1994): 305–37. http://dx.doi.org/10.2307/2600979.

————. *Nuclear Logics: Contrasting Paths in East Asia and the Middle East.* Princeton, NJ: Princeton University Press, 2007. http://www.loc.gov/catdir/toc/ecip0712/2007008396.html.

————. "The Political Economy of Nuclear Restraint." *International Security* 19, no. 2 (1994): 126–69. http://dx.doi.org/10.2307/2539198.

————. *Regional Orders at Century's Dawn: Global and Domestic Influences on Grand Strategy*. Princeton Studies in International History and Politics. Princeton, NJ: Princeton University Press, 1998.

Spagat, Eliot. "Reputed Mexican Drug Lord Teodoro Garcia Simental Is Captured." *Washington Post*, January 13, 2010.

Spruyt, Hendrik. *The Sovereign State and Its Competitors*. Princeton, NJ: Princeton University Press, 1994.

Steinhauer, Jennifer, and James C. McKinley Jr. "U.S. Officials Arrest Suspect in Top Mexican Drug Gang." *New York Times*, August 17, 2006, sec. National. http://www.nytimes.com/2006/08/17/us/17drug.html.

Stevenson, Mark, and Jose Antonio Rivera. "Mexico Chief Pitches Anti-Crime Crackdown: After Disappearances, Beheadings in City of Iguala, Pena Nieto Seeks to Reduce Corrupt Municipal Power." *Houston Chronicle*, November 28, 2014.

Stone, Hannah. "Zetas Splinter Group Announces Mission to Kill Z-40." InSight Crime, October 23, 2012. http://www.insightcrime.org/news-briefs/zetas-splinter-mission-kill-z40.

Stout, David. "D.E.A. Arrests Mexican Drug Ring Leader." *New York Times*, August 16, 2006, sec. National. http://www.nytimes.com/2006/08/16/us/17arrestcnd.html.

"Study: 98.5% of Crimes Go Unpunished in Mexico." *Latin American Herald Tribune*. 2010. http://www.laht.com/article.asp?ArticleId=376423&CategoryId=14091.

Sullivan, John P. "The Barrio Azteca, Los Aztecas Network." *Counter Terrorist*, May 2013. https://www.academia.edu/3246070/The_Barrio_Azteca_Los_Aztecas_Network.

————. "Extreme Narco Violence in Mexico." *Baker Institute Blog*, October 9, 2012. http://blog.chron.com/bakerblog/2012/10/extreme-narco-violence-in-mexico/.

————. *From Drug Wars to Criminal Insurgency: Mexican Cartels, Criminal Enclaves and Criminal Insurgency in Mexico and Central America; Implications for Global Security*. May 3, 2012. https://halshs.archives-ouvertes.fr/halshs-00694083/document.

————. "Los Caballeros Templarios: 'Social Bandits.'" *Counter Terrorist*, December 2012. https://www.academia.edu/11193325/Los_Caballeros_Templarios_Social_Bandits_.

————. "Mexico's Drug War: Cartels, Gangs, Sovereignty and the Network State." Doctoral diss., Open University of Catalonia, 2013.

————. "Transnational Gangs: The Impact of Third Generation Gangs in Central America." *Air & Space Power Journal*, July 1, 2008. http://www.airpower.maxwell.af.mil/apjinternational/apj-s/2008/2tri08/sullivaneng.htm.

———. "Will El Chapo Rule from Prison?" *Daily Beast,* February 24, 2014. http://www.thedailybeast.com/articles/2014/02/24/captured-mexico -s-cartel-kingpin-el-chapo.html.

Sullivan, J. P., and A. Elkus. "State of Siege: Mexico's Criminal Insurgency." *Small Wars Journal* 12 (2008). http://www.smallwarsjournal.com.

Sullivan, J. P., and R. J. Bunker. "Drug Cartels, Street Gangs, and Warlords." *Small Wars & Insurgencies* 13, no. 2 (2002): 40–53. http://dx.doi.org/10.1080/ 09592310208559180.

Sullivan, John P., and Samuel Logan. "La Línea: Network, Gang, and Mercenary Army." *Counter Terrorist,* August 4, 2011. https://www.academia .edu/1123636/La_L%C3%ADnea_Network_gang_and_mercenary_army.

———. "Los Zetas: Massacres, Assassinations and Infantry Tactics." *Security Solutions International,* November 24, 2010. http://www.homeland1.com/ domestic-international-terrorism/articles/913612-Los-Zetas-Massacres -Assassinations-and-Infantry-Tactics/.

Sullivan, Kevin. "Tijuana Gang Figure Held after Slaying of Journalist." *Washington Post,* June 26, 2004. http://www.washingtonpost.com/wp-dyn/articles/ A6989-2004Jun25.html.

"Suspected Tijuana Drug Kingpin Arraigned." News story. KGTV San Diego, May 7, 2001. http://www.10news.com/news/suspected-tijuana -drug-kingpin-arraigned.

Thelen, Kathleen. "Historical Institutionalism in Comparative Politics." *Annual Review of Political Science* 2, no. 1 (1999): 369–404. http://dx.doi .org/10.1146/annurev.polisci.2.1.369.

Thompson, Ginger. "Justice Department Accused of 'Reckless Technique.'" *New York Times,* June 14, 2011. http://www.nytimes.com/2011/06/15/us/ politics/15guns.html?_r=1&pagewanted=print.

———. "US Widens Its Role in Battle against Mexico's Drug Cartels." *New York Times,* August 6, 2011. http://www.nytimes.com/2011/08/07/world/ 07drugs.html?_r=1&nl=todaysheadlines&emc=tha22.

Thompson, Ginger, and Mark Mazetti. "U.S. Sends Drones to Fight Mexican Drug Trade." March 15, 2011. http://www.nytimes.com/2011/03/16/world/ americas/16drug.html?_r=1&partner=rss&emc=rss&pagewanted=print.

Thompson, Grahame. *Between Hierarchies and Markets: The Logic and Limits of Network Forms of Organization.* Oxford/New York: Oxford University Press, 2003. http://dx.doi.org/10.1093/acprof:oso/9780198775270.001.0001.

Thompson, Robert Grainger Ker. "Defeating Communist Insurgency: The Lessons of Malaya and Vietnam." *Studies in International Security,* vol. 10. New York: F. A. Praeger, 1966.

"Tijuana's Cartel Landscape." Stratfor, January 17, 2011. https://www.stratfor .com/analysis/ tijuanas-cartel-landscape.

"Tijuana Police Get Guns Back." *Los Angeles Times,* January 28, 2007. http://articles.latimes.com/2007/jan/28/world/fg-tijuana28.

Tilly, Charles. *Coercion, Capital, and European States, AD 990–1990.* Cambridge, MA: Blackwell, 1990.

———. "War Making and State Making as Organized Crime." In *Bringing the State Back In,* edited by Peter Evans, Dietrich Rueschemeyer, and Theda Skocpol. Cambridge, UK: Cambridge University Press, 1985. http://dx.doi.org/10.1017/CBO9780511628283.008.

"Tortura y corrupción en la municipal." Semanario *Zeta,* January 20, 2015. http://zetatijuana.com/noticias/reportajez/16691/tortura-y-corrupcion-en-la-municipal.

Transnational Organized Crime in Central America and the Caribbean: A Threat Assessment. Vienna: United Nations Office of Drugs and Crime (UNODC), September 2012. http://www.unodc.org/documents/data-and-analysis/Studies/TOC_Central_America_and_the_Caribbean_english.pdf.

"Treasury Designates Additional Sinaloa-Based Drug Trafficking Organization: Action Is the First by the Treasury Department Against the Meza Flores Organization" Press release. US Department of the Treasury. January 17, 2013. www.treasury.gov/press-center/press-releases/Pages/tg1824.aspx.

"Treasury Sanctions Mother-in-Law of Sinaloa Cartel Drug Lord 'El Azul.'" Press release. US Department of the Treasury. December 18, 2014. http://www.treasury.gov/press-center/press-releases/Pages/jl9721.aspx.

"Two Mass Graves Containing 48 Bodies Discovered in the San Fernando Area." Sensitive cable. US Consulate, Matamoros, April 6, 2011. http://www2.gwu.edu/~nsarchiv/NSAEBB/NSAEBB445/docs/20110406.pdf.

United States Department of the Army and United States Marine Corps. *The U.S. Army/Marine Corps Counterinsurgency Field Manual: U.S. Army Field Manual No. 3–24; Marine Corps Warfighting Publication No. 3–33.5.* Chicago: University of Chicago Press, 2007.

United States vs. Tomas Yarrington Ruvalcaba and Fernando Alejandro Cano Martinez. Indictment. United States District Court Southern District of Texas, Brownsville Division, May 22, 2013. http://www.ice.gov/doclib/news/releases/2013/131202brownsville.pdf.

"US Embassy Cables: Mexico Is Losing Drug War, Says US." *Guardian,* January 29, 2010. http://www.theguardian.com/world/us-embassy-cables-documents/246329.

USG Assistance: INSCR Volume 1. US Department of State, 2005. http://www.state.gov/documents/organization/42865.pdf.

Valdez, Diana Washington. "ATF: Most Guns at Mexican Crime Scenes Traced to US." *El Paso Times,* December 27, 2012. http://www.elpasotimes.com/ci_22265245/atf-most-guns-at-mexican-crime-scenes-traced.

Van Schendel, Willem. *The Bengal Borderland: Beyond State and Nation in South Asia*. Anthem South Asian Studies. London: Anthem, 2005.

Van Schendel, Willem, and Itty Abraham. *Illicit Flows and Criminal Things: States, Borders, and the Other Side of Globalization*. Tracking Globalization. Bloomington: Indiana University Press, 2005.

Varese, Federico. *Mafias on the Move: How Organized Crime Conquers New Territories*. Princeton, NJ: Princeton University Press, 2011. http://dx.doi.org/10.1515/9781400836727.

Velasco, J. L. *Insurgency, Authoritarianism, and Drug Trafficking in Mexico's "Democratization"*. New York: Routledge, 2005.

Wagley, John R. *Transnational Organized Crime: Principal Threats and U.S. Responses*. Congressional Research Service, 2006. http://www.fas.org/sgp/crs/natsec/RL33335.pdf.

Walker, Rob. "Tijuana Police Chief Leyzaola: Torturer or Saviour?" BBC News, December 23, 2010. http://www.bbc.co.uk/news/world-latin-america-12070346.

Walser, Ray. "U.S. Strategy against Mexican Drug Cartels: Flawed and Uncertain." Backgrounder #2407. *Heritage Foundation*. April 26, 2010. http://www.heritage.org/research/reports/2010/04/us-strategy-against-mexican-drug-cartels-flawed-and-uncertain.

Waltz, Kenneth Neal. *Man, the State, and War: A Theoretical Analysis*. New York: Columbia University Press, 2001.

———. *Theory of International Politics*. Reading, MA: Addison-Wesley, 1979.

"War in Europe." PBS's *Frontline*, February, 2000. http://www.pbs.org/wgbh/pages/frontline/shows/kosovo/.

Wasserman, Stanley, and Katherine Faust. *Social Network Analysis: Methods and Applications*. Structural Analysis in the Social Sciences. Cambridge/New York: Cambridge University Press, 1994. http://dx.doi.org/10.1017/CBO9780511815478.

Weber, Max. *From Max Weber: Essays in Sociology*, edited by Hans Heinrich Gerth and C. Wright Mills. New York: Oxford University Press, 1958.

Weick, Karl E. "Educational Organizations as Loosely Coupled Systems." *Administrative Science Quarterly* 21, no. 1 (1976): 1–19. http://dx.doi.org/10.2307/2391875.

Wilkinson, Tracy. "Drug Cartel Leader Hector Beltran Leyva Arrested in Mexico." *Los Angeles Times*, October 1, 2014. http://www.latimes.com/world/mexico-americas/la-fg-mexico-drug-cartel-beltran-leyva-20141001-story.html.

———. "Mexico Acknowledges Drug Gang Infiltration of Police." *Los Angeles Times*, December 18, 2008. http://www.latimes.com/world/la-fg-mexbust28-2008oct28-story.html.

Wilkinson, Tracy, and Ken Ellingwood. "Drug Cartels' New Weaponry Means War: Narcotics Traffickers Are Acquiring Firepower More Appropriate to an Army–Including Grenade Launchers and Antitank Rockets–and the Police Are Feeling Outgunned." *Los Angeles Times,* December 31, 2009. http://www.latimes.com/news/nationworld/world/la-fg-mexico-arms-race15-2009mar15,0,7843719,print.story.

Williams, Phil. "Here Be Dragons: Dangerous Spaces and International Security." In *Ungoverned Spaces: Alternatives to State Authority in an Era of Softened Sovereignty,* edited by A. L. Clunan and H. A. Trinkunas. Stanford, CA: Stanford Security Studies, 2010.

———. "Illicit Markets, Weak States and Violence: Iraq and Mexico." *Crime, Law, and Social Change* 52, no. 3 (2009): 323–36. http://dx.doi.org/10.1007/s10611-009-9194-0.

———. "Transnational Criminal Networks." In Arquilla and Ronfeldt, *Networks and Netwars: The Future of Crime and Militancy,* 61–97, 2001.

———. "Transnational Criminal Organizations: Strategic Alliances." *Washington Quarterly* 18, no. 1 (1995): 57–72. http://dx.doi.org/10.1080/01636609509550132.

World Drug Report 2010: Drug Use Is Shifting towards New Drugs and New Markets. United Nations Office of Drugs and Crime, June 23, 2010. https://www.unodc.org/unodc/en/frontpage/2010/June/drug-use-is-shifting-towards-new-drugs-and-new-markets.html.

Zakaria, F. *The Future of Freedom: Illiberal Democracy at Home and Abroad.* New York: Norton, 2007.

Zeller, Tom. "Tijuana's Police Take Up Arms . . . with Slingshots." *The Lede,* January 24, 2007. http://thelede.blogs.nytimes.com/2007/01/24/tijuanas-police-take-up-arms-with-slingshots/.

"The Zetas in Guatemala." Investigative report by Steven Dudley Director of InSight Crime, InSight Crime's Channel YouTube, September 8, 2011. https://www.youtube.com/watch?v=STjiPvDtpb8&feature=youtube_gdata_player.

"'Zetas' usan a pandillas para extender su control." *El Universal,* May 8, 2010. http://www.eluniversal.com.mx/notas/678889.html.

Index

and violence, 43n90; of Zetas, 111–12, 113
Fuentes, Daniel, 121–22n90
Fuerzas Armadas Revolucionarias de Colombia (FARC), 31–32, 91n15, 135
functional specialization, 33, 39, 43n90, 134

Gagne, David, 101
Gallardo, Miguel Ángel Félix "El Padrino," 97, 114; arrest and imprisonment of, 50; as head of Guadalajara cartel, 47–48, 50
Gambetta, Diego, 19–20, 22–23
García Ábrego, Juan, 106
García Simental, Eduardo Teodoro. *See* El Teo
García Simental, Manuel, 65
García Simental, Marco Antonio "El Cris," 61, 62, 82
Gente Nueva, 99
George, Alexander L., 2
globalization, 4, 5, 9
Godson, Roy, 8
Gómez Herrera, Salvador, 107
Gómez Martínez, Servando "La Tuta," 115, 117, 128, 130
González Pizaña, Rogelio "Z-2/El Kelín," 110, 129, 130, 131
Gonzalez-Ruiz, Samuel, 129
Grayson, George W., 47, 48, 115
Grillo, Ioan, 78, 104, 108, 128
Grupo Aeromóvil Fuerzas Especiales (GAFES), 107
Guadalajara, 57–58
Guadalajara cartel, 44n108, 47–48, 77, 97–98
Guatemala, 109
Guerrero Gutiérrez, Eduardo, 23, 140n17

Guerreros Unidos, 101
Gulf cartel, 100, 106–14, 118; cell structure of, 118; disruptive events for, 108–10; fragmentation and internecine conflict within, 110, 113, 118, 127; increasing territorial character of, 99, 113–14, 126–27; origins of, 106–7; recruitment of Zetas by, 53–54, 107, 114; trafficking-oriented nature of, 114, 118; Zetas' conflict with, 109, 118, 126–27
gun walking, 79–80
Gutiérrez Quiroz, Melvin "El Melvin," 66
Gutiérrez Rebollo, José de Jesús, 78
Guzmán, Fernando, 64
Guzmán Decena, Arturo "Z-1," 107, 110
Guzmán Loera, Joaquín "El Chapo," 30, 49, 65, 100, 101, 118; Arellano Félix Organization conflict with, 51–54, 57, 97, 98; arrest and imprisonment of, 130, 131, 140–41n32; and assassination of archbishop, 57–58; escape from prison by, 61, 103; as innovator, 104–5; and trafficking corridors, 99

Hale, Gary, 109
Harrison Act, 106
El H. *See* Beltrán Leyva, Héctor
Hernandez, Anabel, 98, 100, 106
Herrod, David, 81–82
hierarchy, 49; of Arellano Félix Organization, 56; defined, 29; of Sinaloa cartel, 25, 41n42; of territorial drug networks, 24–25, 39, 143
High Intensity Drug Tracking Area (HIDTA) program, 80